TAE KWON DO

ALSO BY RICHARD CHUN

Moo Duk Kwan Tae Kwon Do
Korean Art of Self-Defense

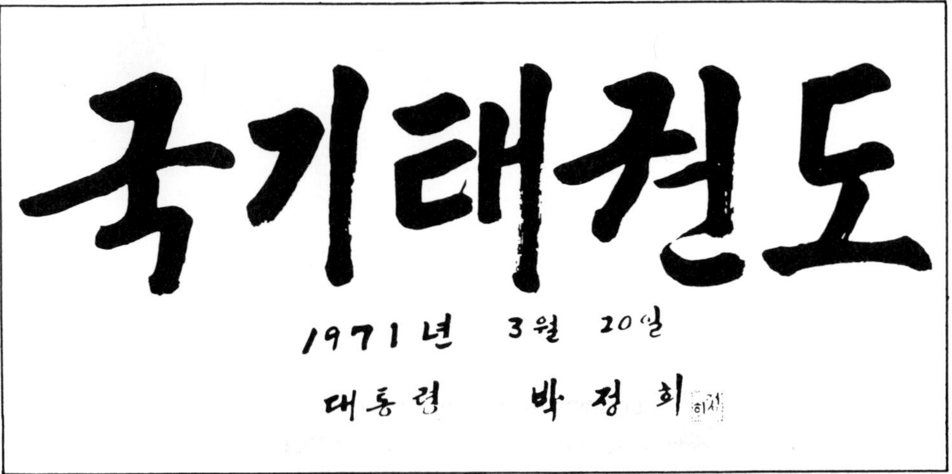

A scroll written and given by H. E. President Park Chung Hee

"A NATIONAL SPORT, TAE KWON DO"

TAE KWON DO

The Korean Martial Art

Richard Chun

with Paul Hastings Wilson

HARPER & ROW, PUBLISHERS, New York
Grand Rapids, Philadelphia, St. Louis, San Francisco
London, Singapore, Sydney, Tokyo, Toronto

PHOTOGRAPHS BY

Marco A. Vega

Designed by Lydia Link

Production Editor: Nancy Gilbert

Library of Congress Cataloging in Publication Data

Chun, Richard.
Tae Kwon Do: the Korean martial art.
Includes index.
1. Karate. I. Wilson, Paul Hastings, joint author.
II. Title.
GV476.C57 1976 796.8'15 74-1799
ISBN 0-06-010779-0

95 MPC 19 18 17

Contents

The techniques and other training programs described in this book, if properly executed, should cause no harm to any person who is physically sound and in good health. However, the publishers can accept no responsibility for accident or injury sustained during their performance and make no representation about their results. Should you have any doubt or question about your health and the advisability of your taking up the programs described, you should consult your doctor.

Richard Chun

DIPLOMA OF PARTICIPATION

Name. Richard Chun (Coach)

Nation. U. S. A.

This Diploma is presented to the above mentioned person for his participation in The First World Tae Kwon Do Championships held in Seoul, Korea, from 25-27 May 1973. Awarded on 27 May 1973.

Un Yong Kim
President
The First World
Tae Kwon Do Championships

CERTIFICATE OF PARTICIPATION

31 August 1975

Nationality. The Republic of Korea
United States of America

Name. Richard Chun

Status: Technical Advisor
U. S. A. TAE KWON DO TEAM

This is to certify that the above-named person has participated in the Second World Taekwondo Championships held in Seoul, Korea between 28-31 August 1975.

Un Yong KIM
President
The 2nd World Taekwondo Championships
The Organizing Committee of the 2nd World Taekwondo Championships

대 한 태 권 도 협 회

Korea Tae Kwon Do Association

OFFICE ADDRESS.
C/OKOREA AMATEUR SPORTS ASSOCIATION
SEOUL, KOREA
TEL 23 - 2374
28 - 5241 - 8

서울특별시중구무교동19번지
대한체육회내609호
전화㉓2374번
㉘5241-8(#65번)

1 February 1972

Dear Mr. Chun:

As President of the Korea Tae Kwon Do Association, I congratulate you for the excellence of your book on Tae Kwon Do, Korea's national sport and martial art.

Your book speaks with authority based not only on your own excellent qualifications, but also with the authority of the Korea Tae Kwon Do Association and the Korea Amateur sports Association since the Richard Chun Taekwondo Center in New York City is fully accredited by us.

I am very pleased to write this letter of congratulation and to wish you and your Taekwondo Center every success.

Sincerely yours,

Un Yong Kim
Un Yong Kim
President

Mr. Richard Chun
Richard Chun Tae Kwon Do Center

New York City

국 기 원

KUK KI WON

San 76, Yuk-Sam-Dong,
Sung-Dong-Ku,
Seoul, Korea
TEL 73-8886

서울특별시 성동구 역삼동 산76번지
전화 73-8886

My dear Rhin Moon Richard Chun,

Congratulations upon an excellent and outstanding achievement. Your book on Tae Kwon Do is the first general treatment of the subject in English, and inasmuch as it presents a clear and authentic introduction of our national sport to Western audiences, it is an important contribution to the exchange of cultural ideas between East and West.

The growing interest in Oriental traditions throughout the world, as evinced in the arts, in medicine, and especially in philosophy, encourages all of us, who are anxious to see the world at peace in our time. Inquiry into the modes of expression of another culture enables one to gain some insight into other ways of viewing the world, and therefore broadens and deepens one's understanding of himself in communion with others.

The Eastern martial art is, when practiced in its true spirit of unself-consciousness, an exercise of participation in the forces of the world around us. It is in this sense that Tae Kwon Do is defensive rather than aggressive. The player of Tae Kwon Do practices the forms and techniques with a sense of the forces within him working as a self-contained harmonious system. And when he is threatened by outside forces, he reacts appropriately, that is, with equal force, to balance and nullify the aggressor.

But you and I have considered these matters at length over the years, since you first came to me in your youth as a student of Tae Kwon Do. I mention them now, in view of the rapidly increasing popularity of Tae Kwon Do in the West, only to say that it gives me great personal pleasure to commend you for the responsible manner in which your book presents our complex and spiritually enhancing martial art.

Yours very sincerely,

Chong Soo Hong
Vice President
Kuk Ki Won

Mr. Richard Chun
The Richard Chun Tae Kwon Do Center
163 East 86th Street
New York, New York 10028

Preface

"Is Tae Kwon Do a technique for killing people?" This question has been put to me many times by those who are first being introduced to the subject. The answer is that Tae Kwon Do is a method of self-defense, and the guiding principle of the art is that the practitioner shall make no attack, except if he be threatened by a dangerous opponent. The disciplines of Tae Kwon Do are designed to make the student nonviolent, to inspire him with feelings of confidence and well-being, and to make his life more meaningful. By studying the art, the individual comes to understand himself and his aggressor: then he can be silent and fearless. The essence of the art of Tae Kwon Do rests in the integrity of the practitioner. Accordingly, the first technique taught in the training academy is the bow of respect, by which the individual attests to his trust in his teacher and in his fellow students, his friends in practice.

The history of humanity is the record of the search for a meaningful existence. "History," the word itself, means "a learning or knowing by inquiry." In the beginning every man was alone, a stranger in the world, insecure and indeterminate. Driven by loneliness, he sought the company of others, and formed society. Society was the pattern men established for mutual protection, but the structure of the pattern was such that men vied with one another for positions of favor. Eventually, those who were stronger usurped power over the weak. Competition developed as a natural course of existence. It took the form of real conflict, on the one hand, and of competitive sport, on the other.

The roots of Tae Kwon Do go very far back in the history of mankind. The originators and practitioners of this art, by mastering its extraordinarily efficient techniques for self-defense, made themselves equal to any personal threat against them. At a time when the strong would attempt to destroy the weak, and conflict meant combat to the death, the practitioners of Tae Kwon Do became far superior to their opponents. And they discovered that, when one is definitely superior in combat, he no longer has the need to kill. He can control his opponent easily without killing.

Fear is restricting. One who is fearful limits himself and tries to impose limitations upon the freedom of others. But when we are free of fear, we no longer seek to dominate others, for we are confident that they cannot dominate us—they have no means of intimidating us. We know that we have a valid "place" in the world: we have explored it, chosen it, taken root, and flowered in it. The study of Tae Kwon Do, by inspiring its practitioner with confidence, enables him to enjoy the benefits of society without being absorbed or overwhelmed by it. He is free to develop and preserve his unique individuality and avoid the danger of being reduced to a faceless cipher, arbitrarily counted and controlled by impersonal forces. There are those who, lacking in true, inner confidence, attempt to assert their individuality by boisterous and belligerent protestations against anything that thwarts them—and that is almost everything. However, there is a theory, essential to Tae Kwon Do, concerning the dialectical concept of "soft and hard," Yin and Yang. The practitioner of Tae Kwon Do becomes mild in manner, insofar as he knows that he can assert himself with force when necessary. He becomes like water, which, because it possesses tremendous inherent force—for generating life as well as for terrible destruction—is all the more beautiful and reassuring when we see it as a gentle stream, flowing around the rough rocks in its path.

This book is the product of the teachings of my masters and the experience of my life. In my own search for a meaningful existence, I entered into the study of Tae Kwon Do in the hope that it should provide me with an answer as to how to conduct my life. As I practiced the techniques over the years, I came to realize that the *art* in Tae Kwon Do rested in the fact that it taught, not answers, but a way in which to explore oneself, so as to discover the correct questions. I practiced movement, and learned the meaning of direction.

At this time, Tae Kwon Do is no longer the concern of Koreans only, but has become a popular endeavor among people throughout the world. It is important, therefore, that there be some guide for these students to follow. This book constitutes the only comprehensive manual of instruction presently available to the general reader in English. It provides, for the first time, texts for the study of the eight Pal-Gwe Forms, which are approved and practiced by the Korea Tae Kwon Do Association and the World Tae Kwon Do Federation, and presents new sparring techniques, which are now practiced in Korea. It is intended to serve as an introduction to an increasingly popular sport, as well as an aid in the practical, everyday need for self-defense. But my main purpose in writing this book is to share with my fellow students the right approach to the practice of Tae Kwon Do, in the firm conviction that without the proper approach, the student, though he practice the techniques exhaustively, will not arrive at the ultimate goal of the art, which is to realize a true and full determination of self. There is an old Oriental saying to the effect that the student who feels a debt of gratitude to his master repays that debt by going on to become greater than his master. The fact that so many young people throughout the world are seriously involved in the study of Tae Kwon Do gives me hope for the future of the art and the benefits it shall continue to bring to mankind.

In conclusion, I would like to take this opportunity to express my deepest appreciation to Marco Vega, photographer, for his energetic and creative contribution; Margaret Ann Sauers for her help as assistant photographer; Leny Delessio for the use of his photographs and for valuable consultations; Gae Hirsch for her drawings and illustrations; and to Dr. Tadashi Akaishi, Vice President of Harper & Row, for the benefit of his assistance in bringing this work to completion. Finally, my special thanks to my students for their endless contribution toward making this book possible.

RICHARD CHUN

Author's Notes

All schools of the Korea Tae Kwon Do Association wear white uniforms, which symbolize purity. It is the tradition of the Moo Duk Kwan School, however, that its members who hold the black belt wear white uniforms trimmed with black, symbolizing dignity. Thus, both styles of uniform appear in the photographs in this book. It should be noted, however, that in all official events sponsored by the Tae Kwon Do Association, in order to keep uniformity and simplicity, all participants are required to wear the pure-white uniform.

Throughout the book, the Korean terminology is given, in parentheses, after the English term for each technique.

This mural, discovered by archeologists in 1935, appears on the ceiling of Muyong-chong, a royal tomb in southern Manchuria built during the Koguryo dynasty, between A.D. 3 and A.D. 427. The painting depicts two men engaged in Tae Kwon Do free sparring.

1

Introduction

HISTORY OF TAE KWON DO

In the city of Kyongju, capital of the ancient kingdom of Silla, two giants face each other in Tae Kwon Do stance. They are incised on the tower wall of a Buddhist temple nearly two thousand years old, and they stand as testimony to the early development of Tae Kwon Do as a national art in Korea.

Tae Kwon Do means, literally, "The Art of Kicking and Punching." This style of fighting derives from more primitive techniques of foot, hand, and head fighting, called Pal Ke, Soo Bak, Kwon Bop, Okinawate, Tae Kyun, and Tang Soo, various forms of which were practiced in many parts of the Orient as early as the first century A.D. They all may have had their beginnings in India two thousand years before the birth of Christ. According to legend, they spread throughout the East with the teachings of the Buddhist monks, who developed a system of self-defense to protect themselves in their travels against the wild animals and unruly marauders of the time.

From the dawn of his species, man's ingenuity was called upon to develop personal skills to fight in order to obtain food and to provide defense against natural enemies. The first era, that is, the first half million years of man's existence, we call "The Instinctive Action Age." It was the time before the invention of weapons, when no conscious action was involved in defense. From the Stone Age to the end of the primitive era, when mankind began to spread from the Central Asian Plateau, the cradle of the birth of his race, into Asia, Europe, and Africa, is called "The Conscious Action Age." In this period, man acted consciously to develop methods of protecting his body and gathering his daily needs, using tools and weapons for the first time. "The Early Age of Systemization," also known as the Iron Age, is the period in which the techniques of self-defense were developed systematically, along with the advancing forms of art, architecture, religion, and government, in the rise of civilizations. During "The Age of the Flowering of the Arts," from about 2,600 years ago up to the modern era, the arts of self-defense reached their fullest development in various forms throughout the world, and it is this age in which we are most interested.

Diverse theories have been offered as to which country first developed the system of unarmed fighting popularly known, in the West, as Karate. It is said that an Indian prince invented the first scientific method of self-defense about 3000 B.C. He jabbed needles into his slaves until he discovered the most vulnerable points of the human body, where a single puncture caused death, and then he developed movements designed to aim blows at these critical points.

In the sixth century A.D., a Buddhist monk, named Bodhidharma, journeyed from India to China and established Zen Buddhism at the temple of Ko San So Rim. When his Chinese followers became physically exhausted by the severe discipline and intense pace that he set for them, Bodhidharma began to teach them a method of physical and mental exercises outlined in the *I-Chin Sutra* to enable them to free themselves from all conscious control in order to attain enlightenment. His followers worked at these exercises, which were abstract forms of the Indian system of open-hand fighting, until they came to be the most formidable fighters in China. They named their system of fighting Kwon Bop. It is suggested

These stone reliefs, dating from the Shil-La dynasty, c. sixth century A.D., are located in the cave of Suck-Kool-Am in southern Korea. The carvings represent the famous warrior, Kum Kang Yuksa, executing early Tae Kwon Do blocking techniques.

that Kwon Bop was spread by later Buddhist monks through Korea, Japan, and Okinawa, and that it is the primary system from which all other forms of open-hand fighting derived.

You will recall, however, the tower wall in Kyongju, in Korea, on which the giants facing each other in Tae Kwon Do position were carved two thousand years ago, that is, five hundred years before Bodhidharma made his journey to China. There are, also, mural paintings of men performing Tae Kwon Do exercises on the walls and ceilings in the tombs of Koguryo, another ancient kingdom of Korea. The construction of these tombs dates back to the period between A.D. 3 and A.D. 427, indicating that Tae Kwon Do was practiced in Korea long before the Chinese fighting forms were introduced there.

These three photos show actual pages from the *Muye Dobo-tongji,* an illustrated textbook of the Korean martial art Soo Bak Do, an early form of Tae Kwon Do. The book was written by Lee Duk Moo by order of King Chongjo in A.D. 1790 as a training manual for military personnel.

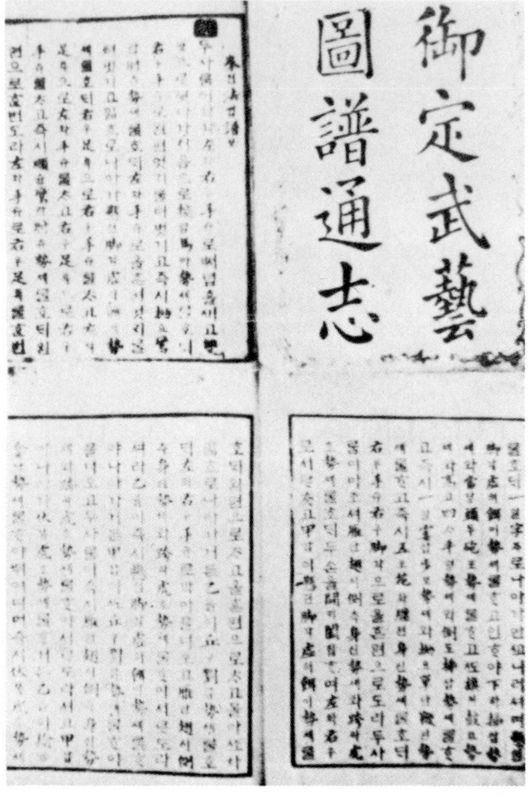
御定武藝圖譜通志

The cover page of *Muye Dobo-tongji*.

Illustrations from the text showing a blocking technique and its application in fighting.

跨驢逐前進乙作丘劉勢
左右手遮退作雁翅側身
勢跨虎勢相廻立乙卽作
懸脚虛餌勢進甲又作丘
劉勢退兩人卽作雁翅側
身勢跨虎勢相廻立

武藝圖譜通志 卷之四

拳法

十一

甲進作伏虎勢乙作擒拿
勢跳越旋作伏虎勢甲亦
作擒拿勢跳越

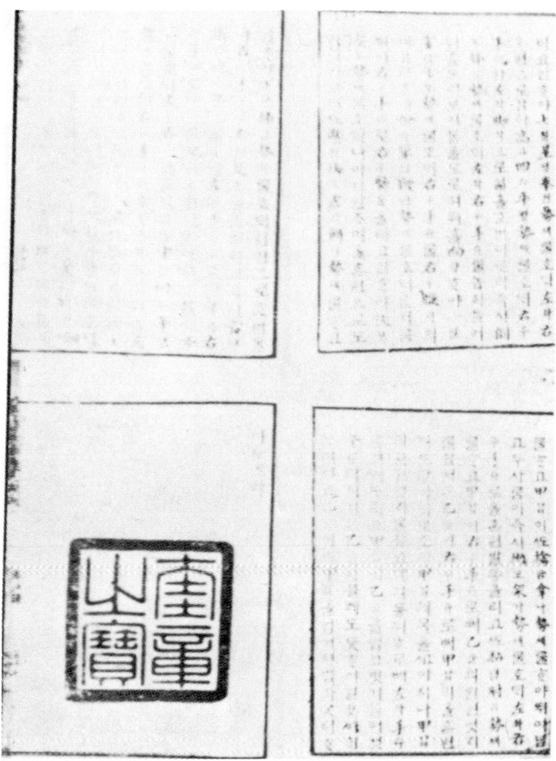

The seal of the author, Lee Duk Moo.

No detailed record is available as to when Karate was initiated in Japan. There are indications that the Japanese fighting style derived from Okinawate, the style indigenous to Okinawa. But *The Historical Record of Choson* gives evidence that there was trade between Choson (the ancient name for Korea) and the Ryukyu Islands (Okinawa), and that the games and customs native to Korea might have been transmitted to Okinawa through the traveling envoys.

It becomes obvious that open-hand fighting did not originate in one country only, but developed naturally in different places, as each people adapted themselves to cope with the dangers of their environment, and that the various styles influenced one another inevitably as trade and politics brought these nations into contact with one another in peace and war.

The primitive method of self-defense in Korea was called Soo Bak, meaning "Punching and Butting." It was popular among the common people and was as old as the nation itself. About 1,400 years ago, in the reign of Chin Heung, twenty-fourth king of Silla, the young aristocrats of the country formed an officers' warrior corps, which they named Hwa Rang Dan, to defend their kingdom against the constant invasions and harassment of their more powerful northern neighbors. They went into the mountains and along the seashore studying the fighting styles of the wild animals to learn what defensive and offensive positions gave each its most formidable advantage. These positions were adapted and then combined

A painting by Hong Do Kim, a famous artist of the Yi dynasty, representing a Soo Bak Do (early Tae Kwon Do) sporting competition held on the royal palace grounds.

with the traditional method of self-defense. Incorporating the disciplines taught by the Buddhist monks, rigorous exercises in intense concentration conditioned these young warriors to coordinate mind and body into one harmonious system, called Soo Bak Do, or Tae Kyun ("The Art of Kicking, Punching, and Butting"), the most effective unarmed martial art in the world. The Hwa Rang Dan became renowned for their courage and skill in battle, and their heroism, which became legendary, inspired the people of Silla to rise and eventually conquer their enemies. With Silla's victory, the Korean peninsula was united as one country for the first time in its history.

Soo Bak Do retained its popularity through the Silla and Koguryo dynasties and achieved its greatest preeminence during the succeeding Koryo dynasty, which was established in A.D. 935 and ruled for 457 years. It was from the Koryo dynasty that the peninsula gained its modern name, Korea. The kingdom under these rulers was strictly militaristic in spirit, a fact dictated by the necessity of defending the country against continual foreign invasions. The soldiers of the Koryo dynasty were among the finest the country has ever produced, and their martial spirit and bravery has been a source of inspiration ever since. At this time, Soo Bak Do was practiced not only as a martial art, but also as a skill to improve health and to enjoy competitively as a sport. An extract from the historical record of Koryo says that "King Uijong admired the excellence of Yi Ui-min in [the sport of] Soo Bak and promoted him [in military rank] from Taejong to Pyolchang."

During the reign of King Uijong, in the years between the end of the Sung dynasty in 1279 and the beginning of the Ming dynasty in 1368, Kwon Bop became popular in China as a national sport with two styles, Neikya and Weikya. These styles differed chiefly in that one emphasized defensive and the other offensive skills.

With the rise of the Yi dynasty in Korea, founded by Yi Sung Kye in 1392, Soo Bak Do, which had been the special province of the military society of the Koryo period, became more popular as a national sport among the general public. Those who aspired to be employed by the military department of the royal government had to learn Soo Bak Do, as it was included as part of the test given to the applicants. During this time, King Chongjo published an illustrated textbook on the martial arts, *Muye Dobo-tongji*, which included a major study of Soo Bak Do as one of the most important.

Nevertheless, in the latter half of the Yi dynasty, the time being generally peaceful, except for internal political struggles at the royal court, the feudal lords encouraged the development of literature and painting, at the expense of the martial arts, and Soo Bak Do declined in popularity, to become the pastime of a few devotees, mainly among the younger people.

From the Sino-Japanese War of 1894 through World War II, Korea was involved in continual military conflicts between China and Japan. During this period, the foreign fighting styles influenced that of Korea, and Soo Bak Do came to be called Tang Soo Do, that is, "The Art of the China Hand."

After the liberation of Korea, in 1945, a number of Koreans began a conscientious effort to revitalize the art of Tae Kwon Do as a national sport. The art regained its prominence among the people, and the enthusiastic support of its many practitioners eventually led to the inclusion of Tae Kwon Do as one of the official events of the Forty-Third Annual National Athletic Meet in 1962. From that point on, the popularity of Tae Kwon Do has spread throughout the world, and in May 1973, more than thirty countries competed in the First World Tae Kwon Do Championships, held in Seoul.

WHAT IS TAE KWON DO?

"Karate" is the generic term most commonly used in the West to refer to any of several forms of unarmed self-defense developed in the Orient. There are three main categories of this martial art. "Karate" is a Japanese word, meaning "Empty Hand," and indicates, specifically, the Okinawan-Japanese style of fighting, with its abrupt movements along straight lines. Kung Fu, literally "tasks" and Chuan Fa, literally "system of boxing" are the Chinese styles, which use flowing, circular movements. Tae Kwon Do, "The Art of Kicking and Punching," incorporates the abrupt, linear movements of Karate and the flowing, circular patterns of Kung Fu

with its own incomparable kicking techniques to form an integrated system unique to Korea.

Tae Kwon Do is an exact system of symmetrical body exercises designed for unarmed self-defense and counterattack. The significance of this definition, however, is only physical and superficial, for Tae Kwon Do means, more importantly, a state of mind. Thus, the control of one's mind, self-restraint, kindness, and humility must accompany physical grace. Tae Kwon Do develops in a man the speed and power to kill instantly with his bare hands and feet. But it is the art of the discipline to develop, also, such control, coordination, and balance that the punching and kicking movements can be stopped just centimeters short of their mark on the opponent's body. A Tae Kwon Do master can make a punch, forcible enough to smash a two-inch board, touch a sheet of rice paper without breaking it.

An essential difference between Eastern and Western attitudes toward self-defense lies in the fact that the Eastern approach does not limit itself to proficiency in technique as an end in itself, as does the Western idea, but goes further, to integrate the art as a way of being-in-the-world. The word "technique" derives from both the Greek *technikos*, meaning "of art, skillful," and the Sanskrit *taksati*, "he forms, constructs." "Art" derives from the Latin *ars*, meaning "skill"—and more basically "arm"—and the Greek *harmos*, "joint," and *arariskein*, "to fit." The basic meaning of the English word "art" is "joining, fitting." But the Korean word *Do* (*Do* in Japanese, *Tao* in Chinese), which is translated here as "art," means more literally "Way"—the *W* is capitalized to indicate that this means "Way-of-Being-in-the-World," as opposed to a "method" one practices or a "direction" one takes arbitrarily. "The Way" is not chosen arbitrarily, but in accordance with one's own temperament, as qualified by the notion of the Good, that is, what is creative, rather than destructive, and in harmony with the Universe. It is the object of technique to make, form, or impose a change on the environment. Art, on the other hand—that is, *Do*—does not impose, it nurtures.

Self-preservation involves a striving against those things in the world which inhibit one's own growth and development. But one must be able to distinguish necessary from unnecessary antagonisms in order to avoid wasting energy in fear and wanton destruction. It is the beginning of wisdom for one to know what he contains already complete within himself, and therefore has no need to seize from another. Thus, thought is made clear, action efficient, and human life, which consists in the integration of these two things, is enhanced. The ultimate goal is to live.

OUTLINES AND TECHNIQUES OF TAE KWON DO

1. Composition of Tae Kwon Do

A. Form Divisions

(1) Pal-Gwe (eight forms)
(2) Tae-Kook (eight forms)
(3) Black Belt (nine forms)
(4) Other Traditional Forms
  (a) Ki-Cho
  (b) Black Belt Traditional
  (c) Stick and Weapon

B. Sparring Divisions

(1) Three-Step Sparring
(2) One-Step Sparring
(3) Arranged Free Sparring
(4) Free Sparring

C. Breaking Divisions

(1) Hand, Foot, and Head Breaking
(2) Jumping, Turning, and Flying Breaking

D. Self-Defense Divisions

(1) Practical Daily Self-Defense
(2) Self-Defense Against Weapons
(3) Basic Falling and Throwing

2. Tae Kwon Do Techniques

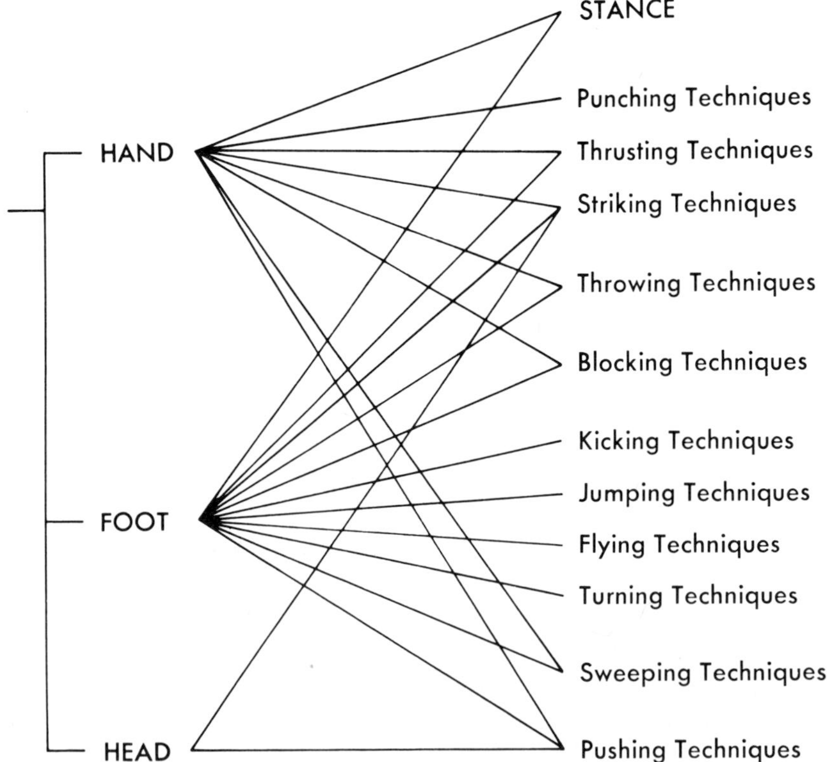

3. Hand Attacking Techniques

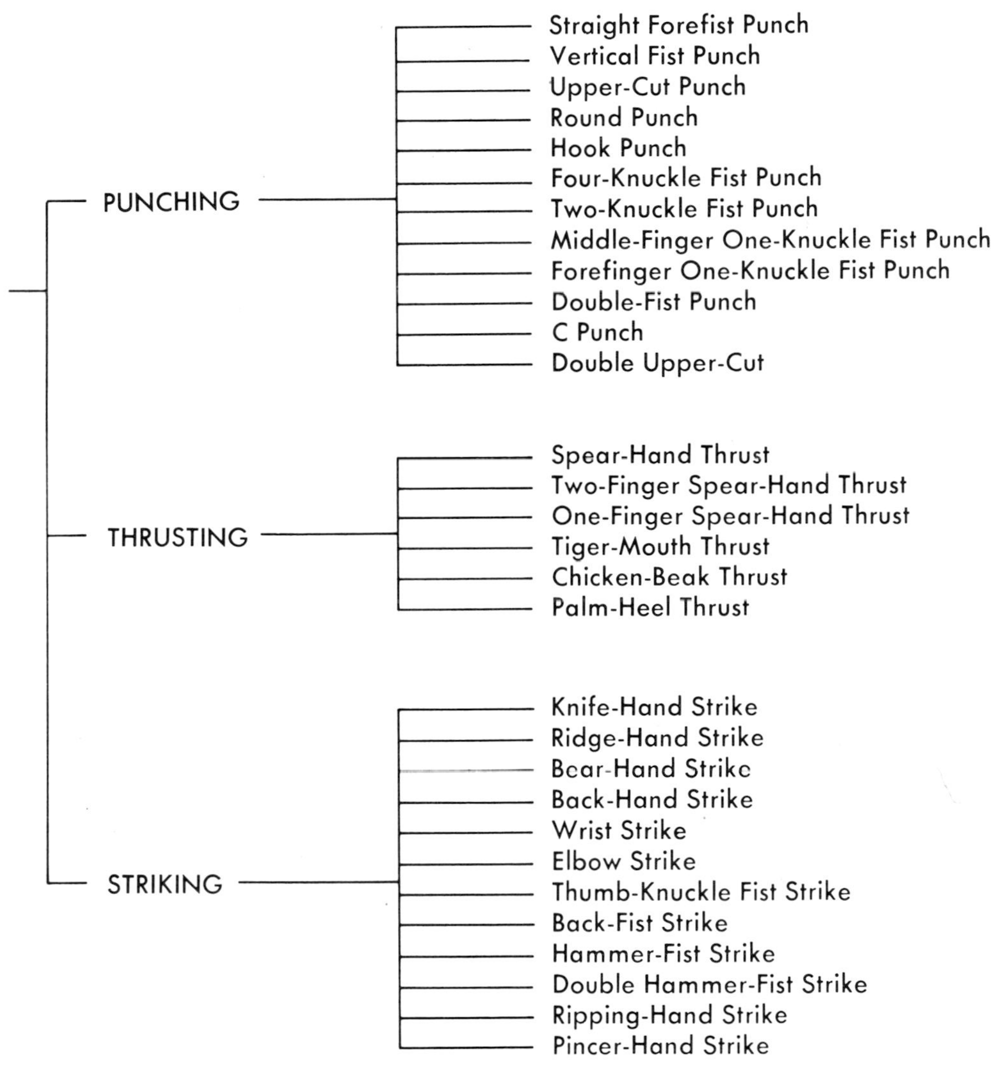

4. Blocking Techniques

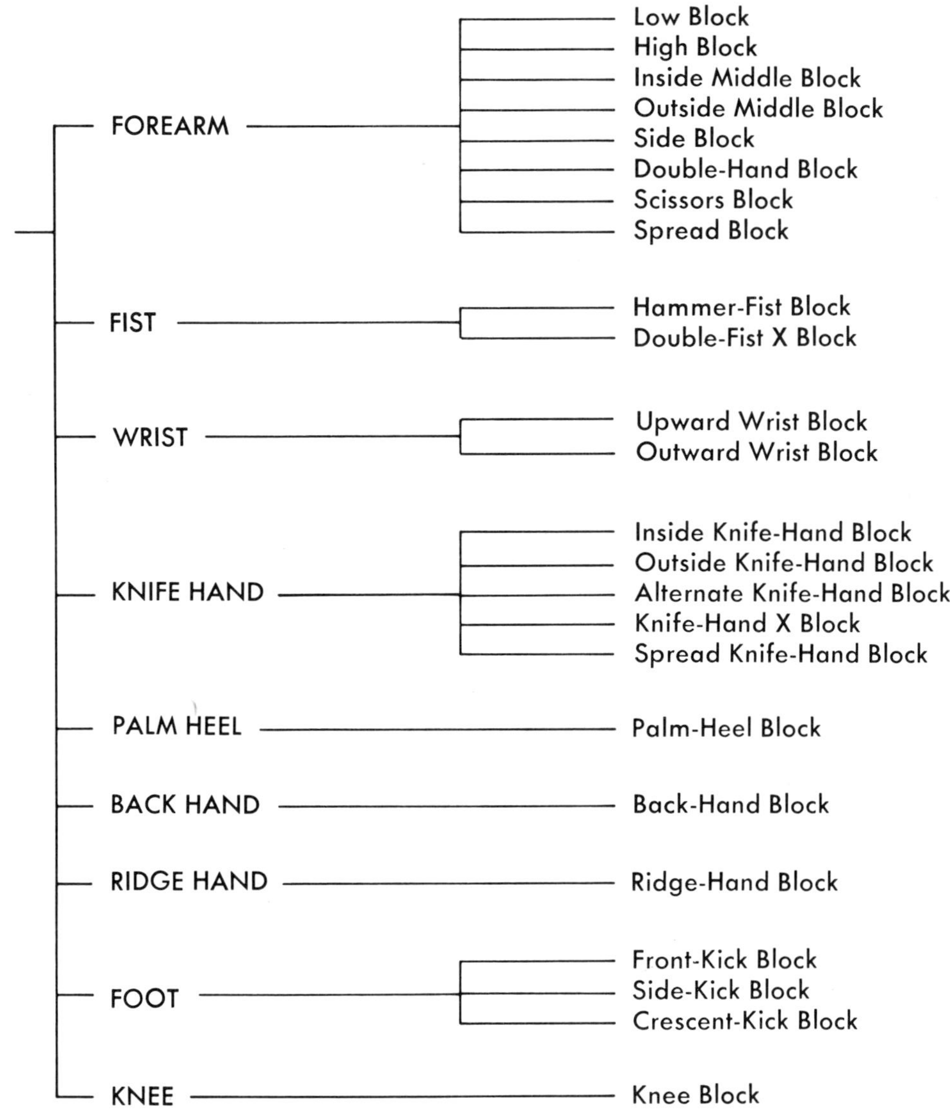

5. Kicking Techniques

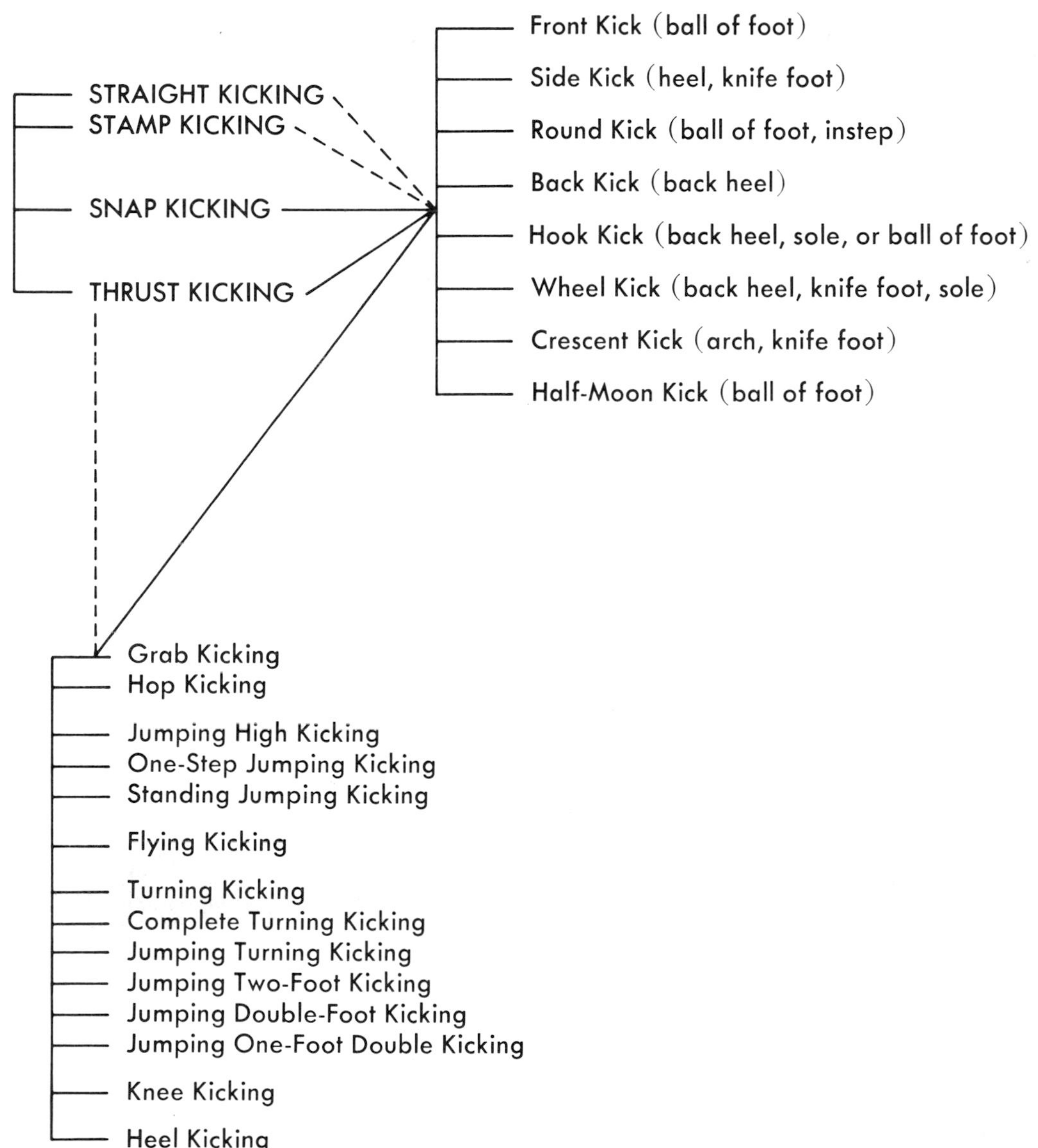

6. Main Targets of Attack

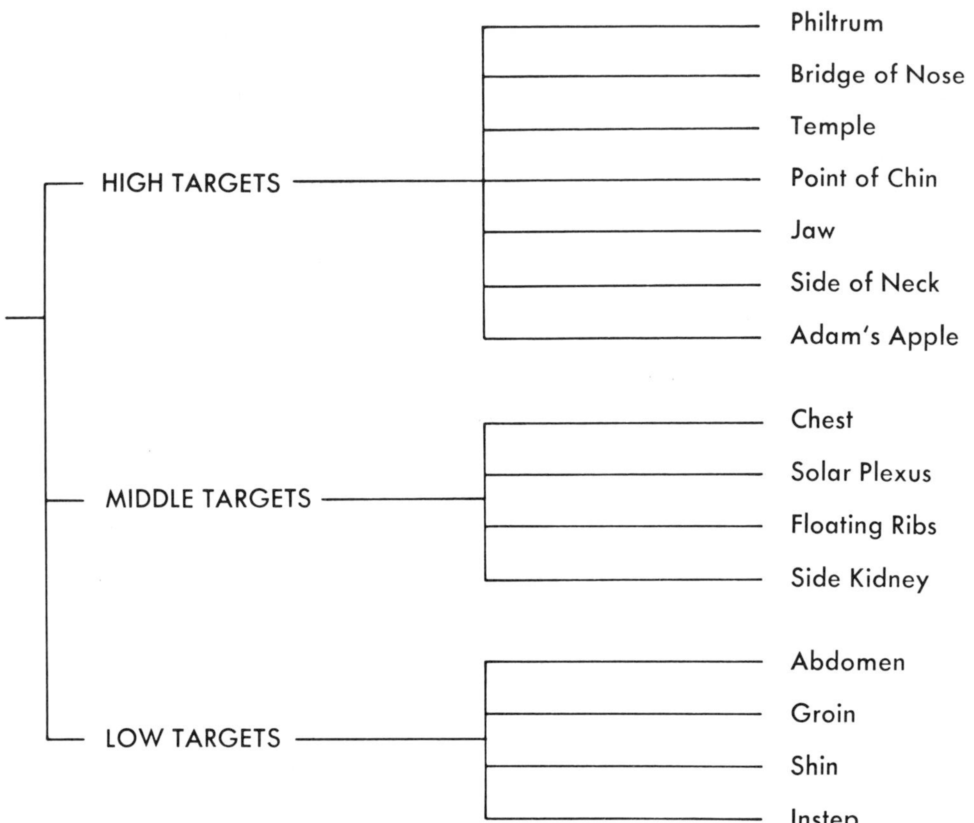

7. Basic Training Commands

Sequence	Command	Stance and Application
1.	Ready (*Choon-Bi*)	Assume Normal Attention Stance, eyes focused front, fists palm in in front of abdomen.
2.	Horseback-Stance Punch (*Ju-Choom-So-Ki Ji-Lu-Ki*)	Assuming Horseback Stance, execute (a) single, double, or triple punches at middle, high, or low level; or (b) Elbow Strikes upward, backward, inward, or outward.
3.	Low Block (*A-Le Mak-Ki*)	Assuming Front Stance, execute Low Blocks walking forward or backward by count.
4.	Regular Punch (*Pa-Lo Ji-Lu-Ki*)*	Execute Middle, High, or Low punches walking forward or backward in Front Stance.
5.	Middle Block (*Mom-Tong Mak-Ki*)	Execute Outside-to-Inside or Inside-to-Outside Middle Blocks walking forward or backward in Back Stance or in Front Stance.
6.	Front Kick (*Ap Cha-Ki*)	Execute Front Kicks walking forward in Front Stance.
7.	Knife-Hand Strike (*Sohn-Nal Chi-Ki*)	Execute Inside Knife Hand Strikes (palm up) walking in Front Stance.
8.	High Block (*Ol-Gool Mak-Ki*)	Execute High Blocks walking in Front Stance.
9.	Round Kick (*Dol-Rio Cha-Ki*)	Execute Round Kicks walking forward in Back Stance.
10.	Side Kick (*Yop Cha-Ki*)	Assuming Horseback Stance, facing to left or right side, shift into Cross Stance and execute side kicks, moving sideways.
11.	Knife-Hand Block (*Sohn-Nal Mak-Ki*)	Execute Knife-Hand Blocks (usually Middle Blocks, but may be High or Low Blocks when indicated) walking in Back Stance or Cat Stance.
12.	Reverse Punch† (*Ban-De Ji-Lu-Ki*)	Execute Reverse Punches (usually middle level) walking in Front Stance.

* What is termed "Regular Punch" in English is called "Reverse Punch" in Korea.
† What is termed "Reverse Punch" in English is called "Regular Punch" in Korea.

13.	Variations	Execute any of various techniques in different stances, as indicated.
14.	Intermediate and Advanced Applications	As indicated, the application of more advanced techniques in different stances or in sequence.

8. Miscellaneous Terminology

English	Korean
High (Upper) Part	*Ol-Gool*
Middle Part	*Mom-Tong*
Low Part	*A-Le*
Punch	*Ji-Lu-Ki*
Thrust	*Jji-Lu-Ki*
Strike	*Chi-Ki*
Block	*Mak-Ki*
Kick	*Cha-Ki*
Bow	*Kyong-Ne*
Attention	*Cha-Riot*
At Ease (Rest)	*Shi-Yo*
Ready	*Choon-Bi*
Start (Begin)	*Shi-Jak*
Stop	*Koo-Man*
Separate	*Kal-Lyo*
Continue	*Kye-Sok*
One-Step Sparring	*Han-Bon Kyo-Lu-Ki*
Three-Step Sparring	*Se-Bon Kyo-Lu-Ki*
Arranged Free Sparring	*Ma-Chu-O Kyo-Lu-Ki*
Free Sparring	*Kyo-Lu-Ki*
Form (Formal Exercise)	*Poom-Se*
Counting: 1	*Hana*
2	*Dool*
3	*Set*
4	*Net*
5	*Da-Sot*
6	*Yo-Sot*
7	*Il-Kop*
8	*Yo-Dol*
9	*A-Hop*
10	*Yol*

2

Basic Principles

One day, as a Zen master strolled through a field with his student, a pheasant started from a bush in front of them and ran awkwardly into a thicket. The student laughed and said, "Birds are so silly and defenseless." The Zen master swung his walking staff and struck the student across the shins. "Fly," he commanded.

All things have their weaknessses—and their strengths. Stone grinds scissors, scissors cuts paper, paper wraps stone. People think themselves weak because they do not know how to use their strength. The essence of Tae Kwon Do is to make the individual aware of his natural strengths and of how to apply them to the greatest advantage. In this way, the individual overcomes his only real weakness: his lack of faith in himself.

Patience is required. Wise men have said that he who finds it easy in the beginning has all the more difficulty later on. For some, even patience requires practice. The impatient may rush to develop flashy techniques to impress themselves and others of equal shallowness—only to discover, upon confronting one who is truly valorous, that all their tricks are to no avail. When one commits himself sincerely to the practice of Tae Kwon Do, he enters a reciprocal relationship, in which moral courage is enhanced by physical development, and vanity is exchanged for genuine confidence.

The mind must be calm, and the will determined. A troubled or distracted mental attitude will blur perception. It is better to react spontaneously in response to the opponent's threat, rather than to act hastily in anticipation of a move he may not make. To this end, the mind must be relaxed and open to perceive the opponent's intentions clearly, and one must practice the techniques relentlessly to develop a responsiveness which is instantaneous and correct, an intuitive reflex, requiring no thought or preparation. Response should be synchronized with perception: defense should begin *as* the opponent's attack begins. And one must respond without self-consciousness: attention must be wholly fixed on the opponent and the actions necessary to thwart his attack—without concern for any injury one may necessarily suffer in the process. One must realize and accept the fact that to stand and defend his life means to risk losing it. Once he has accepted the likelihood of death, fear cannot distract him, the opponent cannot intimidate him, and he is free to perceive and concentrate on the opponent's weaknesses, rather than his own. This is the total absorption of the *person* into the *act*, the enthusiasm of the unified spirit, which naturally triumphs over the spirit in disorder. It is the basic meaning of "focus" in this book.

Tae Kwon Do is a method of self-defense without weapons. Flesh and bone, the natural, vulnerable equipment of the body, are the only resources of the Tae Kwon Do practitioner. Therefore, the techniques of Tae Kwon Do are designed to train all the muscles and joints of the body to develop their ultimate capacities toward an integrated and totally efficient mechanism for defense. By applying the Yin and Yang principle to the soft and hard areas of the body, the very natures of these areas are exploited to advantage. What is "soft" is pliable, and is therefore not used to resist an attack so much as to give way before the onslaught, allowing the opponent's own momentum to carry him off balance, thus placing him in a poor position for continuing the assault and at the same time making him vulnerable to counterattack. What is "soft" is also movable, and is therefore trained to react with maximum speed and agility. What is "hard" is naturally resistant, and is therefore used to fend off blows to which the soft parts of the body should be vulnerable. What is "hard" is also forcible, and is thus a logical striking point, in which to concentrate one's strength for a counterattack.

The center of force is in the abdomen, and it is at this point that the flow of energy begins, and from which it goes outward, through the body, to the extremities. Thus, concentration—the integration of strength, speed, and muscular coordination, which is necessary to the execution of all the techniques in Tae Kwon Do—begins at the center.

3

Calisthenics, Breathing, and Meditation

The word "calisthenics" comes from the Greek *kallos*, meaning "beauty," and *sthenos*, meaning "strength." Calisthenics are the means to an end, the necessary preparation of the mind and body toward a graceful performance. Grace is economy of motion, speed, strength, and accuracy achieved with minimal effort. The practice of Tae Kwon Do requires that the joints and muscles of the body be limber and strong to avoid injury and to coordinate maneuvers effectively. One should give complete attention to these exercises while doing them in order to gain their full benefits and to prepare the mind for the concentration necessary in the performance of Tae Kwon Do.

It is recommended that at least ten to twenty minutes be devoted to the following exercises at the beginning of each practice session. If these calisthenics are done every day, including days when no Tae Kwon Do practice session is planned, the body will make rapid progress toward, and will sustain, an excellent condition for performance.

STRETCHING EXERCISES
(in the recommended order of performance)

1. Neck

a. Rotation: Stand normally, feet parallel, hands on hips, and roll head in a circular motion clockwise, keeping neck as relaxed as possible. Repeat several times, then reverse direction.

b. Direct Motion: Bend head straight forward, then straight back, then from side to side.

2. Shoulders

a. Raise each arm overhead in turn, and first pull it to the opposite side with the other hand, then push the elbow straight back.

b. Rotate the shoulders by extending the arms straight forward at shoulder level, fists clenched, and then swinging the arms out, then forward and up overhead, then down and around in a circular motion, returning to the front.

3. Side Stretching

a. Raise arms in front of chest at shoulder level, elbows bent and fists clenched, and twist at the hip as far as possible to each side, swinging the arms in the direction of the twist. In doing this exercise, stand with feet parallel and two shoulder-widths apart, and keep torso erect.

b. Standing normally, with feet one shoulder-width apart and hands on hips, bend at the hip straight over to each side, stretching as far as possible. *[upper right]*

c. Standing normally (as in b, above), with one hand on hip and other hand, open and palm down, held high over head—arm slightly bent—bend straight over to the side that has hand on hip, stretching as far as possible. Reverse position of hands and bend alternately to each side.

4. Back and Stomach

Standing normally, bend forward at the hips, keeping the knees locked straight, and touch the palms of both hands to the floor, then raise up and bend over backward as far as possible, bracing hands on buttocks.

5. Sides and Back

a. Spread feet two and a half shoulder-widths apart and, keeping knees locked straight, bend forward at the hips and twist to each side, swinging the arms to touch each hand to the opposite foot in turn.

b. Standing with feet spread two shoulder-widths apart and arms extended downward together, rotate the torso 360°, bending over at the hips as far as possible in each direction. Complete several rotations clockwise, then reverse direction. *[upper right]*

6. Knees

a. Standing with feet together and hands braced on knees, bend the knees, lowering the body with the torso erect, then rise up, bending forward at the hips to push the knees back straight with both hands.

b. Standing with feet together and hands braced on knees, as above, bend the knees slightly and rotate in each direction, pushing the knees back straight on each completion of the circular motion.

7. Fingers

Clasp hands in front of chest and open the palms, bending the fingers back. Then place fingertips of both hands together and press the palms together, bending the fingers back as far as possible.

8. Wrists

Grasp the extended fingers of each hand, in turn, with the other hand and press the extended hand backward toward the forearm, stretching the front of the wrist. Grasp the back of each hand, in turn, and press the hand forward toward the inside of the forearm, stretching the back of the wrist.

9. Leg Stretching

a. Stand with one leg straight back and the other, bent at the knee, one long step forward, placing the forward hand on the bent knee and the other hand on the hip. Stoop forward as low as possible, keeping the torso erect and the heel of the front (bent) leg on the floor. Then shift the forward hand down inside and around to the outside of the front foot and stoop forward as low as possible, trying to touch the elbows of both arms to the floor next to the front foot. Reverse legs and repeat.

b. Front and Side Splits: Extend one leg straight forward and the other straight back as far as possible, supporting yourself on your hands, and bend forward, touching your head to the front knee. Reverse legs and repeat. Turn to the front, keeping each leg extended straight out to the side as far as possible, and touch your head to the floor in front.

c. Sit with torso erect and knees bent outward, placing the soles of both feet together in front of you and holding them as close to the groin as possible. Use elbows to press knees outward and down as close to the floor as possible. Bend forward and try to touch your head to your toes.

d. Sit with one leg extended straight out in front and the other bent back behind you. Grasp the ankle in front with both hands and bend forward, touching your head to your knee. Reverse legs and repeat. *[upper right]*

e. Sit with one leg out straight and grasp the heel of the other leg, bent inward with the foot just in front of you, in one hand (when exercising the left leg, hold left heel in left hand; when exercising right leg, hold right heel in right hand). Straighten the bent leg, pulling it up and back as far as possible, then bend it again, bringing the foot back in front of you. Repeat several times in this manner, then with the other hand on the exercising knee, helping to push it straight. Reverse legs and repeat.

f. Front-Kick Stretch: Stand straight, with one leg extended straight up in front on the shoulder of an assistant, and have him grasp your foot and raise it as high as possible, while you keep your balance. Keep torso erect and inclined slightly forward.

g. Side-Kick Stretch: Stand straight, with one leg extended straight out and up on the assistant's shoulder, and have him raise the leg as high as possible. Keep the toes turned down, as if you were kicking with the heel. Keep your balance, holding your torso as erect as possible and twisted forward in the direction of the extended leg.

(*continued*)

h. When working without an assistant, stand straight and extend each leg, in turn, straight up and slightly outward, grasping the heel in the hand on the same side, pulling the leg up and out as much as possible while maintaining your balance, and placing the other hand on the extended knee to keep it locked straight.

10. Legs and Back

a. Sit with legs extended together straight forward, and have an assistant place his hands on your shoulders and press you forward to touch your head to your knees.

b. Standing back to back with an assistant, have him lock his arms in yours and bend forward, lifting you over on his back. In this position, the supporting assistant shifts from side to side and up and down gently, stretching your back muscles and joints.

c. Sit with legs extended out in front and roll backward, lifting legs straight overhead and back until toes touch the floor. Hold this position for a moment and breath deeply, using the diaphragm rather than the chest. Bend the legs until the knees touch the floor. Roll back slowly, until you are sitting up again with legs straight out on the floor in front of you.

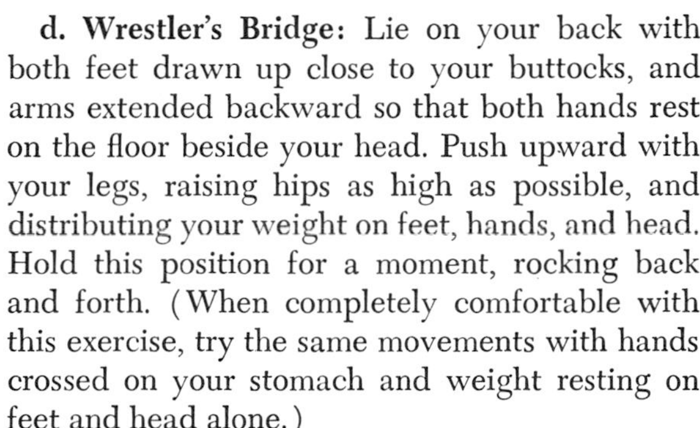

d. Wrestler's Bridge: Lie on your back with both feet drawn up close to your buttocks, and arms extended backward so that both hands rest on the floor beside your head. Push upward with your legs, raising hips as high as possible, and distributing your weight on feet, hands, and head. Hold this position for a moment, rocking back and forth. (When completely comfortable with this exercise, try the same movements with hands crossed on your stomach and weight resting on feet and head alone.)

STRENGTHENING EXERCISES

1. Push-Ups

a. Lie face down, with legs together and straight back and forefists at sides of chest, palm in. Raise the body by extending both arms together until they are straight, and lower it again to the floor. Do this several times, increasing repetitions in each subsequent session. Note that the weight must be carried on the first and second knuckles of the forefinger and middle finger, only, of both fists.

b. Repeat this exercise, placing weight on the five fingertips of both hands.

(*continued*)

c. Three-Finger Push-Ups: Repeat as above, placing weight on thumb, forefinger, and middle finger of both hands.

d. Two-Finger Push-Ups: Repeat as above, placing weight on thumb and forefinger, only, of both hands.

e. Rocking-Horse Push-Ups: Place weight on balls of feet and palms of both hands, with arms straight, and hips raised up and back. Rock forward, scooping chin, chest, and hips, in sequence, close to the floor, bending arms to do so, and then straighten arms, raising head and shoulders up and forward, and then rock back with arms straight, raising hips up and back into original position.

2. Sit-Ups

a. Lie on your back with feet together and drawn in slightly, knees bent upward, and clasp hands behind head. Sit up, keeping feet flat on floor, and bend straight forward, touching elbows to knees, then lie back again. Repeat several times in this manner, and again with legs straight.

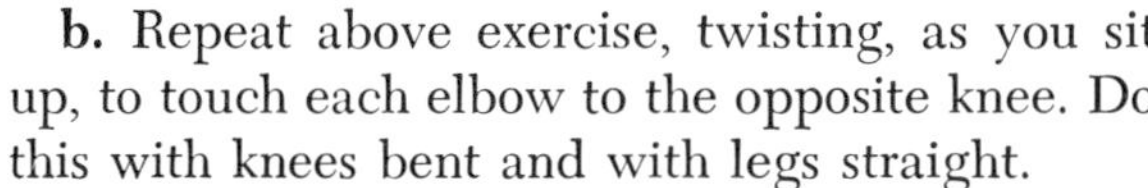

b. Repeat above exercise, twisting, as you sit up, to touch each elbow to the opposite knee. Do this with knees bent and with legs straight.

3. Handstand

Stoop down and place palms of both hands on the floor, and push up with both legs, keeping arms straight, until both legs are straight up over head. Have an assistant catch your ankles to help you keep your balance. Hold this position for a moment, and try walking on your hands, with the assistant holding your ankles.

BREATHING

Breath is essential to life. This statement may appear more simple than it really is. It implies that to live well, to be healthy, to be active and resilient, requires that one breathe correctly. Fresh air restores energy that is depleted in activity. The circulation of nutrients in the blood is enhanced by proper breathing. Inadequate air supply and improper breathing hamper restoration and cause mental weariness and muscular fatigue.

The practice of Tae Kwon Do places special demands on proper breathing, for it requires continuous mental alertness and sometimes involves considerable muscular effort over extended periods of time. In order to maintain a condition of optimum responsiveness, one must learn how to conserve his breath, and how to use it to advantage for added power. The following points should be borne in mind:

1. Breathe using the diaphragm rather than the chest. Animals and infants naturally breathe correctly this way, but people, as they grow older, sometimes develop tensions of which they are unaware in response to stressful situations in life. The muscular effects of these tensions center in the solar plexus, making the diaphragm tense and breathing, therefore, shallow. Practice breathing. Imitate the attitudes of sleep and of smelling. Make a conscious effort to smell the air you are breathing. When you are smelling or sleeping you are breathing correctly.

2. When performing calisthenics and the other Tae Kwon Do exercises, breathe rhythmically, conscious of all the parts of your being working harmoniously together: exhale at the moments of stress and inhale at the moments of relaxation. Inhale through the nostrils; the mouth may be used for exhaling when special emphasis is desired.

3. When you are practicing breathing, be conscious of all the space within your body that can contain the air: when inhaling, expand (relax) your muscles completely; when exhaling, contract the solar plexus completely, forcing all the used air out.

Deep-Breathing Exercise

1. Stand naturally, feet one shoulder-width apart, legs straight, hands crossed in front of abdomen.

2. Raise arms slowly forward and up, simultaneously inhaling slowly, using the diaphragm only, and taking air in through the nostrils, not the mouth.

3. Continue the smooth motion of the arms up, overhead, and outward to the sides, inhaling —when the diaphragm has expanded to the utmost—with the expanding chest, until the lungs are filled to capacity.

4. Slowly lower the arms to the sides, and simultaneously contract the diaphragm, exhaling as forcibly as possible (from the bottom up, so that the air leaves the abdomen first and the upper chest last). Exhale through the open mouth and, as you lower your arms, press the palms down, as if forcing the air out with the downward pressure of your hands.

5. Continue pressing the palms downward and inward, until the lungs are completely empty.

6. Return to the original position, with hands crossed in front of abdomen, and repeat the process.

Note: The exhalation is forcible, but not fast. The force may be increased by retarding the outward flow of air: press the tongue against the roof of the mouth and force the expelled air to pass out between them.

MEDITATION

The training of the mind is as fundamental to Tae Kwon Do as the training of the body. Concentration is critical to a successful performance. But the sort of concentration required in Tae Kwon Do is very special. One must concentrate on what he is doing, but one must not be self-conscious: the *person* must be absorbed in the *act*. On the other hand, life is continuously in flux, and one's attitude must be flexible and responsive to change, prepared for the unexpected. This is to say that you must be aware of what you are doing, but not to the exclusion of whatever is going on around you: Be aware of everything, and distracted by nothing.

In order for the average person to attain this state of concentration, it is necessary for him to train his mind to perceive without self-consciously thinking. One does this through meditation. The forms of Tae Kwon Do, as, for example, those illustrated in this book, are more than physical exercises: they are vehicles for active meditation.

Meditation is also possible with the body at rest. In this case, when you practice meditation, do not force your mind to concentrate on any one thing, but allow your mind to find its own focus. Open yourself to any awareness, but avoid distraction. Surrender curiosity and analysis. Make no effort to find meaning or significance in your perceptions. *Think* of nothing: let your mind reflect itself to you.

The following are two positions for meditation at rest. If you find that you require some focus to help you begin, focus upon your own feelings, literally, physically. If this is still too vague, then focus on your breathing: imagine the air as a silver thread.

Meditation Positions

1. Sitting

Sit with legs crossed in front, knees as close to the floor as is possible with comfort, and hands, clenched into fists, palm down on knees. Keep torso erect, in good posture; do not slump.

2. Kneeling

Kneel with knees together and sit back on your ankles. (Feet may be resting on insteps, with soles turned up, or resting on the balls of the feet, with toes bent back. This last position is a good exercise in stretching the toes, to facilitate curling them back when kicking with the balls of the feet.) Place hands on thighs, palm down. Keep torso erect, in good posture.

Note: Meditation is also possible while standing naturally, feet one shoulder-width apart, legs straight, and hands crossed on the belt, in front of the abdomen.

In any of these positions, one may meditate with eyes open or closed, whichever is most effective at the time. It is sometimes helpful to have the eyes half-closed, and focused at a point in space about three to five feet directly ahead.

4

Basic Stances

To practice Tae Kwon Do one must be able to move quickly and easily. But agility begins with balance. To walk, jump, kick, punch, and block effectively one must start from a stable position and be able to maintain proper balance in the transition from one technique to another. In sparring with another person of equal ability, for example, in order to get through his defense it is advisable to draw him off balance first, physically or psychologically, and thus provide an "opening" for your attack. In attacking, you yourself must be properly balanced so that your weight and strength are coordinated to move in the chosen direction. It follows that you must stand, walk, and turn in such a manner as to permit you to shift into a position of defense and counterattack in any direction at an instant's notice.

The basic stances shown below are essential to this art, and they must be practiced diligently until they are mastered, before any real progress can be made in the techniques of movement.

ATTENTION STANCES *(Pyun-Hi-So-Ki)*

1. Normal Stance *(Choon-Bi-So-Ki)*

a. Stand straight, eyes focused front, body relaxed.

b. Place feet one foot-length apart and parallel, with toes pointed forward and legs straight. Weight is evenly distributed on both legs.

c. Hold fists, tightly clenched, in front of abdomen, palm in, with elbows slightly bent.

2. Open Stance *(Pal-Ja-So-Ki)*

a. Stand straight, eyes focused front.

b. Place feet with heels one foot-length apart, toes pointed outward at about 30° angle.

3. Pigeon-Toe Stance ***(An-Jong-So-Ki)***

Same as Open Stance, but toes pointed inward at about 30° angle.

INFORMAL STANCES (*Mo-A-So-Ki*) (feet together)

1. Normal Stance ***(Mo-A-So-Ki)***

a. Stand straight, eyes focused front.

b. Place feet together, toes pointed forward.

2. V Stance ***(Cha-Riot-So-Ki)***

a. Stand straight, eyes focused front.

b. Place feet with heels together, toes pointed outward at about 30° angle.

HORSEBACK STANCE *(Ju-Choom-So-Ki)*

a. Place feet two and a half foot-lengths apart and parallel, toes pointed forward.

b. Bend both knees outward in a half-squat, feeling the tension of your legs pushing outward against your feet, weight evenly distributed on both feet.

c. Pull buttocks back slightly, keep upper torso erect, shoulders back.

d. Place clenched fists close to hips, palm up, elbows straight back.

DIAGONAL HORSEBACK STANCE (*Ap-Ju-Choom*)

Note: This is similar to Horseback Stance, twisted forward.

a. Place feet two foot-lengths apart, side to side, and one step apart, front to back, both feet pointed forward and slightly inward.

b. Bend back knee outward, and front knee slightly inward.

c. Tilt torso slightly forward.

d. Weight is evenly distributed (on heel of front foot and ball of back foot).

FRONT STANCE (*Ap-Ku-Bi*)

a. Place feet one and a half steps apart, front to back, with heels one foot-length apart, side to side. Point toes of front foot straight forward and toes of back foot out about 45°.

b. Bend front knee forward until it is directly over toes of front foot, and lock back leg straight.

c. Keep upper torso centered and erect, shoulders back, eyes focused front.

d. Weight is distributed 70 percent on front leg and 30 percent on back leg, with both feet flat on the floor.

HIGH FRONT STANCE (*Ap-So-Ki*)

Note: This is similar to Front Stance, but:

a. Feet are one step apart, front to back.

b. Both knees are very slightly bent.

c. Weight distribution is same as Front Stance.

BACK STANCE (*Duit-Ku-Bi*)

a. Place feet one step apart, front to back, with front foot pointed straight forward and back foot turned out 90°—heel of back foot in a direct line with heel of front foot.

b. 80 percent of weight is on back leg, with both feet flat on floor.

c. Bend both knees outward.

d. Eyes are focused front, and upper torso is held erect and turned obliquely away from the front, providing a minimal target to attack.

CAT STANCE (*Bom-So-Ki*)

Note: This is similar to Back Stance, but:

a. Front foot is one very short step in front of back foot, with only the surface between the ball and the toes of the front foot touching the floor (heel of front foot is raised one fist-width above floor).

b. Heel of back foot is in direct line with ball of front foot, but toes of back foot are turned out 45°.

c. Weight is 100 percent on back foot, with both knees bent outward.

CROSS STANCES (*Ko-A-So-Ki*)

1. Forward Side-Cross Stance

a. Place 90 percent of weight on supporting foot.

b. Slide other foot into position across and in front of supporting foot.

2. Backward Side-Cross Stance

a. Place 90 percent of weight on supporting foot.

b. Slide other foot into position across and in back of supporting foot.

3. Front Cross Stance

a. Place 90 percent of weight on supporting foot, which is in front, with toes pointing forward.

b. Bend knee of front (supporting) leg sharply forward.

c. Hook back foot around the heel of front foot, with only the ball of the back foot touching the floor.

d. Bend knee of back leg outward.

CRANE STANCES (*Hak-Da-Ri-So-Ki*)

1. Foot at the Side

a. Place 100 percent of weight on supporting leg, with knee bent slightly forward and toes pointing forward.

b. Raise other foot into position beside knee of supporting leg.

2. Foot Behind

a. Place 100 percent of weight on supporting leg, with knee bent slightly (as above).

b. Raise other foot into position with instep hooked behind knee of supporting leg.

5

Walking, Turning, Lunging

When you have practiced the basic stances until you can assume them comfortably, begin seriously practicing the patterns of walking, turning, and lunging. It is necessary to perfect these fundamental maneuvers before the techniques of blocking, striking, and kicking can be made truly effective. Stability is essential. This cannot be stressed too strongly. To achieve a balanced stance is only the beginning. Balance must be maintained while moving—and in practicing Tae Kwon Do, one is moving most of the time. When standing still, one is merely poised between the completion of one technique and the beginning of the next. And when moving in one direction, one must be prepared—i.e., balanced and always ready—to change direction at an instant's notice. The basic stances and maneuvering patterns of Tae Kwon Do are designed to prepare one to expect the unexpected.

The patterns of movement shown below should be practiced diligently at the beginning of every session, before one goes on to the forms or other techniques.

When executing these maneuvers, concentrate on the following points:

1. Keep your balance well centered always (have someone test your balance by pushing you gently from the front, back, and each side).

2. Shift your weight smoothly, avoid awkward transitions. When one foot is being extended, your weight should be firmly balanced on the foot that is still in place.

3. Keep your torso erect and centered above the hips. Do not lean in the direction you intend to move: this would telegraph your intention and overcommit you, preventing you from changing direction quickly and easily.

4. Keep hips and shoulders parallel to the floor and moving in a straight line from one position to the next: your progress should not be noticeable, except in the movement of your feet.

5. Slide your feet forward, backward, or to the side very close to, but not quite touching, the floor (just high enough, ideally, to allow a single sheet of rice paper to lie undisturbed on the floor beneath you), and bring them to rest in the new position smoothly and silently, without a visible jerk or audible thump.

FRONT STANCE

1. Walking Forward

side view

a. Assume Ready Stance (stand straight, feet parallel and one foot-length apart, toes pointed forward).

side view

b. Slide one foot straight forward one long step (one and a half steps in length).

side view

c. Assume Front Stance (70 percent of weight on front leg, which is bent forward at the knee; back leg locked straight).

(*continued*)

side view

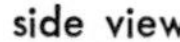

d. Slide back foot forward one long step, i.e., one and a half steps (past front foot), describing a concave arc (as you slide back foot forward, shift it in, to pass one-half foot-length near stationary foot, and out to the side again, one foot-length, as it extends forward). The knee of the stationary foot stays slightly bent until the moving foot slides into the new position—at which instant, the knee of the stationary foot locks straight in back, as the front leg, bent forward, assumes 70 percent of your weight.

Note: The concave arc described by the advancing foot serves the purpose of keeping your weight centered, enabling you to shift your balance smoothly.

side view

2. Walking Backward

This is similar to walking forward, except that the front foot slides, in a concave arc, backward one long step past stationary foot.

3. Turning About-Face*

a. Assume Front Stance.

b. Shift back foot straight across, sideways, into position behind and one foot-length to the opposite side of front foot.

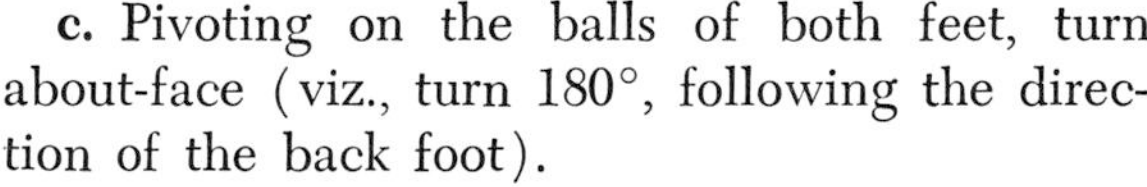

c. Pivoting on the balls of both feet, turn about-face (viz., turn 180°, following the direction of the back foot).

d. Immediately assume Front Stance (70 percent of weight on front leg, bent forward, and back leg locked straight).

* The directions given above are for beginners only. Beyond the beginner level, the turn is accomplished by lifting the back foot slightly, pivoting on the ball of the front foot, and turning about-face while simultaneously shifting the back foot—now the front foot—into the new position, one long step forward and one foot-length to the side of the pivoting foot.

4. Quarter Turn

a. Assume Front Stance, left foot forward.

b. Bend right knee, shifting your weight onto right (back) leg. Simultaneously slide left foot back (describing a concave arc), passing close to right foot, and out one long step (one and a half steps in length) to the left, pivoting on right foot and turning 90° to face left.

c. Assume Front Stance (left foot forward).

5. Three-Quarter Turn

a. Assume Front Stance, right foot forward.

b. Pivoting on right (front) foot, slide left (back) foot out, back, and around in a wide arc, turning 270° to the left (three-quarters of a circle), to face right.

c. Assume Front Stance, left foot forward.

6. Full Turn*

a. Assume Front Stance.

b. Bend back knee, shifting weight onto back leg and lift front foot slightly and swing it around backward.

c. Simultaneously pivoting on the ball of back foot, turn 180° (following the direction of the swinging foot) to face the opposite way.

d. Slide swinging foot forward one long step, into position one and a half steps in front and one foot-length to the side of pivoting foot. Immediately assume Front Stance, bending front leg forward at the knee and locking back leg straight.

* The essential differences between this Full Turn and Turning About-Face (see page 47) are:

- In the Full Turn, the foot that was in front at the beginning is in front at the end.
- In the Full Turn, in addition to turning, one simultaneously advances one long step forward in the new direction.

BACK STANCE

side view

1. Walking Forward

a. Assume Back Stance (feet one step apart, with heels in a direct line, front to back; toes of front foot pointing straight ahead, toes of back foot turned out at 90° angle to front foot; 80 percent of weight on back leg, both knees bent out).

side view

side view

b. Shifting weight forward, pivot on the ball of front foot and slide back foot forward one step (past pivoting foot). Keep both knees bent as you move, so that hips, shoulders, and eyes do not rise above their original level but proceed in smooth, straight lines parallel to floor. Keep eyes focused front.

c. Simultaneously, as back foot slides forward, turn hips and torso in the direction of the pivoting foot.

side view

side view

d. Immediately assume Back Stance.

side view

2. Walking Backward

This is similar to Walking Forward, except that you pivot on back foot and slide front foot backward one step past pivoting foot.

3. Turning About-Face

a. Assume Back Stance.

b. Shift weight to front foot and simultaneously shift back foot out and back. Simultaneously pivoting on the ball of front foot, turn (180° in the direction of the shifting back foot) about-face.

c. Immediately assume Back Stance.

Note: For Quarter Turn, Three-Quarter Turn, and Full Turn in Back Stance, the same principles apply as in Front Stance (see pages 48–50).

HORSEBACK STANCE

Note: Walking in Horseback Stance is, in effect, walking to the left or the right side, rather than forward or backward. Horseback Stance is occasionally used in attacking to the front, as in punching, or striking with elbows or hands, but it is a difficult position to defend to the front, as it presents the whole breadth of the body to the opponent. One moves out of this position quickly, therefore, and uses Horseback Stance more effectively to advance, or go back and counterattack, to either side, in free sparring because it offers only a narrow target to the opponent.

1. Full-Step Advance

a. Assume Horseback Stance. Focus eyes to the right (toward an imaginary opponent).

b. Shift weight to right foot and simultaneously lift left foot (into position near right knee), pointing raised left knee forward and to the right.

c. Simultaneously, i.e., continuing in one smooth action, turn hips and torso 180° to the right (about-face), pivoting on ball of right foot and sliding left foot out to the left side one long step (two foot-lengths) toward opponent. Throughout, keep eyes focused toward opponent.

Assume Horseback Stance, eyes focused to the left (toward opponent).

2. Full-Step Back

This is similar to Full-Step Advance, except that front foot is lifted and swung around backward and hips and torso turn 180° backward, following the direction of the retreating foot.

3. Close-Step Advance

a. Assume Horseback Stance, eyes focused to the right.

b. Shift weight to right foot and simultaneously slide left foot into position next to right foot, keeping knees bent.

c. Immediately shift weight to left foot and slide right foot out one long step to the right.

d. Immediately assume Horseback Stance.

4. Cross-Step Advance—Crossing in Back

a. Assume Horseback Stance, eyes right.

b. Shift weight to right foot and simultaneously slide left foot in to cross just in back of right foot, keeping knees bent. (Mainly used as preparation for Back Kick—to the right—with right foot.)

c. Immediately shift weight to left foot and slide right foot out (crossing in front of left foot) one long step to the right.

d. Assume Horseback Stance, eyes right.

5. Cross-Step Advance—Crossing in Front

a. Assume Horseback Stance (as above).

b. Shift weight to right foot and simultaneously slide left foot in to cross just in front of right foot. (Mainly used as preparation for Side Kick—to the right—with right foot.)

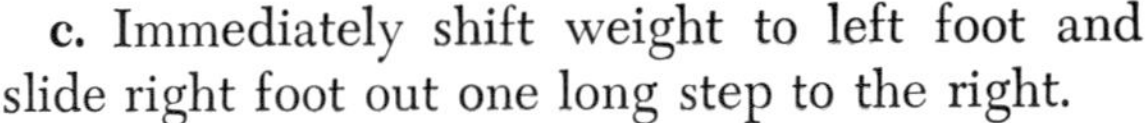

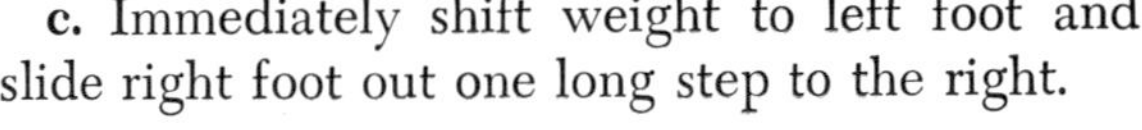

c. Immediately shift weight to left foot and slide right foot out one long step to the right.

d. Assume Horseback Stance, eyes right.

LUNGING

Note: A lunge is a sudden, quick movement toward a point some distance away, requiring an extension of the body in order to reach it. The lunge is used in Tae Kwon Do as a technique of attacking an opponent out of normal reach with a punch, strike, or kick.

1. Lunge to the Front

a. Assume Ready Stance, eyes front.

b. Slide right foot one quick long step forward.

c. Immediately assume Front Stance.

Note: Sliding forward into Front Stance constitutes a lunge in that the body is extended one long step. This lunge may be used from an original position in Front Stance or in Back Stance by sliding the back foot forward.

2. Leap to the Front

a. Assume Ready Stance.

b. Leap forward one quick long step, bring weight down on right foot, toes pointing forward.

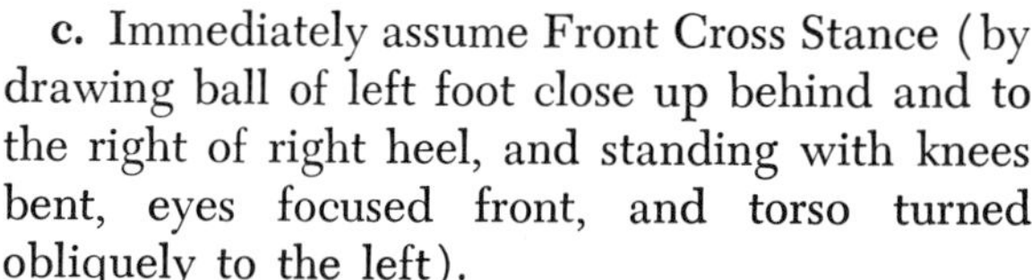

c. Immediately assume Front Cross Stance (by drawing ball of left foot close up behind and to the right of right heel, and standing with knees bent, eyes focused front, and torso turned obliquely to the left).

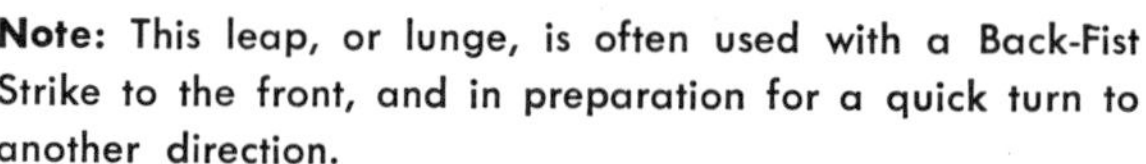

Note: This leap, or lunge, is often used with a Back-Fist Strike to the front, and in preparation for a quick turn to another direction.

3. Lunge to the Side

a. Assume Ready Stance, eyes focused to the right.

b. Slide right foot out one quick long step to the right.

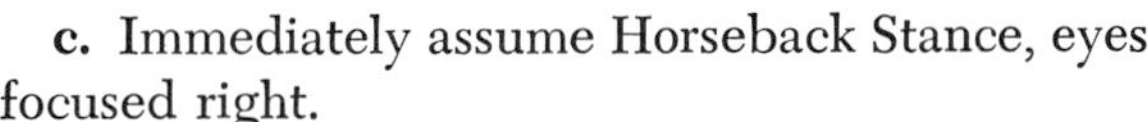

c. Immediately assume Horseback Stance, eyes focused right.

Note: The lunge may be further extended from Back Stance or from Horseback Stance by taking a quick short step, or hop, forward with the back foot before extending the front foot.

6

Basic Striking Weapons, and Vital Points

Since the only physical defense of the Tae Kwon Do practitioner is his own body, considerable attention is given to developing the hard areas of the body as striking weapons. Any hard area could, theoretically, be used for this purpose, but the techniques of Tae Kwon Do focus on those areas, such as the hands, feet, elbows, and knees, in which strength can most readily be concentrated to the greatest effect. To convert them into effective weapons takes years of conscientious training and discipline.

HANDS (*Sohn*)

1. Closed-Fist Strikes

a. Forefist (*Chu-Mok*)

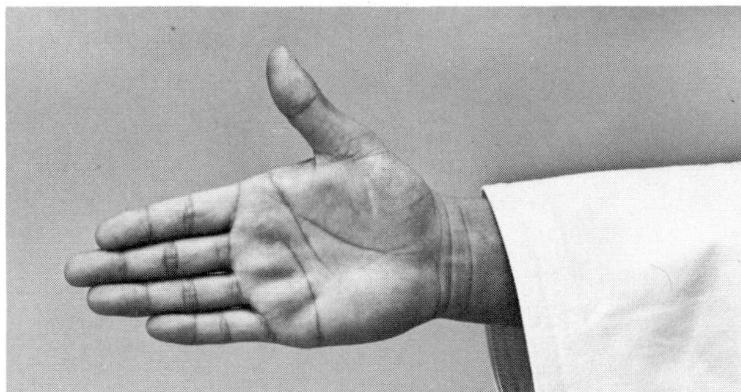

This is the most basic and frequently used striking weapon. The first two knuckles of the forefinger and the middle finger constitute the striking surface. It is necessary to practice constantly to develop the tight, rigid fist and to toughen the skin covering the knuckles, all of which go toward forging an effective striking weapon.

The Forefist is made by tightly clenching the four fingers—beginning with the little finger, and closing the other fingers in succession—and then closing the thumb down firmly against the forefinger and middle finger. The fingers must be closed as tightly as possible, so that none may be jarred out of place by the force of contact.

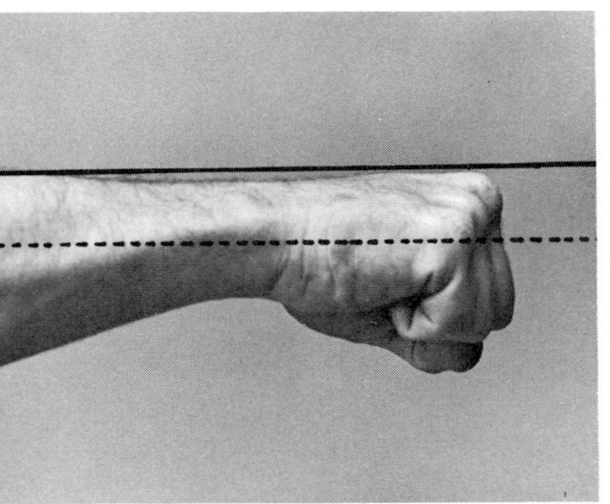

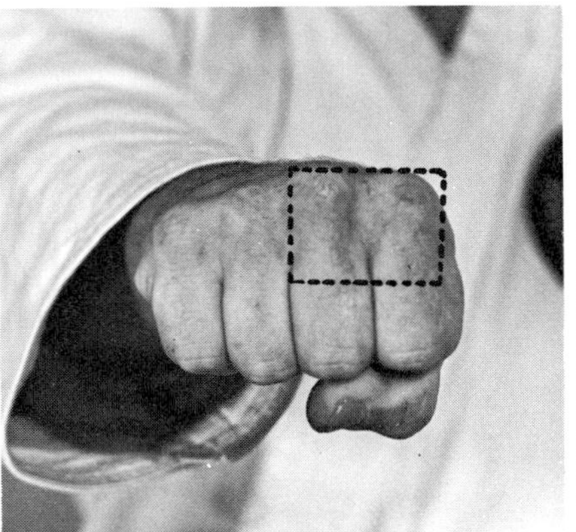

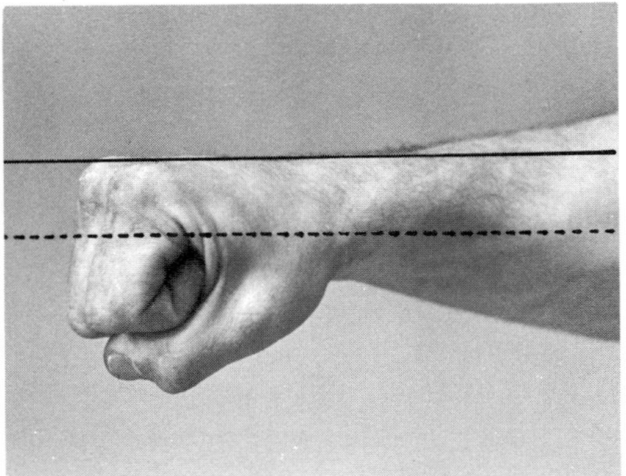

The fist, wrist, and forearm are held rigidly in a straight line—from the center of the forearm through the wrist to the center of the striking surface (between the knuckles of the forefinger and middle finger), and from the center of the forearm through the wrist to the horizontal level of the first knuckles of both forefinger and middle finger.

When punching, the Forefist normally starts, palm up, at the hip, and is thrust with as much speed and force as possible to the full extent of the arm—and at the last instant before contact, the wrist is snapped around, so that the palm is down when striking, and the fist, wrist, and elbow form a straight line.

The Forefist is useful in strikes to the face, chin, chest, stomach, or abdomen, and is also effective in blocking kicks, strikes, and punches.

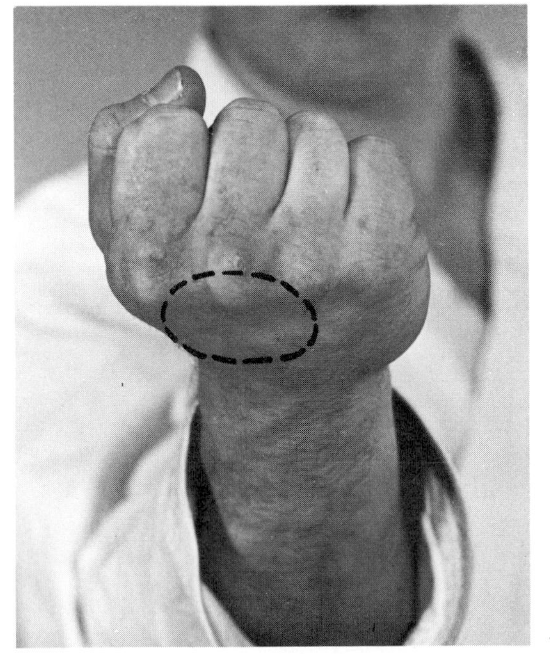

b. Back Fist (*Doong-Chu-Mok*)

Make a Forefist, but bend the wrist slightly back. The striking point is the backs of the first knuckles of the forefinger and middle finger.

This is effective in strikes to the face, temples, and abdomen, and in blocking.

(*continued*)

c. Hammer Fist *(Me-Chu-Mok)*

Clench the fingers as in Forefist, but the striking surface is the outer edge of the fist, between the wrist and the little finger.

This is the most powerful downward strike. It is effective in striking downward or outward to the head, face, elbow, ribs, collarbone, and other hard surfaces, and in blocking.

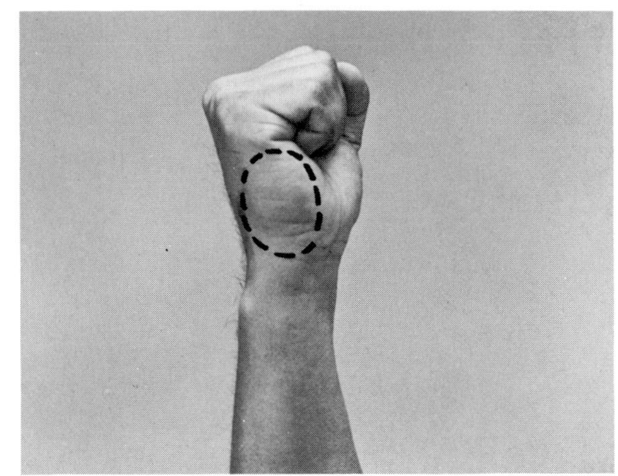

d. Forefinger One-Knuckle Fist *(In-Ji-Chu-Mok)*

Clench fingers as in Forefist, but jut the second knuckle of forefinger outward to make a point, supporting it with the thumb.

Effective in attacks to the temple, between the eyes, the point where the nose meets the upper lip, and other small areas of vulnerability.

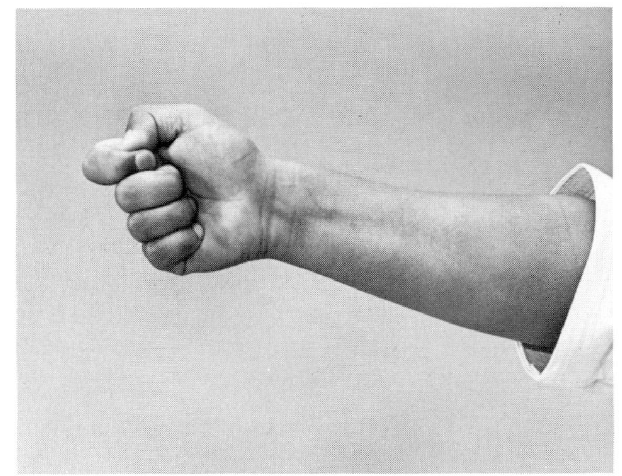

e. Middle-Finger One-Knuckle Fist
(Bam-Chu-Mok)

Same as Forefinger One-Knuckle Fist, but jut out second knuckle of middle finger.

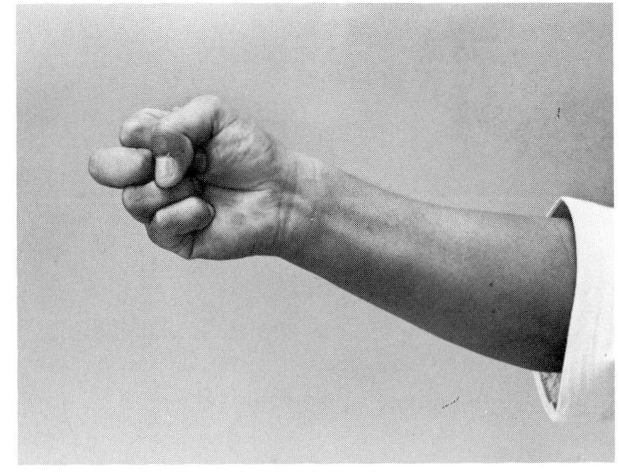

f. Two-Knuckle Fist (*Doo-Bam-Chu-Mok*)

Jut out second knuckles of both forefinger and middle finger. Uses are the same as One-Knuckle Fist.

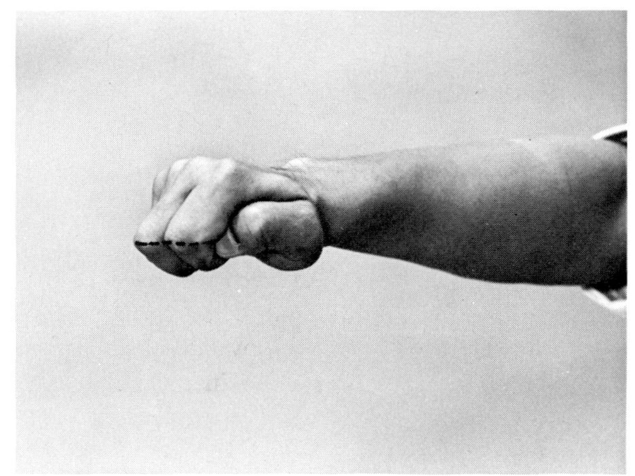

g. Four-Knuckle Fist (*Pyun-Chu-Mok*)

Jut out second knuckles of four fingers, with middle finger forming the outermost point. Uses are the same as One-Knuckle Fist. May also be used in attacks to solar plexus.

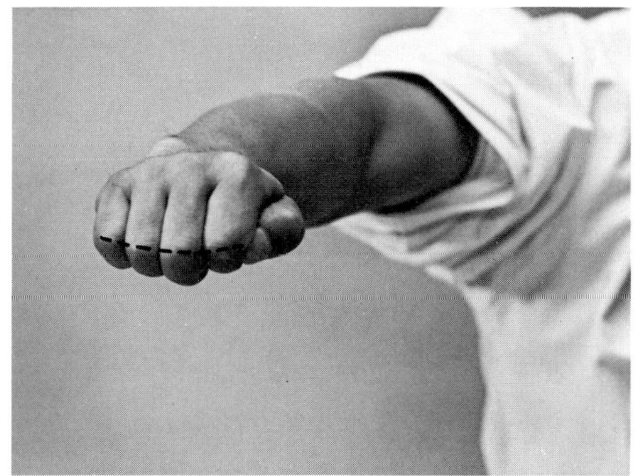

h. Thumb-Knuckle Fist (*Om-Ji-Chu-Mok*)

Close four fingers tightly, as in Forefist, but press the tip of the thumb against the side of the second knuckle of the forefinger, jutting the second knuckle of the thumb out to the side. The striking point is this second knuckle of the thumb, and it is used, with the fist palm down, in attacks to the temple, the point where the nose meets the upper lip, and the ribs.

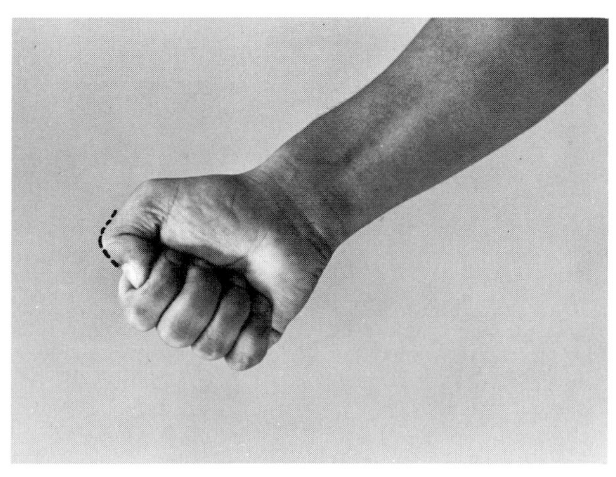

2. Open-Hand Strikes

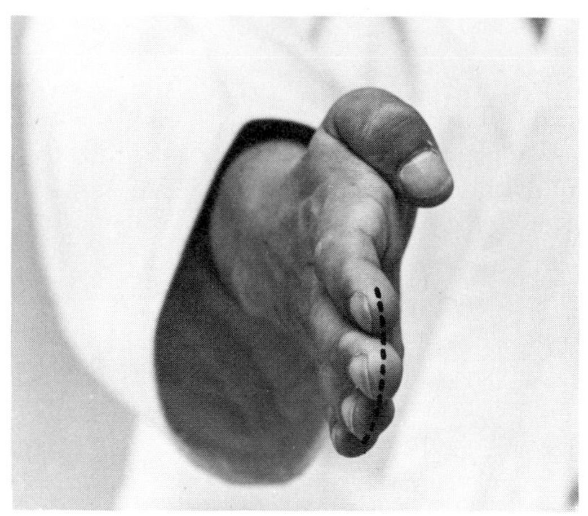

a. **Spear Hand** (*Pyun-Sohn-Koot*)

Hold hand rigid, with fingers straight out together and thumb close against palm. The striking area is the tips of the fingers.

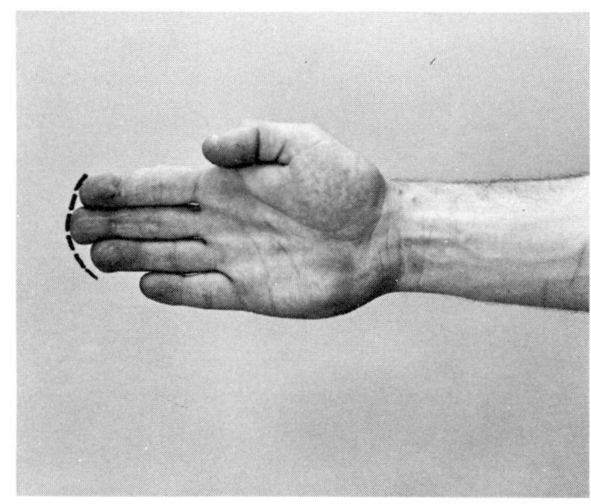

(1) Vertical Spear Hand: holding the hand thumb uppermost. This is effective in attacks to the solar plexus.

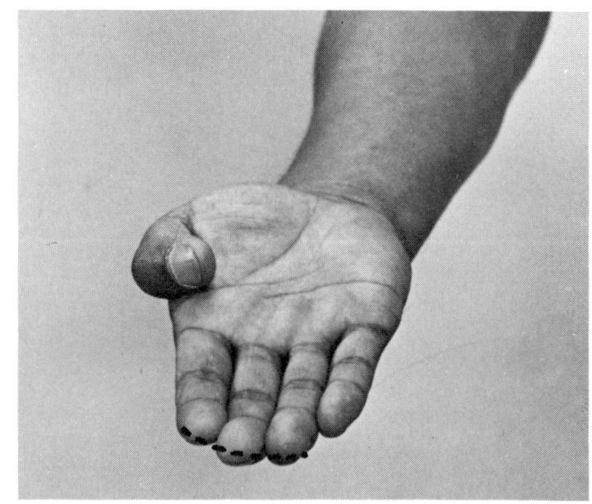

(2) Horizontal Spear Hand: holding the hand palm up. Effective in attacks to the ribs, and throat.

(3) Two-Finger Spear Hand *(Ka-Wi-Sohn-Koot)*: Extend forefinger and middle finger in **V** position, with other fingers closed and the palm down. Effective in attacks to the eyes.

(4) One-Finger Spear Hand *(In-Ji-Sohn-Koot)* Extend the forefinger, with other fingers closed. Effective in attacks to the solar plexus and throat.

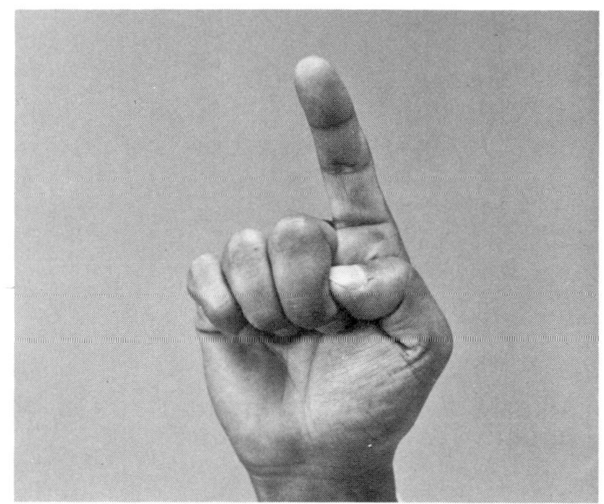

b. Tiger-Mouth Hand (*A-Kum-Sohn*)

Extend the four fingers together and the thumb open and opposite. The striking area is the curve between the thumb and forefinger. Useful in scissors-like thrust to the throat, with the palm down.

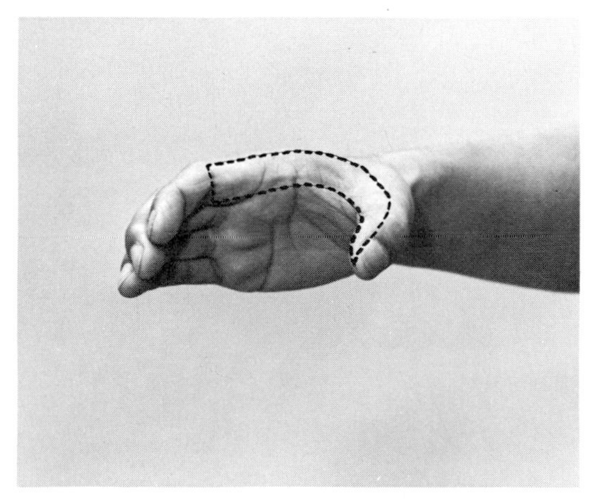

(*continued*)

c. **Chicken-Beak Hand** (*Sohn-Koot-Jo-Ki*)

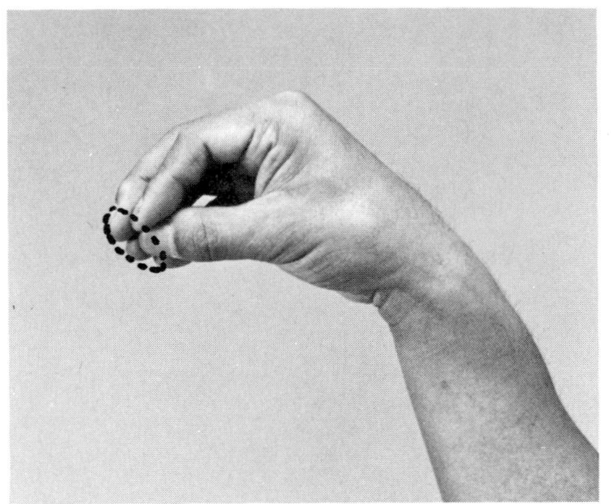

Extend the fingers so that all five fingertips meet together in a point (the striking point). Useful in attacking downward or straight ahead, especially in attacking the eyes.

d. **Knife Hand** (*Sohn-Nal*)

Extend the four fingers, keeping the hand rigid—especially tensing the ring finger and pinkie—and press the thumb down against the palm. The striking area is the outer edge of the hand, between the base joint of the pinkie and the heel of the hand. (The closer to the heel of the hand one strikes, the more force at the instant of contact.)

The Knife Hand is very effective in strikes to the face, neck, temple, collarbone, ribs, and abdomen. It is also used in blocking arm and leg attacks.

Depending on the angle of attack, the Knife Hand may be used:

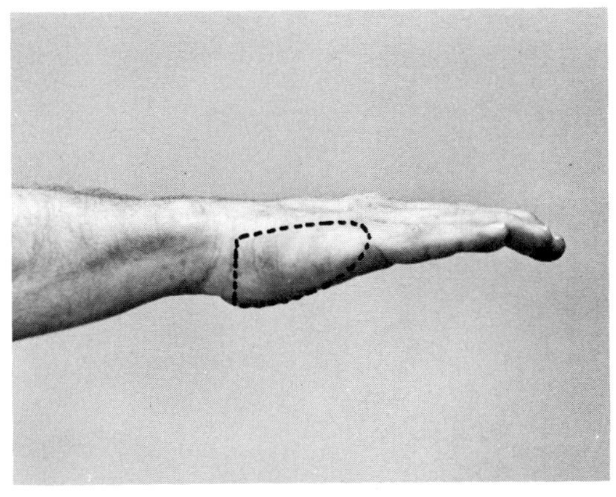

(1) Palm down (striking outward).

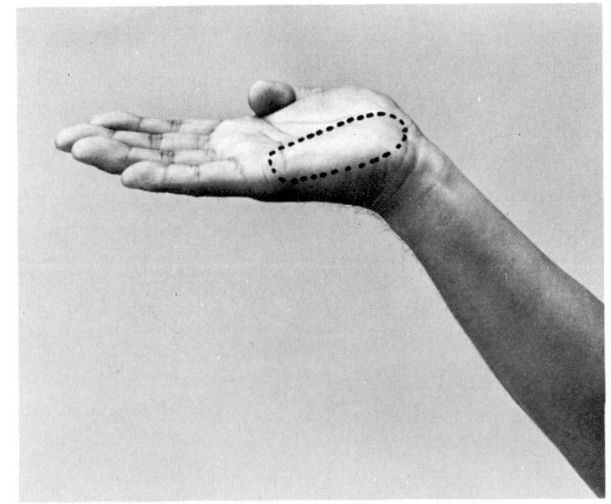

(2) Palm up (striking inward).

(3) Vertically (striking downward).

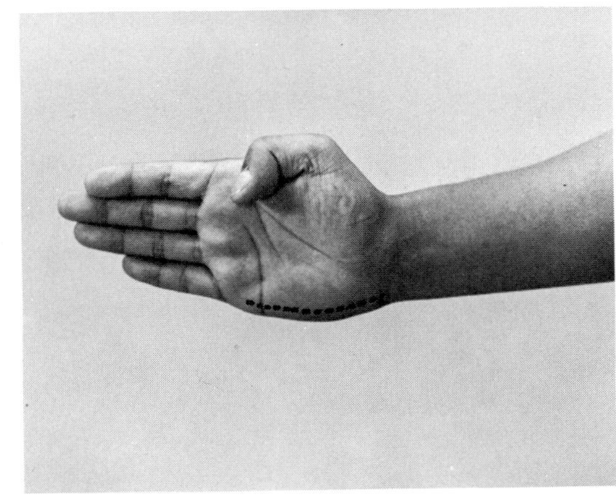

e. Ridge Hand *(Sohn-Nal-Doong)*

Extend the four fingers straight out, holding them rigidly together, and bend the thumb down against the palm.

The striking edge is the first knuckle of the forefinger, with the palm held up or down. This is used in strikes to the head or abdomen.

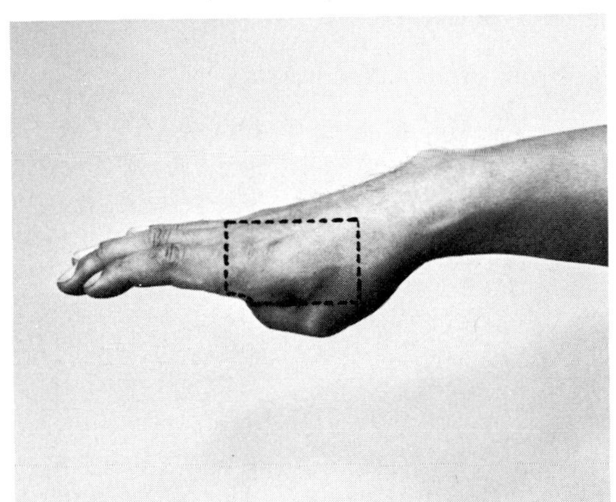

f. Palm Heel *(Ba-Tang-Sohn)*

Hold the hand open, bent back at the wrist. The fingers and thumb are curved and held away from the palm.

The striking area is the heel of the palm and the base of the thumb. The hand is held with the fingers up or down. The Palm Heel is used in strikes to the face, especially the chin, stomach, and the abdomen. It is also effective in blocking.

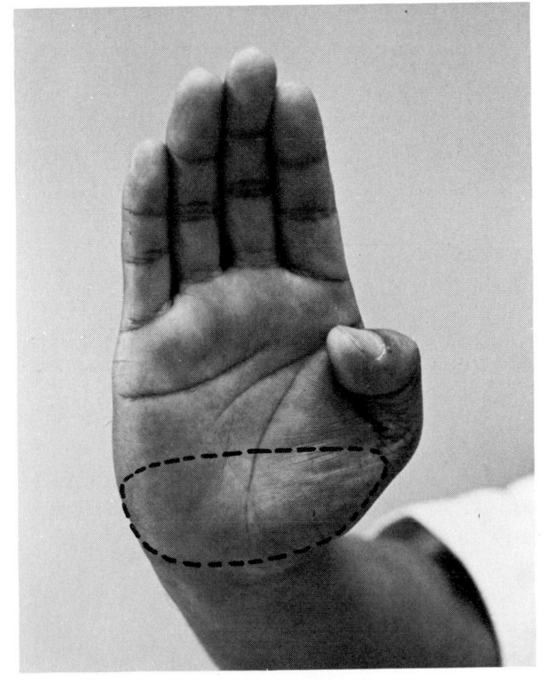

g. Bear Hand (*Gom-Sohn*)

Jut out the second knuckles of the fingers, as in the Four-Knuckle Fist. The striking area is the circle formed by the thumb, fingertips, and palm. It is used in ripping strikes to the ears and face.

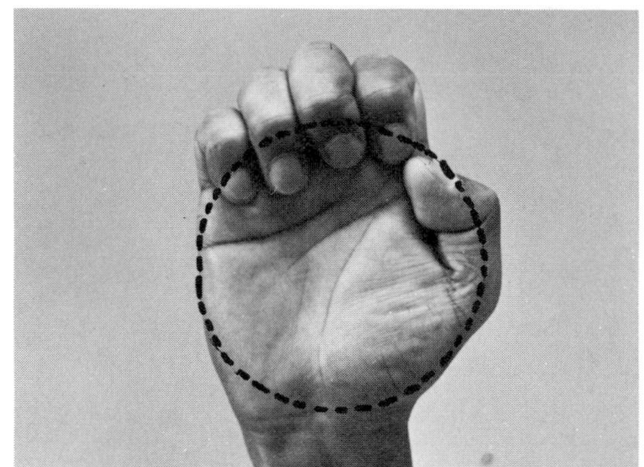

h. Back Hand (*Sohn-Doong*)

Extend the fingers together with the thumb closed. The striking area is the back of the hand up to the first knuckles of the fingers. It is useful in strikes to the face and ears, and in blocking.

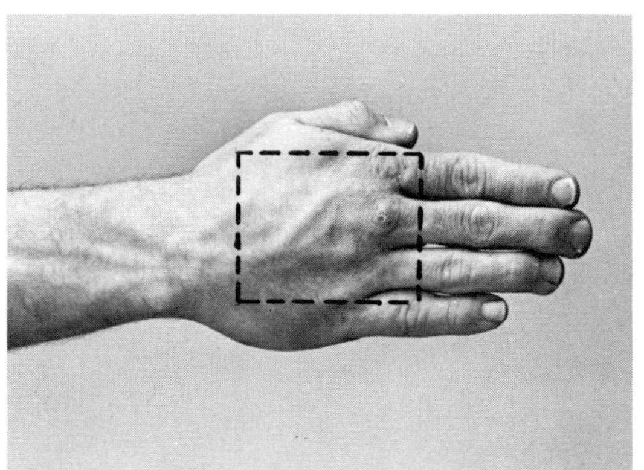

i. Ripping Hand (*Gal-Kwi-Sohn*)

Hold the five fingers half-bent toward the palm. The tips of the fingers (the striking points) are used in grabbing and ripping attacks to the eyes, face, neck, and ribs.

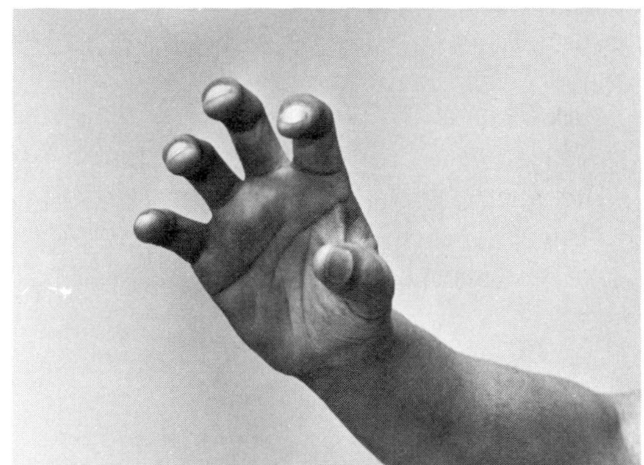

j. Pincers Hand *(Jip-Ke-Sohn)*

Close the other fingers against the palm, holding the forefinger and thumb half-bent toward each other. The striking points are the tips of the forefinger and thumb. The Pincers Hand is used in attacks to the eyes, nose, and throat.

WRISTS

Ox Jaw *(Sohn-Mok)*

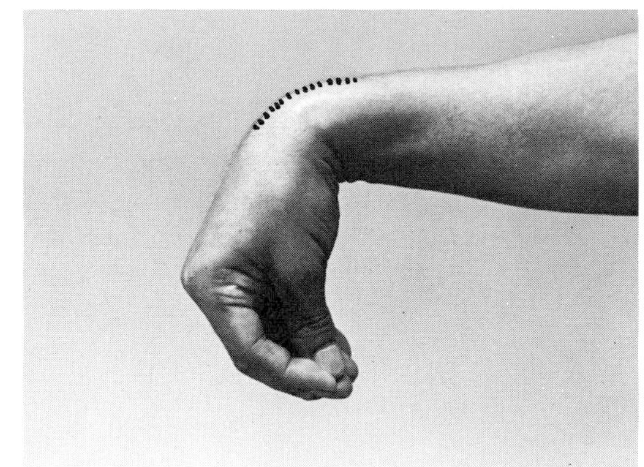

Hold fingers loosely in position similar to the Chicken Beak. Bend the wrist so that the palm of the hand is moved toward the inner forearm.

The striking area is the back of the wrist. It is used in upward, downward, or side-to-side strikes. It is also used in advanced blocking techniques.

FOREARMS *(Pal-Mok)*

The four surfaces of the lower forearm are very effective in blocking hand strikes and kicks, and may also be used in striking.

Close the hand tightly in a Forefist and hold the wrist straight. The striking surface depends on the blocking position:

1. Back Forearm *(Doong-Pal-Mok)*

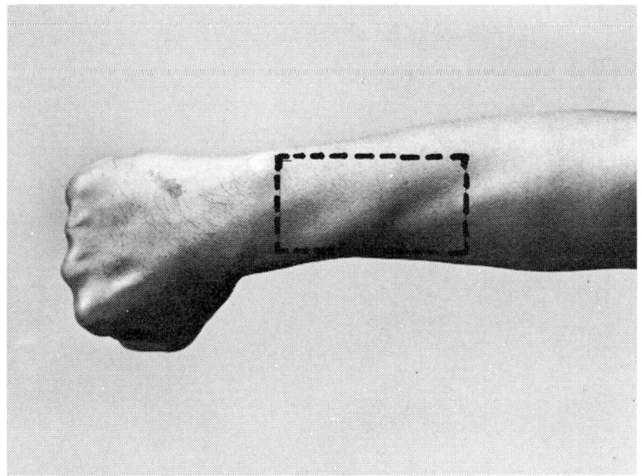

The striking area is the flat back surface of the lower forearm. This is called Back Forearm Strike when used as a striking weapon.

2. Front Forearm *(Mit-Pal-Mok)*

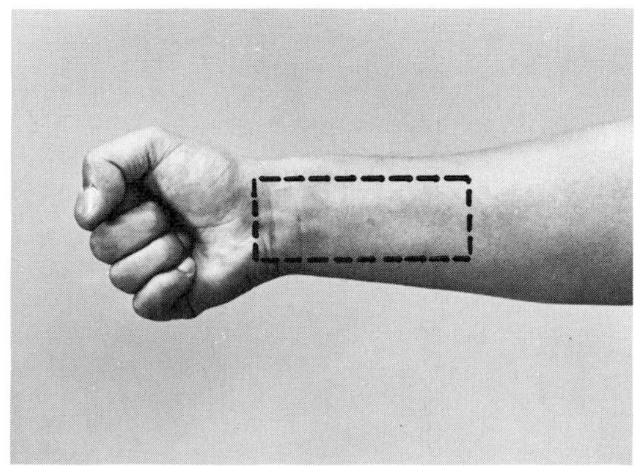

The striking area is the flat undersurface of the lower forearm. This is called Front Forearm Strike when used as a striking weapon.

3. Inner Edge *(An-Pal-Mok)*

The striking area is the inner, or thumb-side, edge of the lower forearm. This is called Inner Edge Forearm Strike when used as a striking weapon.

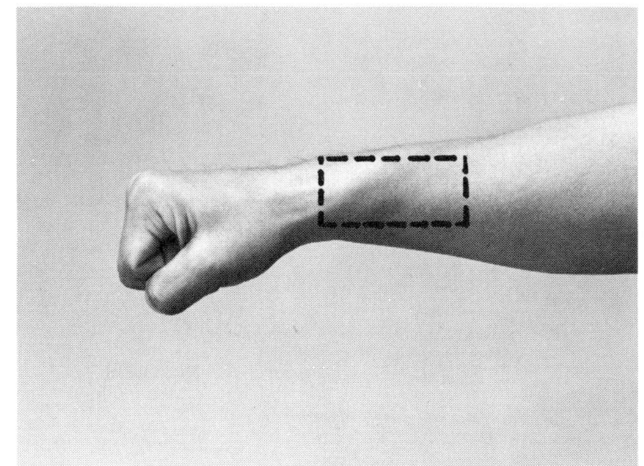

4. Outer Edge *(Bakat-Pal-Mok)*

The striking area is the outer, or pinkie-side, edge of the lower forearm. This is called Outer Edge Forearm Strike when used as a striking weapon.

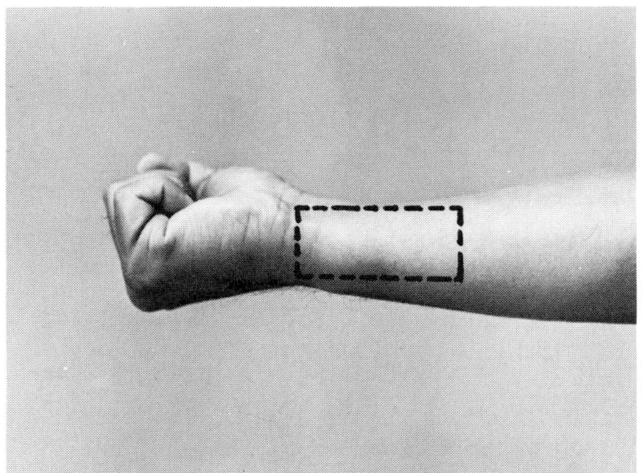

ELBOWS *(Pal-Kup)*

Bend the arm sharply and strike with the point of the elbow:

1. Forward and Upward

or

2. Backward

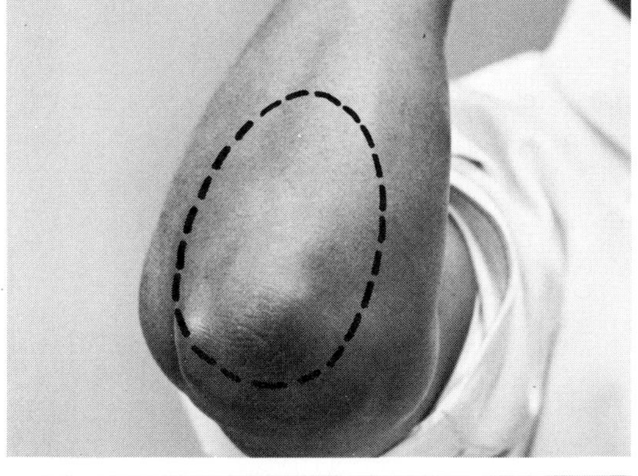

3. Forward and Inward

or

4. Outward to the Side

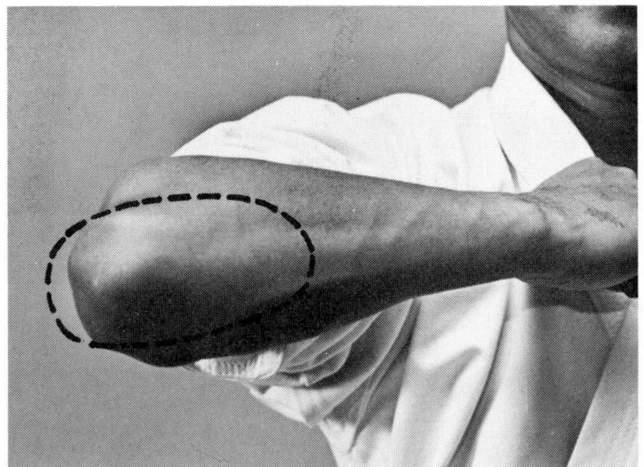

5. Downward

FEET (*Bal*)

1. Ball of the Foot *(Ap-Chook)*

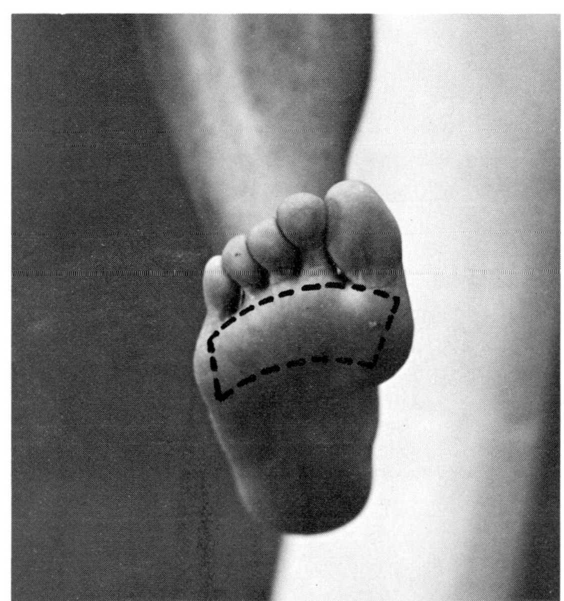

With the toes curled back, the ball of the foot is used in Front Kicks and Round Kicks to the face, temple, neck, chest, stomach, abdomen, groin, and knee.

2. Heel *(Dwi-Chook)*

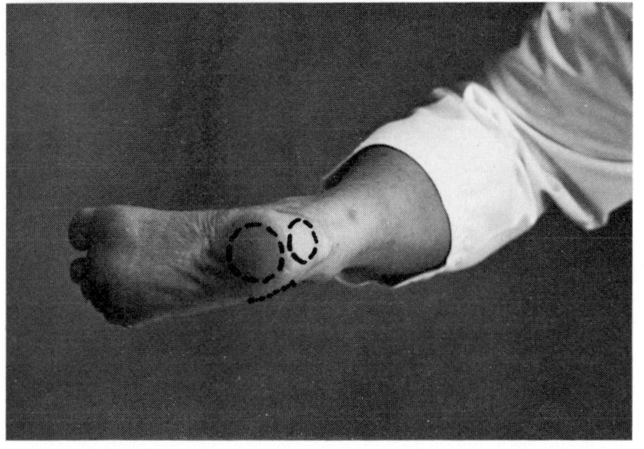

Used in attacks to the face, temple, neck, chest, abdomen, ribs, groin, knee, and instep.

a. Back of the Heel: Striking point in Hook Kicks, Back Kicks, and Wheel Kicks.

b. Side of the Heel: Striking point in Wheel Kicks.

(*continued*)

c. Bottom of the Heel: Striking point in kicking downward or stamping.

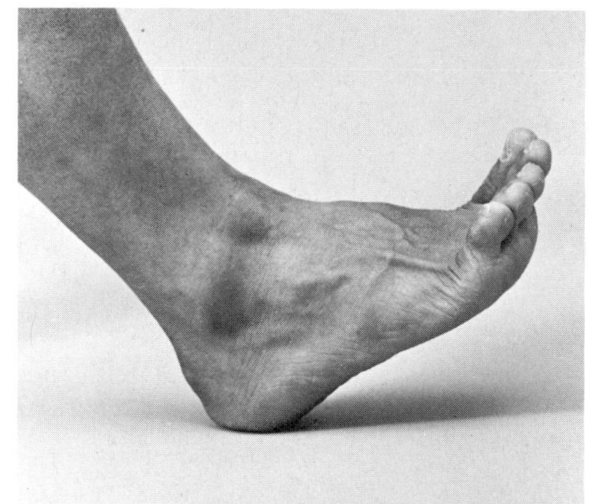

3. Knife Foot *(Bal-Nal)*

Striking area is the outer edge of the foot. It is used in Side Kicks, Wheel Kicks, and Outward Crescent Kicks to the head, neck, ribs, abdomen, knee, and instep, and may also be used against the arms and legs in blocking.

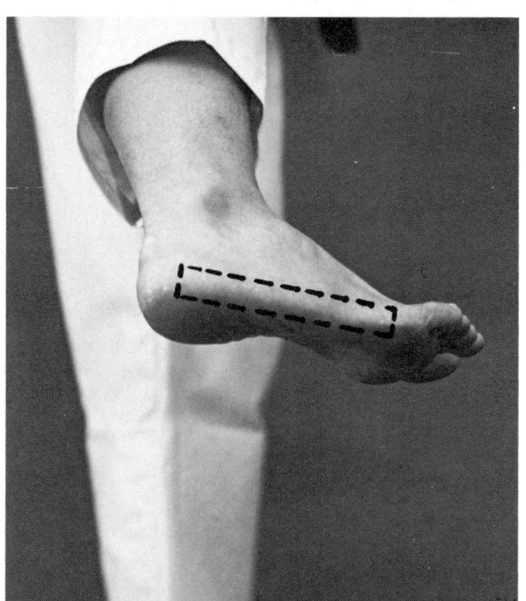

4. Instep *(Bal-Doong)*

Effective in Front Kicks and Round Kicks to the groin, abdomen, neck, temple, and face.

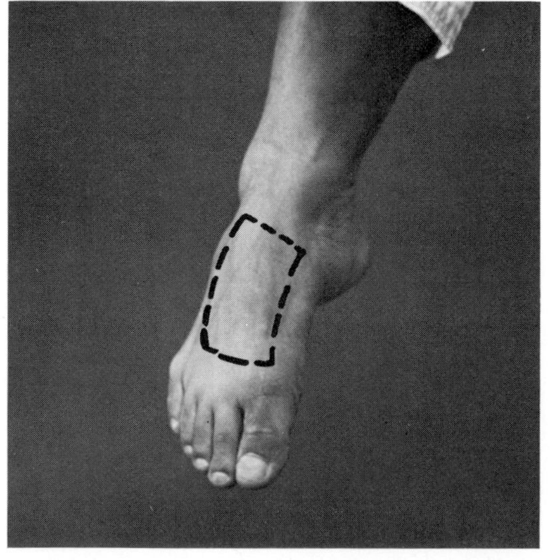

5. Arch *(Bal-Bong-O-Ri)*

Used in Crescent Kicks, the arch is effective in strikes to the face, arms, and abdomen, and in blocking attacks by the arms and legs.

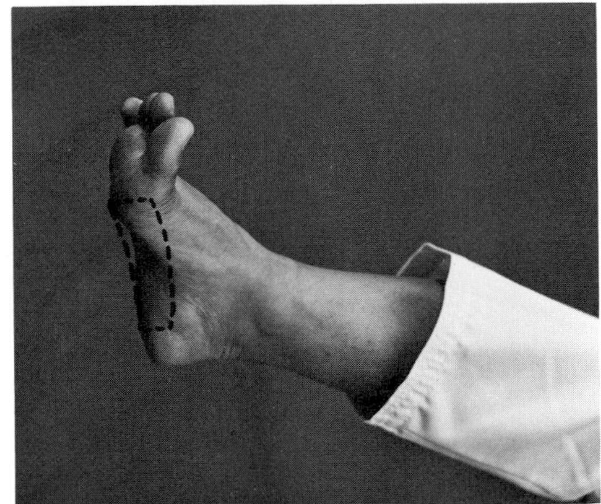

KNEES *(Moo-Roop)*

The knee is effective in close combat for strikes to the face, stomach, abdomen, and groin.

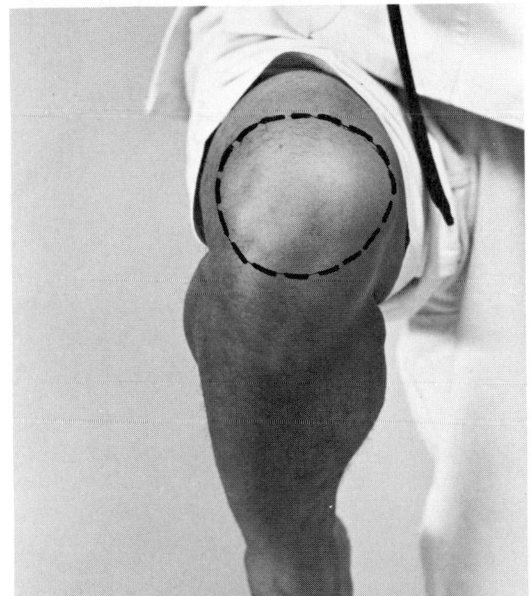

HEAD *(Moh-Ri)*

The head may be used in strikes to the face. Because the head is vulnerable, it should be used only when one has mastered timing and is in an effective position.

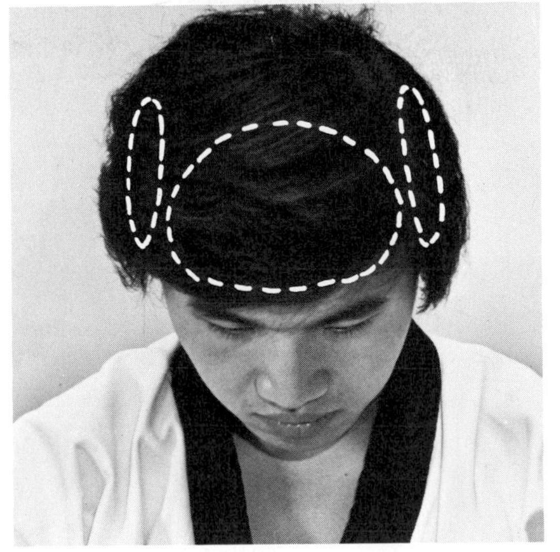

VITAL POINTS

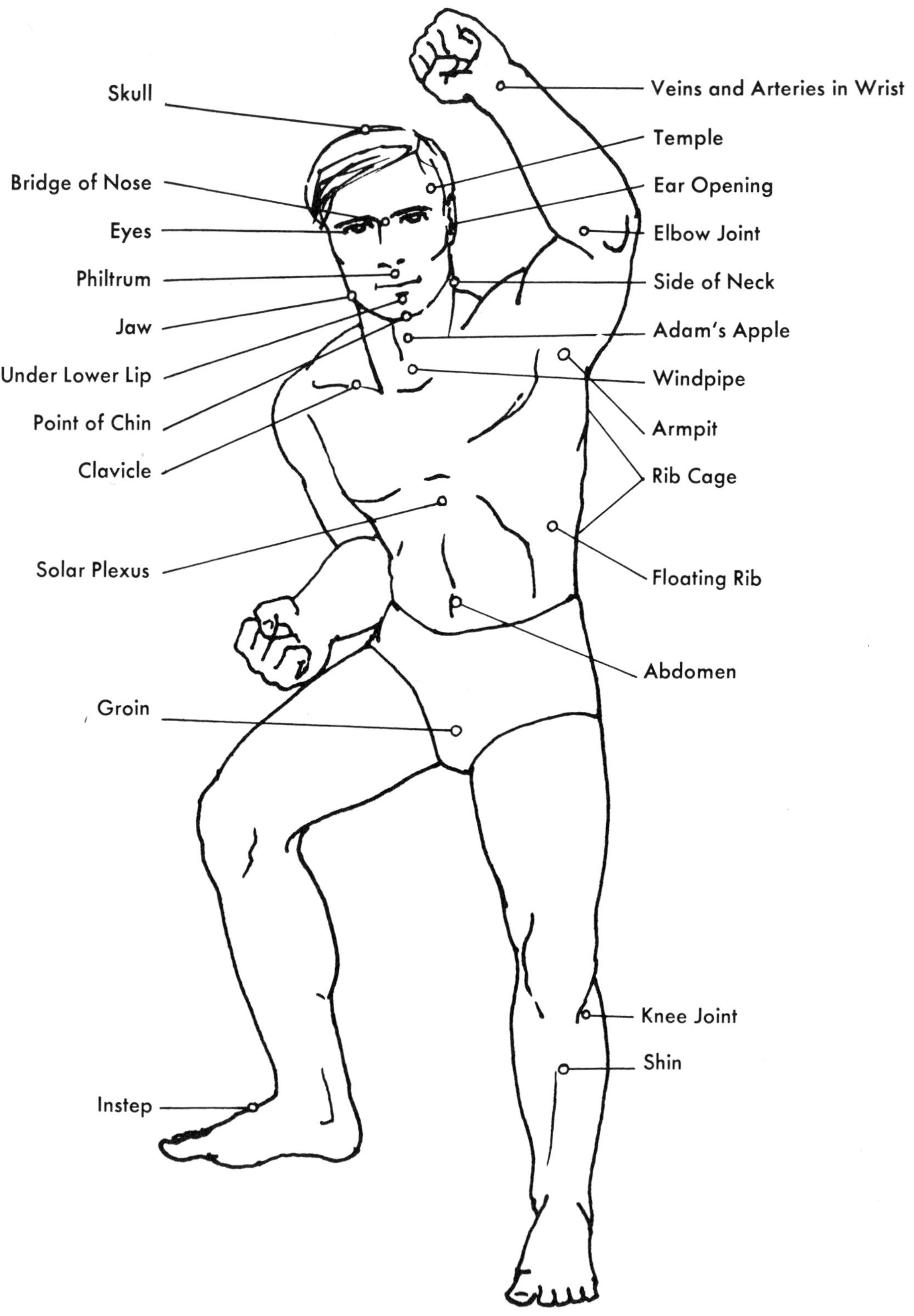

VITAL POINTS

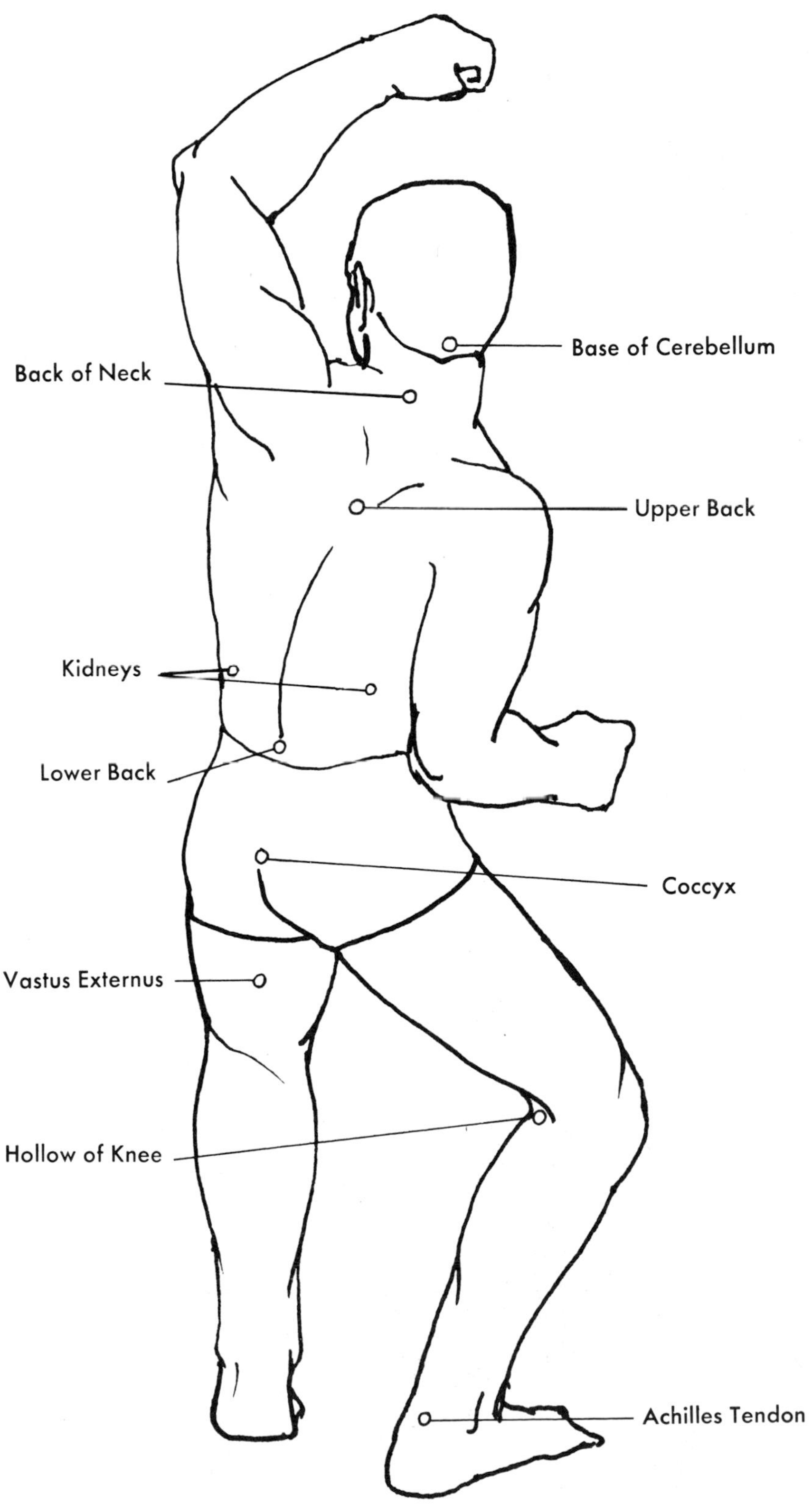

7

Hand, Arm, and Head Attacking Techniques

Tae Kwon Do has highly developed offensive techniques employing the hands, arms, and head. Because these techniques are very forcible and can inflict serious injury, they ought to be used only on the occasion when blocking techniques are insufficient to discourage the attack of a strong opponent.

Punching, thrusting, and striking are three categories used in this chapter to differentiate the methods of attack. A *punch* is a blow with the closed fist moving more or less in a straight line to the striking point. A *thrust*, like a punch, moves in a straight line, but the blow is delivered with the hand open. A *strike* is a blow whose force is transmitted through an arc. In all cases, the blows are focused and, where appropriate, the action should begin in the hip for added power, with the hip twisting slightly in advance of the striking hand.

These techniques are difficult to control, and if the student does not execute them properly, he may unintentionally injure his practice mates or even himself. The techniques should be practiced diligently thousands of times. They will be perfected only after years of study.

STRAIGHT FOREFIST PUNCH (*Chu-Mok Ji-Lu-Ki*)

This is the most basic striking method in Tae Kwon Do and, as is the nature of basic things, appears deceptively simple. When properly executed, the Forefist Punch is extremely fast and strong, and very effective in close combat. It is used especially for strikes to the face, solar plexus, and lower abdomen.

The following points are essential to this technique:

1. Punch to the center. A basic principle of Tae Kwon Do is that the greatest force can most readily be concentrated in the direction of the center of the body. When facing an opponent directly, his most vulnerable points are located along a vertical line at the center of his body. A punch to the center is most difficult to parry.

2. Keep shoulders and arms relaxed as your fist moves into position. Do not attempt to add force by tensing the muscles or throwing your weight into the punch. Force, in Tae Kwon Do, is the result of speed, coordination, and concentration. Speed is inhibited by muscular tension, and your weight will be of little use against a larger and stronger opponent. Tension also wastes energy. The punch is made more forcible by the fact that your energy is conserved until, at the instant of impact with the opponent, your whole being is concentrated against him at the striking point.

3. Punch straight. Shift the hip, *slightly*, but not the shoulder. In practicing the basic straight punch, do not attempt to extend your reach by throwing the shoulder forward, but aim at a target just at arm's length. Do not raise or lower the shoulder, for this breaks the line of greatest concentration. Start the punch with the fist, palm up, at the hip and the elbow straight back; move the fist forward in a straight line to the target, always keeping the fist in a straight line with the forearm and not bending the wrist; extend the arm forward until the elbow is straight, snapping the wrist around at the last moment, so that, on impact, the fist is palm down and in a straight line, through the wrist, forearm, and elbow, to the shoulder.

4. Focus. Make a tight fist. Know your target, the exact point you intend to strike, before your fist moves. Take a good stance, one that will support the force of impact. Pull the opposite fist sharply back to the hip, snapping the wrist palm up, simultaneously, as you punch. This adds great force to the blow, in accordance with the physical law that every action has an equal and opposite reaction. Concentrate your whole body and will into the point of impact. Snapping the striking fist palm down adds shock force to the punch, and as it happens at the last moment, it is the signal for the whole body to lock into a strong and rigid posture. This rigidity is related immediately upon the completion of the punch.

5. Maintain a serious mental attitude, even in practice. Be aware that you are forging a deadly weapon. If you do not concentrate, you will not develop proper control, your technique will not become truly effective, and you may even cause yourself injury.

Examples of the Straight Forefist Punch

1. High Punch *(Ol-Gool Ji-Lu-Ki)*

(continued)

2. Chin Punch (*Tok Ji-Lu-Ki*)

3. Neck Punch (*Mok Ji-Lu-Ki*)

4. Middle Punch (*Mom-Tong Ji-Lu-Ki*)

5. Low Punch ***(A-Le Ji-Lu-Ki)***

6. Downward Punch ***(Ne-Rio Ji-Lu-Ki)***

7. Side Punch ***(Yop Ji-Lu-Ki)***

Note: The Straight Forefist Punch must be directed to the center, that is, to the vertical line running through the center of the opponent's body, whether it is a High Punch, Middle Punch, or Low Punch. In order to visualize the proper position of the fist in striking to the center, assume a stance in which the feet are parallel—e.g., Horseback Stance—and extend both fists, palm down, forward and to the center until the base knuckles of the forefingers and thumbs meet at arms' length.

Straight Forefist Punch Exercises

1. Horseback-Stance Punch *(Ju-Choom-So-Ki Ji-Lu-Ki)*

a. Assume Horseback Stance.

b. Simultaneously extend left fist forward, palm down, and pull right fist back to hip, palm up, making sure both fists are properly formed and clenched tight.

c. Shifting the hip slightly to add power, thrust right fist out, with as much speed as possible, to arm's length, punching at the level of your own solar plexus (and toward the center, directly in front), and snapping wrist palm down at the last instant.

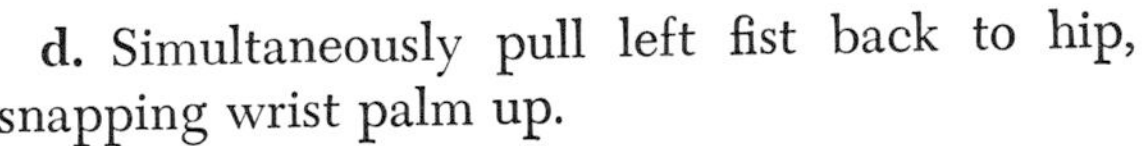
d. Simultaneously pull left fist back to hip, snapping wrist palm up.

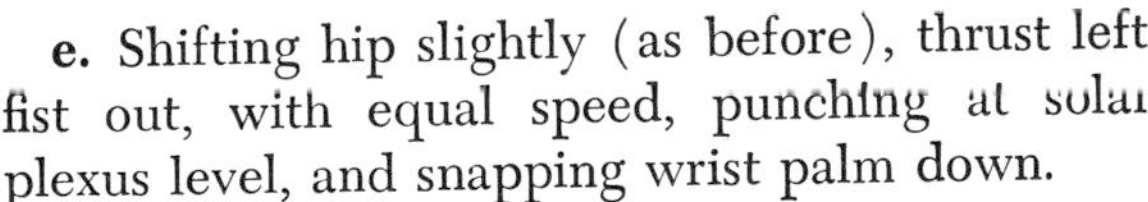
e. Shifting hip slightly (as before), thrust left fist out, with equal speed, punching at solar plexus level, and snapping wrist palm down.

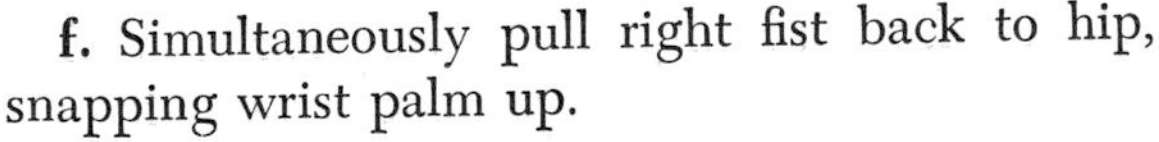
f. Simultaneously pull right fist back to hip, snapping wrist palm up.

Note: Breathe regularly during this exercise, exhaling sharply with each punch, and inhaling before the next. Repeat this exercise several times, punching alternately, with right and left fist, at solar plexus level. Then, maintaining Horseback Stance, punch to face level, then groin level. Finally, punch alternately at all three levels.

Proceed to double punching (punching twice in rapid sequence with alternate fists), triple punching, then four punches.

2. Walking Punch ***(Ba-Ro Ji-Lu-Ki)***

a. Assume Front Stance, left foot forward (two-thirds of weight on front leg, back leg locked straight).

b. Place clenched fists at hips, palm up.

c. Slide right foot forward one long step.

d. Immediately assume Front Stance.

e. Simultaneously (as right foot comes to rest) execute a Middle Punch with right fist (punching at solar plexus level, and snapping wrist palm down).

f. Slide left foot forward one long step.

g. Immediately assume Front Stance.

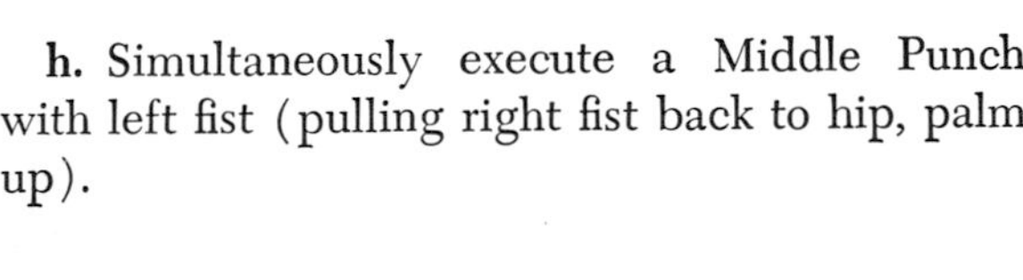

h. Simultaneously execute a Middle Punch with left fist (pulling right fist back to hip, palm up).

Repeat this exercise several times, walking forward, then walking backward. After practicing with the Middle Punch, practice High (face level) and Low (groin level) Punches in the same manner.

REVERSE PUNCH (*Ban-De Ji-Lu-Ki*)

The Reverse Punch is a punch executed with either fist while the alternate leg is forward—e.g., punching with the right fist while the left leg is forward in Front or Back Stance.*

In Reverse Punching, the hip plays an especially important role, adding considerable power to the thrust. The Reverse Punch may be directed to a high, middle, or low target, as Reverse High Punch, Reverse Middle Punch, and Reverse Low Punch.

Different forms of Reverse Punch may be used, depending on the distance to be covered between you and the opponent:

1. Normal Reverse Punch

Punching to the full length of the arm.

2. Reverse Thrust Punch

Turning the shoulder to extend the punch over a greater distance.

3. Reverse Snap Punch

A punch delivered at close range, in which the fist is immediately pulled back to the hip in preparation for the next technique.

Practice Reverse Punching walking forward and backward several times in Front as well as in Back Stance.

* In Korean terminology, "Reverse Punch" means what is called here Regular, or Walking, Punch, and "Walking Punch" means what is known here as Reverse Punch. In order to avoid confusion, we use, in this book, the terminology which is more familiar to Western students. The reader should, however, be aware of this discrepancy.

Walking Reverse Punch in Front Stance

A

B

C

D

E

F

(*continued*)

Walking Reverse Punch in Back Stance

A

B

C

D

VERTICAL FIST PUNCH *(Got-Jang Ji-Lu-Ki)*

Essentially, this is like the Straight Forefist Punch, except that the wrist is snapped around only 90° (from palm-up position, at the hip) to strike with the fist in a vertical position, thumb side uppermost. This technique is particularly effective when attacking at close range, and may be applied with either hand, that is, as a regular or as a reverse punch.

ROUND PUNCH *(Dol-Rio Ji-Lu-Ki)*

This punch begins as a straight punch, but the fist arcs outward slightly and then snaps back to strike, palm down, at the opponent's temple. It may be used as a regular or a reverse punch, and with the Forefist, One-Knuckle, Two-Knuckle, or Four-Knuckle Fist.

This punch should be used only against an opponent directly in front of you. Use the hip for added power, but do not throw your shoulder forward or swing past a direct frontal position.

HOOK PUNCH (*Koon-Dol-Jo-Ki*)

This is a short, circular punch for close-range attacks to the face, temple, jaw, solar plexus, or ribs. It is effective as a counterattack when side-stepping the opponent's attack.

Thrust fist slightly outward and snap it around to the front, striking with the fist palm down and the elbow bent outward at about a 45° angle.

UPPER-CUT PUNCH (*Chi Ji-Lu-Ki* or *Chi-Chi-Ki*)

This punch is especially useful in attacking the chin or solar plexus at close range.

Thrust the fist forward and up, keeping the elbow bent down, and striking with the fist palm up.

BACK-FIST STRIKE (*Doong-Chu-Mok Chi-Ki*)

This is effective in close-range attacks to the face, solar plexus, and ribs. The striking area is the back, or top, of the first two knuckles of the Forefist.

The movement is mostly in the elbow, and is a quick, snapping action rather than a thrust. The fist strikes palm in, with the wrist bent back slightly to advance the points of the knuckles.

HAMMER-FIST STRIKE (*Me-Chu-Mok Chi-Ki*)

This technique is very strong in striking downward or laterally outward. It is effective in attacks to the head, face, collarbone, chest, solar plexus, ribs, and kidneys, and in blocking kicks and punches it can be used to strike the leg or break the elbow. The striking surface is the bottom, or pinkie side, of the Forefist.

THUMB-KNUCKLE FIST PUNCH (*Om-Ji-Chu-Mok Ji-Lu-Ki*)

Effective in strikes to the temple, the point where the nose meets the upper lip, and the ribs. The striking point is the second knuckle of the thumb, which juts out to the side of the Forefist.

FOREFINGER ONE-KNUCKLE FIST PUNCH
(In-Ji-Chu-Mok Ji-Lu-Ki)

Useful in attacks to the temple, between the eyes, the point where the nose meets the upper lip, and other small areas of vulnerability. The striking point is the jutting second knuckle of the forefinger, with the other fingers closed into a fist. It may be applied as a Walking or Reverse Straight Punch, Round Punch, or Hook.

MIDDLE-FINGER ONE-KNUCKLE FIST PUNCH
(Bam-Chu-Mok Ji-Lu-Ki)

The striking point is the jutting second knuckle of the middle finger, with the other fingers closed into a fist. Its uses are the same as the Forefinger One-Knuckle Punch.

TWO-KNUCKLE FIST PUNCH
(Doo-Bam-Chu-Mok Ji-Lu-Ki)

The striking points are the jutting second knuckles of the forefinger and middle finger together. This punch is used in the same way as the One-Knuckle Punch.

FOUR-KNUCKLE FIST PUNCH
(Pyun-Chu-Mok Ji-Lu-Ki)

This is effective in attacks to the smaller points of vulnerability, such as the point between the eyes, the temple, the chin, the point where the nose meets the upper lip, the throat, and the solar plexus. It may be applied as a Walking or Reverse Punch and in combination with the movements of the Straight Punch, Upper-Cut, Round Punch, or Hook.

DOUBLE-FIST PUNCHES
(Doo-Chu-Mok Ji-Lu-Ki)

A Double-Fist Punch is one in which both fists are used to strike the opponent simultaneously, thus doubling the force of the attack. It is a very strong technique, but must be used with caution since it leaves one open to counterattack.

1. Double-Fist Straight Punch *(Doo-Chu-Mok Ba-Ro-Ji-Lu-Ki)*

Thrust both Forefists forward simultaneously to strike the same target with palms down. Do not lean forward, but keep the torso erect in order to maintain balance and focus correctly.

2. C Punch *(Di-Koot-Ja Ji-Lu-Ki)*

Thrust both fists forward simultaneously, executing a Straight Forefist Punch to the face and an Upper-Cut to the groin, abdomen, or solar plexus at the same time, so that your two arms form the pattern of the letter **C**. Lean forward slightly—just enough to enable you to strike with both fists on a vertical line through the middle of the body.

3. Double Upper-Cut Punch *(So-Sum Ji-Lu-Ki* or *So-Sum Chi-Ki)*

Thrust both fists forward simultaneously, to strike the same target with palms up. Keep torso erect. This punch is used especially in close-range attacks to the solar plexus and to the chin. Also, both Middle-Finger One-Knuckle Fists can be applied for the same results.

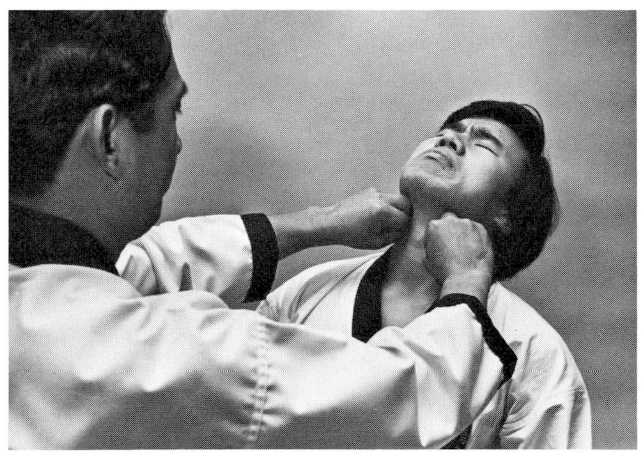

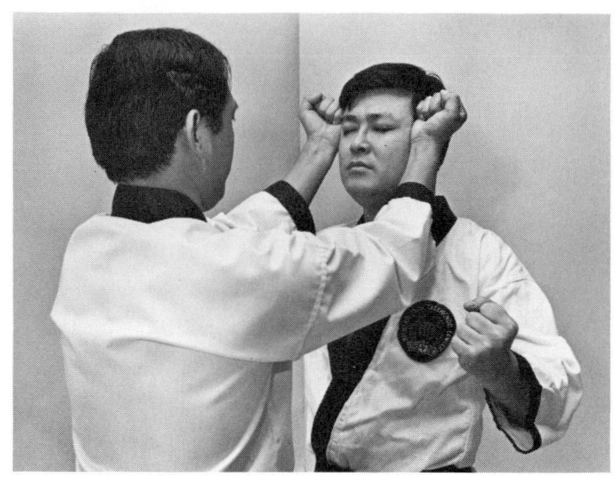

4. Double Hammer-Fist Strike *(Ho-Li Chi-Ki)*

Thrust both fists forward and out simultaneously and swing them inward and down to strike opponent on both sides of the head, collarbone, or ribs at the same time.

SPEAR-HAND THRUST
(Pyun-Sohn-Koot Jji-Lu-Ki)

This technique is effective in strikes to the eyes, throat, ribs, and solar plexus, depending on the position of the hand and the fingers employed. The striking area consists of the tips of the fingers, and the main purpose is to puncture and penetrate to the inner organs.

1. Vertical Spear-Hand Thrust *(Pyun-Sohn-Koot Se-Wo-Jji-Lu-Ki)*

Keeping all four fingers extended and close together, and the hand rigid, thrust forward to strike the solar plexus with the hand held vertically (thumb side uppermost).

2. Horizontal Spear-Hand Thrust *(Pyun-Sohn-Koot Je-Cho-Jji-Lu-Ki)*

Keeping fingers extended and hand rigid, as above, thrust forward, with the hand held palm up, to strike between or just under the ribs (**a**), or to strike the throat (**b**).

3. Two-Finger Spear-Hand Thrust *(Ka-Wi-Sohn-Koot Jji-Lu-Ki)*

Keeping ring finger, pinkie, and thumb closed, thrust forward to strike the eyes with rigidly extended forefinger and middle finger, with hand palm down.

4. One-Finger Spear-Hand Thrust *(In-Ji-Sohn-Koot Jji-Lu-Ki)*

Keeping all other fingers closed, thrust forefinger forward to solar plexus, neck, throat, or eye.

TIGER-MOUTH THRUST (*A-Kum-Sohn Jji-Lu-Ki*)

With the four fingers extended together and the thumb open and opposite, thrust forward to attack opponent's throat (striking with the curved surface between the thumb and the forefinger).

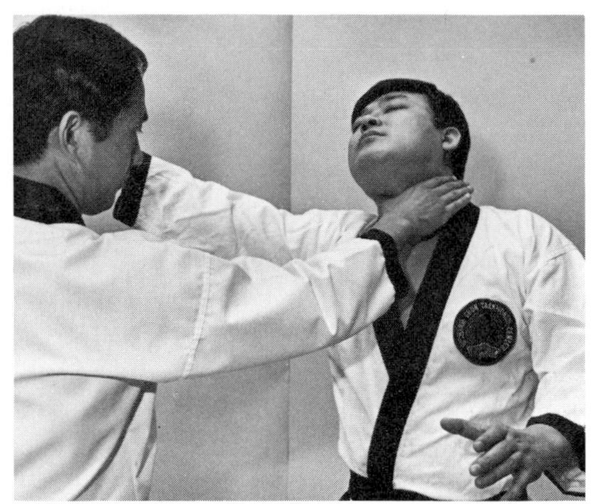

CHICKEN-BEAK STRIKE (*Sohn-Koot-Jo-Ki*)

Extend the fingers so that all five fingertips meet in a point (the striking point), and thrust forward to attack the opponent's eye, striking with the hand palm down.

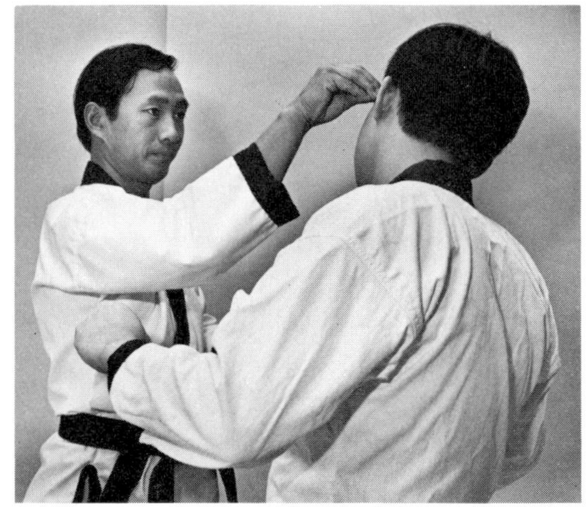

PALM-HEEL STRIKE (*Ba-Tang-Sohn Chi-Ki*)

This is effective in attacks to the chin and solar plexus. The striking area is the base of the palm, with the fingers curved back and turned upward, downward, or to the side, depending on the angle of attack. When attacking, snap the wrist back to advance the Palm Heel.

KNIFE-HAND STRIKE (*Sohn-Nal Chi-Ki*)

This is a strong breaking technique, effective in blocking, and in strikes to the head, temple, neck, collarbone, ribs, elbows, and spleen. The striking surface is the outer edge of the open hand, from the base joint of the pinkie to the heel of the hand, with the four fingers extended together, the thumb closed against the palm, and the hand rigid.

1. Knife-Hand Strike—Palm Up *(Sohn-Nal Je-Cho-Chi-Ki)*

Raise Knife Hand up and back, into position near the ear, with palm facing outward and elbow sharply bent; then swing Knife Hand forward and around in a slight arc, snapping wrist palm up, to strike temple, neck, ribs, etc., of opponent in front.

2. Knife-Hand Strike—Palm Down *(Sohn-Nal O-Po-Chi-Ki)*

Raise forearm across chest with Knife-Hand palm in, then swing Knife Hand sharply outward, snapping wrist palm down, to strike opponent standing at the side or in front.

3. Vertical (Downward) Knife-Hand Strike *(Sohn-Nal Se-Wo-Chi-Ki)*

Raise Knife Hand straight up over your own shoulder and swing it down sharply to strike opponent's collarbone with Knife Hand held vertically—i.e., thumb uppermost.

RIDGE-HAND STRIKE *(Sohn-Nal-Doong Chi-Ki)*

This is similar to the Knife-Hand Strike, but the striking edge is the base knuckle of the forefinger, with the thumb closed against the palm and the hand held rigidly open. It is effective in blocking, and in attacks to the temple, face, under the chin, the neck, throat, ribs, solar plexus, and groin.

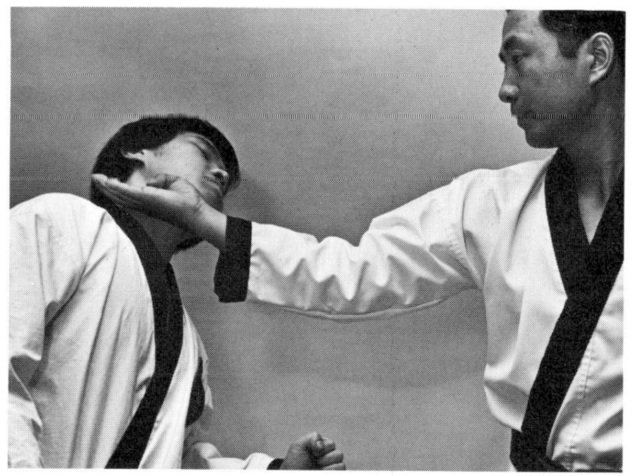

1. Ridge-Hand Strike—Palm Up (striking outward)

Raise forearm across chest, holding Ridge Hand palm down, and then swing Ridge Hand out and up, snapping wrist around to strike opponent palm up. This is effective in blocking hand attacks.

2. Ridge-Hand Strike—Palm Down (striking inward)

Beginning with Ridge Hand palm up at hip, swing Ridge Hand forward, up, and around in a slight arc, snapping wrist around to strike opponent palm down (as Ridge Hand arcs inward) on the face, temple, neck, throat, or ribs.

BEAR-HAND STRIKE (*Gom-Sohn Chi-Ki*)

Holding the hand with all five fingertips curled back against the palm, the striking surface is the circle formed by the thumb, fingertips, and palm. It is especially effective in striking and ripping attacks to the face and ears.

FINGERTIP THRUSTS (*Sohn-Ka-Rak-Koot Jji-Lu-Ki*)

1. Ripping-Hand Thrust *(Gal-Kwi-Sohn Jji-Lu-Ki)*

With all five fingers curved toward the palm, the fingertips are used to strike and rip the face, neck, ribs, or groin.

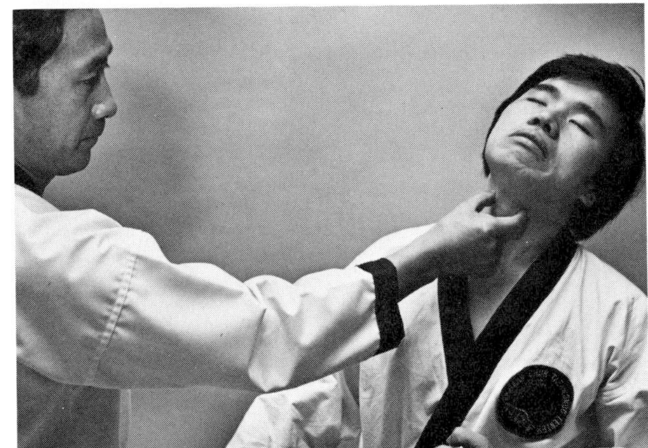

2. Pincers-Hand Thrust *(Jip-Ke-Sohn Jji-Lu-Ki)*

The striking points are the tips of the forefinger and thumb, curved toward each other, with the other fingers closed against the palm. The Pincers Hand is used to attack the eyes, ears, nose, or Adam's apple.

BACK-HAND STRIKE (*Sohn-Doong Chi-Ki*)

Holding the hand open, the striking area is the back of the base knuckles of the fingers. It is effective in strikes to the face, ribs, and abdomen, and may be used against an opponent standing to the front or to the side of you.

WRIST (OX-JAW) STRIKE (*Sohn-Mok Chi-Ki*)

Holding the fingertips loosely together, as in the Chicken-Beak Hand, but bending the palm down toward the inner forearm, the striking surface is the point of the back of the wrist. Effective in attacks to the temple, face, chin, and solar plexus, especially at close range. This is also effective in blocking hand attacks.

ELBOW STRIKES (*Pal-Kup Chi-Ki*)

The striking surface is the point of the elbow, with the elbow sharply bent. It is a very effective attacking technique for close-range strikes to the chin, the top of the head, face, ribs, and solar plexus.

1. Forward and Upward Elbow Strike

Swing elbow forward and up to strike chin of opponent in front, keeping elbow sharply bent and fist, palm down, close above shoulder.

2. Backward Elbow Strike

Thrust elbow straight back—passing close against your own ribs—to strike solar plexus or ribs of opponent standing behind you.

3. Inward Elbow Strike

Swing elbow forward, up, and inward (arching toward your own opposite side), to strike face of opponent in front.

4. Outward Elbow Strike

Swing elbow outward to strike face of opponent standing to the side.

5. Downward Elbow Strike

Swing elbow downward to strike head or neck of opponent beneath you.

HEAD STRIKES (*Moh-Ri Chi-Ki*)

This is a strong surprise technique for attacking opponent's face, chin, and solar plexus when fighting at close range, and is especially useful when your hands and feet are bound or pinned.

1. Forehead Strike

(*continued*)

2. Striking with the Back of the Head

3. Striking with the Side of the Head

Applied in a manner similar to 1 and 2 above. (Not illustrated.)

8

Blocking Techniques

Inasmuch as Tae Kwon Do is an art of defense, blocking is especially important. Effective blocking techniques can not only resist an attack, but turn the attacker's strength and momentum against himself. Also, it is the nature of many blocking methods of Tae Kwon Do that they are executed with as much focus as a punch or kick; that is to say, the energy of the defender is concentrated to meet the attack with shock force at the point of contact, inflicting severe pain or injury to the offending arm or leg, and thus discouraging the opponent from attacking again. With effective blocking, counterattack may be unnecessary.

The Tae Kwon Do practitioner ought to be prepared, nonetheless, for any eventuality. In executing a block, he must maintain such balance, posture, and alertness as to be ready, instantly, to follow up with another technique.

Most blocking is done with the arms or hands, though the feet are also used. In this chapter, the four most fundamental blocks are described first: Low Block, High Block, Middle Block (Inside-to-Outside and Outside-to-Inside), and Knife-Hand Block. Other blocking methods follow, and more advanced actions and combinations will be found in the forms and free-sparring techniques illustrated in later chapters. Note that all blocks may be executed as regular or reverse blocks, viz., with either arm or either leg, in any stance in which one foot is forward. However, for practice purposes, the basic blocks are illustrated here as regular blocks (executed with the arm on the same side as the forward foot).

LOW BLOCK *(A-Le Mak-Ki)*

This is a focused block. It is used against kicks and low punches to the lower abdomen and to the groin area. It has slight variations, depending on the stance in which it is employed, but the most basic form is that executed in Front Stance.

Walking Low Block

a. Assume Front Stance, left foot forward (two-thirds of weight on front [left] leg, bent forward at the knee, right leg locked straight in back).

b. Simultaneously cross forearms in front of chest, left fist palm in near right ear, and right fist palm down under left elbow.

c. Sweep left forearm downward, across abdomen and groin (the blocking action), and snap the wrist around at the last instant, bringing left fist into position, palm down, two fist-widths above left knee. (The blocking surface is the outer edge of lower left forearm.)

d. Simultaneously pull right fist back to right hip, snapping wrist palm up.

Note:

• In blocking with either hand, snap both wrists around simultaneously at the last instant as the block is being completed. This snapping motion at the last instant—viz., at the instant of contact with the opponent's arm or leg—provides much of the force of the block, and is used in all "focused" blocks.

• Pulling the other, "idle," fist back sharply to the hip simultaneously with the blocking motion of the active hand provides more impetus to the blocking action, in accordance with the physical rule that every action has an equal and opposite reaction. It serves the second purpose of putting the hand into the position of being ready immediately for use in another technique.

• The blocking forearm should sweep into position with as much speed and force as possible, and for this purpose the hip should twist slightly (in this case, to the right and back to the left)—and slightly in advance of the downward-sweeping forearm—to add power.

• Do not raise the shoulders, or tighten the muscles in any way, *during* the sweeping action, which should be made with the body relaxed, for tightness inhibits speed. It is only at the last instant of blocking—viz., the instant of contact with the opponent—that the whole body must be focused, that is, rigidly locked into position for the block. The instant after the block has been executed, the body relaxes again, ready to move into the next position.

Practice this block repeatedly while walking forward and backward in Front Stance. Block with the right forearm when the right foot is forward, and the left forearm when the left foot is forward. Execute the block simultaneously as you step forward or backward, so that the blocking forearm locks into position at the same instant that the moving foot comes to rest, and the whole body is focused and stable.

HIGH BLOCK (*Ol-Gool Mak-Ki*)

This is a focused block. It is used against straight punches and overhead strikes to the head and face.

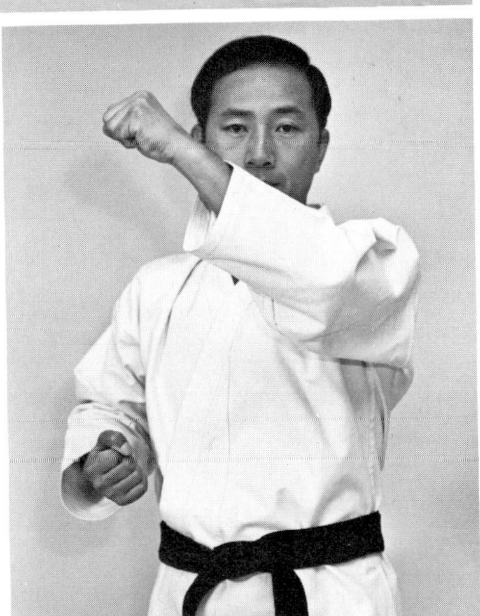

(*continued*)

Walking High Block

a. Assume Front Stance, left foot forward.

b. Simultaneously cross forearms in front of chest, right fist palm down above left shoulder, and left fist palm up under right elbow.

c. Sweep left forearm up—outside right forearm—and snap fist around, palm out (the blocking action), bringing left wrist into position two fist-widths above and two fist-widths in front of forehead, with left forearm at 45° angle to floor. (The blocking surface is the outer edge of lower left forearm.)

d. Simultaneously pull right fist back to right hip, snapping wrist palm up.

Practice this block repeatedly while walking forward and backward in Front Stance. Block with the right forearm when the right foot is forward, and the left forearm when the left foot is forward. Execute the block simultaneously as you step forward or backward, so that the blocking forearm locks into position at the same instant that the moving foot comes to rest.

Note: As with Low Block, use a slight twisting motion of the hip to add power to the block, and do not raise the shoulders or tighten the muscles during the sweeping action, which should be made with the body relaxed—and rigidly focused only at the last instant of blocking.

MIDDLE BLOCK (*Mom-Tong Mak-Ki*)

This is a focused block. It is used against attacks to the chest, ribs, and solar plexus.

1. Inside (Outside-to-Inside) Middle Block (*Mom-Tong Ahn Mak-Ki*)

Walking Inside Middle Block in Back Stance

a. Assume Back (or Front) Stance.

b. Simultaneously, swing blocking forearm out to the side (holding it vertically), into position with elbow sharply bent behind and below shoulder (about 30° to shoulder), and fist, palm out, to the side and just above shoulder. (**Note:** Block with the forearm on the same side as the advanced foot—e.g., block with the right forearm when the right foot is forward.)

c. Simultaneously move other fist, palm down, a little out in front of solar plexus.

d. Sweep blocking forearm strongly forward and down, snapping wrist palm in (the blocking action), into position with elbow, bent down, close beside and in front of body (90° to shoulder), and fist out in front of chest and level with shoulder. (The blocking surface is the outer edge —pinkie side—of the lower forearm.)

e. Simultaneously pull other fist back to hip, snapping wrist palm up.

Walking Inside Middle Block in Front Stance

2. Outside (Inside-to-Outside) Middle Block *(Mom-Tong Pakat Mak-Ki)*

a. Assume Back (or Front) Stance.

b. Simultaneously cross forearms in front of solar plexus and parallel to floor, with both fists palm down and the blocking forearm underneath the other forearm. (**Note:** Block with the left forearm when the left foot is forward, and the right forearm when the right foot is forward.)

c. Swing blocking (lower) forearm up and outward, snapping wrist palm in (the blocking action), into position with fist out in front of, and on a level with, shoulder. (The proper position can be attained when swinging the forearm up and out by rotating the elbow without moving the upper arm in relation to the chest.) At the end of the blocking motion, the elbow should be pointing down close beside and just in front of the body. (The blocking surface is the inner edge —thumb side—of the lower forearm.)

d. Simultaneously pull the other fist back to the hip, snapping wrist palm up.

Practice these Middle Blocks (Inside-to-Outside and Outside-to-Inside) repeatedly while walking forward and backward in Front and Back Stances. Execute the block simultaneously as you step forward or backward, so that the blocking forearm locks into position at the same instant the moving foot comes to rest.

(*continued*)

Walking Outside Middle Block in Front Stance

KNIFE-HAND BLOCK (*Sohn-Nal Mak-Ki*)

This is a focused block. It is usually used against an attack to the solar plexus, ribs, or chest (Middle Block) when the defender is in Back Stance, but may also be used, in Front or Back Stance, against attacks to the groin or abdomen (Knife-Hand Low Block) or attacks to the head or neck (Knife-Hand High Block). When the Knife-Hand Block is executed in Back Stance, the other hand is most often used to assist the blocking action by moving into position—as a Knife Hand—Palm Up—in front of the solar plexus. The special advantages of the Knife-Hand Block are that it is very fast, easy to use when a quick change of positions is required, and is a posture in which one is ready to launch an immediate counterattack.

The Knife-Hand Middle Block is explained below, inasmuch as it is the basic, most common form. It is the same in Front Stance as in Back Stance, except that it may be executed in Front Stance with or without the other Knife Hand assisting.

(*continued*)

1. Knife-Hand Middle Block—Back Stance

a. Assume Back Stance (80 percent of weight on back leg, both knees bent outward).

b. Simultaneously raise blocking Knife Hand to opposite ear, palm in. (**Note:** Block with left Knife Hand when left foot is forward, and with right Knife Hand when right foot is forward.)

c. Simultaneously place other (assisting) Knife Hand at hip, palm down.

d. Sweep blocking Knife Hand outward and down, snapping wrist palm out (the blocking action), into position with elbow bent downward and fingertips of Knife Hand extended, at shoulder level, out to a point at side of face (eyes focused front). The blocking surface is the outer edge of the Knife Hand, between the base of the pinkie and the wrist. (Do not bend the wrist. The outer edge of the Knife Hand should form a straight line with the outer edge of the forearm.)

e. Simultaneously thrust assisting Knife Hand forward, snapping wrist palm up, into position just in front of, but not touching, solar plexus.

2. Knife-Hand High Block—Back Stance

Applied in a manner similar to Knife-Hand Middle Block.

3. Knife-Hand Low Block—Back Stance

Applied in a manner similar to Knife-Hand Middle Block.

4. Knife-Hand Middle Block (Outside-to-Inside)—
Back Stance

This is a variation of the normal Knife-Hand Block, in which the blocking Knife Hand is raised out and back, palm out, with elbow sharply bent, and then swung forward and inward, snapping the wrist around to block with the outer edge of the Knife Hand. (This technique may be used with or without the other Knife Hand assisting.)

5. Knife-Hand High Block (Outside-to-Inside)—Back Stance

Applied in a manner similar to Knife-Hand Middle Block (Outside-to-Inside).

6. Knife-Hand Low Block (Outside-to-Inside)—Back Stance

Applied in a manner similar to Knife-Hand Middle Block (Outside-to-Inside).

7. Alternate Forms of Knife-Hand Block in Front Stance

These blocks are executed the same as the basic Low Block, High Block, and Outside Middle Block (see pages 112, 115, and 120), except that the blocking hand is held open, as a Knife Hand, and not closed into a fist.

a. Knife-Hand Middle Block—Front Stance

(continued)

(1) Cross forearms in front of solar plexus and parallel to floor, with blocking Knife Hand palm up and other hand, closed into a fist, palm down. (The blocking forearm is underneath the other forearm when they are crossed. Block with the hand that is on the same side as the advanced foot.)

(2) Swing blocking Knife Hand up and outward, snapping wrist palm out (the blocking action), into position with elbow bent downward and fingertips of Knife Hand extended, at shoulder level, in front of body.

(3) Simultaneously pull other fist back to hip, snapping wrist palm up.

b. Knife-Hand High Block—Front Stance

c. Knife-Hand Low Block—Front Stance

DOUBLE-HAND BLOCK (*Gho-Du-Lo Mak-Ki*)

This is a focused block, and is used in Front Stance or Back Stance. It is stronger than the normal Middle Block, and has the advantage of having one hand (the assisting hand) in position to defend against a further attack or to move into the counterattack.

The Double-Hand Middle Block is explained below, as it is the most common form. Block with the forearm that is on the same side as the advanced foot.

1. Double-Hand Middle Block

(*continued*)

a. Cross blocking forearm in front of chest, level with shoulders and parallel to floor, with fist palm down in front of opposite shoulder.

b. Simultaneously move other (assisting) fist to hip, palm down.

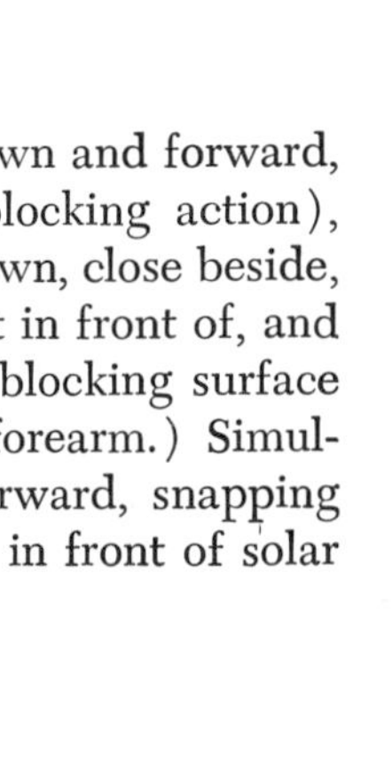

c. Sweep blocking forearm down and forward, snapping wrist, palm in (the blocking action), into position with elbow, bent down, close beside, and in front of body, and fist out in front of, and on a level with, shoulder. (The blocking surface is the inner edge of the lower forearm.) Simultaneously thrust assisting fist forward, snapping wrist palm up, into position just in front of solar plexus.

2. Double-Hand High Block

Applied in a similar manner to block a high attack.

3. Double-Hand Low Block

In defending against a low attack, this block may be applied in either of two ways:

(*continued*)

a. with the fist of the blocking forearm palm up, as in the Double-Hand Middle Block, or

b. with the fist of the blocking forearm palm down.

4. Double-Hand High Middle Block (*Kum-Kang Mom-Tong Mak-Ki*)

This technique is used to defend against attacks from two different angles at the same time, such as a high punch from the front and a middle punch from the side, or a round kick to the face and a middle punch from the side. Generally, this block is used against simultaneous attacks, and so it would be practiced with both arms moving simultaneously into blocking position, as is shown in the illustration. It may also be used

against two attacks launched in rapid sequence, in which case your arms should move into blocking position in rapid sequence, corresponding to the sequence in the angles of attack. The Double-Hand High Middle Block is usually used in Back Stance, and may be employed to the left side (blocking a high attack from the front and a middle attack from the left), or to the right side (blocking a high attack from the front and a middle attack from the right). Blocking to the right is illustrated as an example.

a. Pivoting on left foot, turn 90° to the left and slide right foot forward a half-step.

b. Assume Back Stance.

c. Simultaneously, execute a Double-Hand High Middle Block by sweeping right forearm up and out into position with fist, palm in, held out from right shoulder, as in normal Middle Block; simultaneously sweep left forearm up into position with left fist, palm out, held above and a little in front of forehead, as in normal High Block—except that head is turned to the right. (The blocking surfaces are the inner edge of the lower right forearm and the outer edge of the lower left forearm.)

SCISSORS BLOCK (*Ga-Wi Mak-Ki*)

This is a focused block. It is used against a simultaneous attack to the face or to the solar plexus and the groin. It consists of a Low Block and an Outside Middle Block executed simultaneously. The blocking surfaces are the inner edge (thumb side) of the middle-blocking forearm and the outer edge (pinkie side) of the low-blocking forearm.

a. Cross forearms in front of chest, low-blocking fist near opposite ear, palm in, and middle-blocking fist palm down under opposite elbow.

b. Swing middle-blocking forearm up and outward—outside low-blocking forearm—snapping wrist palm in (the blocking action), into position with fist out in front of, and on a level with, shoulder.

c. Simultaneously sweep low-blocking forearm down—inside middle-blocking forearm—across abdomen, snapping wrist palm down (the blocking action), into position with fist in front of knee.

DOUBLE-FIST X BLOCK (*Ot-Ko-Lo Mak-Ki*)

This is effective against a Front Kick to the groin (Low Block form) or an overhead strike (High Block form).

1. Double-Fist Low X Block

Thrust both fists forward and down simultaneously until arms lock straight with wrists crossed, left under right, at groin level. (The blocking surface is the point at which the backs of the wrists cross, with the fists palm out.)

2. Double-Fist High X Block

Thrust both fists forward and up simultaneously, into position with wrists crossed, right over left, above and in front of forehead.

KNIFE-HAND X BLOCK
(Sohn-Nal Ot-Ko-Lo Mak-Ki)

This is essentially the same as the Double-Fist X Block (above), except that the hands are held in open Knife Hand position.

1. Knife-Hand High X Block

Thrust Knife Hands forward and up, crossing wrists to block a high attack.

2. Knife-Hand Low X Block

Thrust Knife Hands forward and down, crossing wrists to block a low attack.

SPREAD BLOCK (*He-Cho Mak-Ki*)

This is a focused block. It is useful against an opponent who attempts to grab your lapels or your throat with both hands. Of the two forms blocking with the outer edges of the forearms or with the inner edges of the forearms, either may be used, depending on the technique with which you intend to follow up.

1. Spread Middle Block—Outer Edges of Forearms

a. Cross wrists in front of chest, fists palm in.

b. Sweep both forearms outward simultaneously, snapping both wrists palm up (the blocking action), into position with fists out in front of, and level with, shoulders.

2. Spread Middle Block—Inner Edges of Forearms

a. Cross wrists in front of chest, fists palm down.

b. Sweep both forearms outward simultaneously, snapping both wrists palm in (the blocking action).

3. Spread Knife-Hand Block *(Sohn-Nal He-Cho Mak-Ki)*

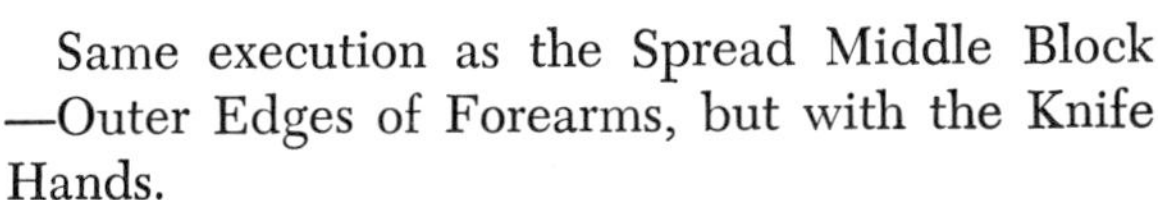

Same execution as the Spread Middle Block —Outer Edges of Forearms, but with the Knife Hands.

4. Spread Low Block

This technique is effective in blocking kicks to the solar plexus or abdomen. It is especially useful, in that as you block, you sweep the opponent's leg to the side, throwing him off balance. The Spread Low Block is usually used in Front Stance, with either foot forward.

Spread Low Block

a. Slide left foot forward one step.

b. Assume Front Stance.

c. Simultaneously, execute a Spread Low Block with both forearms, crossing both wrists, right over left, in front of the chest, fists palm in, then sweeping both forearms down and outward, snapping wrists around, into position with fists palm out at arm's length a little in front and out to the sides of the thighs. (The blocking surfaces are the outer edges of both lower forearms.)

SIDE BLOCK (*Yop Mak-Ki*)

Essentially, this is an Inside Middle Block (see page 117) in Horseback Stance, used to block an attack from an opponent standing to the side. It is a focused block, and is very effective when used in combination with an immediate follow-up counterattack.

a. Swing blocking forearm out to the side (holding it vertically), into position with elbow sharply bent behind and below shoulder, and fist, palm out, to the side and just above shoulder.

b. Sweep blocking forearm strongly forward and down, snapping wrist palm in (the blocking action), into position with elbow, bent down, out to the side, and fist, out to the side, level with, and a little in front of, shoulder. (The blocking surface is the outer edge of the lower forearm.)

PALM-HEEL BLOCK (*Ba-Tang-Sohn Mak-Ki*)

This is useful when you wish to grab the attacking arm or leg and pull the opponent off balance (pulling him in the direction of his attack, and thus using his own momentum to your advantage). It may be applied in three ways.

1. Palm-Heel Center Block

Striking downward, palm down.

2. Palm-Heel Upward Block

Striking upward, palm up.

3. Palm-Heel Side Block

Striking across horizontally, palm facing the direction of movement.

WRIST BLOCK (*Sohn-Mok Mak-Ki*)

This is useful in blocking a high punch, but is especially effective when you wish to counter-attack immediately with a Palm-Heel Strike to the face or solar plexus.

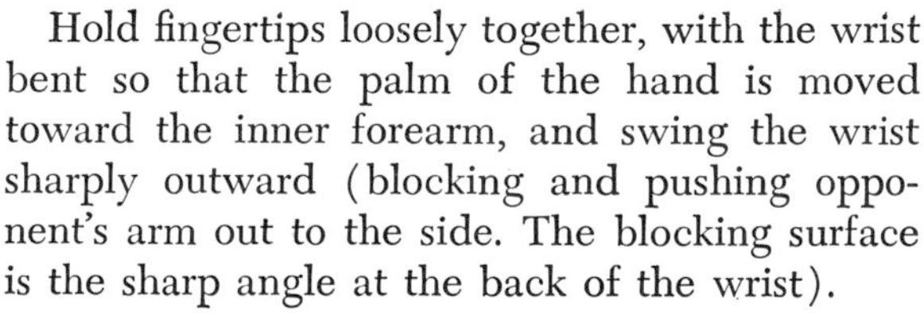

Hold fingertips loosely together, with the wrist bent so that the palm of the hand is moved toward the inner forearm, and swing the wrist sharply outward (blocking and pushing opponent's arm out to the side. The blocking surface is the sharp angle at the back of the wrist).

BACK-HAND BLOCK (*Sohn-Doong Mak-Ki*)

This is useful in blocking a punch when you wish to move in quickly and grab opponent with the same hand.

Swing open hand outward, palm out (blocking and pushing opponent's arm out to the side. The blocking surface is the flat back of the hand).

RIDGE-HAND BLOCK (*Sohn-Nal-Doong Mak-Ki*)

This is a focused block. As a variation of the basic Low Block, High Block, and Outside Middle Block (see pages 112, 115, and 120), it has many uses, and is especially applicable in combination with an immediate counterattack with the same hand. Only one of many possibilities is illustrated here.

HAMMER-FIST BLOCK (*Me-Chu-Mok Mak-Ki*)

This is a focused block. The striking edge is the pinkie side of the fist. It is used mainly in blocking kicks, by striking the instep, shin, or calf.

KNEE BLOCK (*Moo-Roop Mak-Ki*)

By raising the knee high and turning it inward, the knee and thigh may be used very effectively to block punches or kicks to the lower abdomen and groin. The tactic has the added advantage of placing your leg in position to counter immediately with a kick.

KICKING BLOCKS (*Cha-Ki-Lo Mak-Ki*)

Many kicks may be used for blocking purposes, and some are illustrated here. (For detailed instructions on kicking, see the chapter entitled "Kicking Techniques," which follows.)

1. Front-Kick Block *(Ap-Cha-Ki-Lo Mak-Ki)*

This may be used very effectively in blocking kicks by striking the opponent's leg with the ball or the sole of your foot before he can raise it sufficiently to execute his attack.

2. Side-Kick Block *(Yop-Cha-Ki-Lo Mak-Ki)*

This may be used, in much the same way as the Front Kick, to block the opponent's kick by striking with your Knife Foot (outer edge of the foot) to his thigh, knee, or lower leg before he can extend his kick toward you.

3. Crescent-Kick Block *(Pyo-Jok-Cha-Ki-Lo Mak-Ki)*

This is effective in blocking kicks or punches, by striking the offending arm or leg away to the side, using the arch of the foot.

9

Kicking Techniques

Tae Kwon Do places special emphasis on kicking, and techniques for utilizing the feet as striking weapons have been developed and refined into a unique and highly efficient system, in which it is possible to inflict pain, injury, or death at a single blow. Thus, it is fortunate that many years of practice are required to master the almost surgical precision with which the various striking areas of the feet are conditioned and employed in combination with different kicks to produce such deadly effects. These years spent in practice provide time in which one examines his spirit as he discovers his ability. When body and spirit develop together, confidence and clarity flow inward and outward, and the individual is enhanced, raised above the mean needs for boastful display and irresponsible violence. In this manner, one achieves prudence, knowing that life is the private possession of no one, but is the correspondence which inspires all things.

Among the physical techniques of Tae Kwon Do, effective kicking methods are the most difficult to perfect, for they involve the whole body in such a manner as to apply the greatest possible force in positions having the least available base of support. In effect, they call for a dancer's stretch and agility, in combination with such speed and concentration of force as is unparalleled in any other combative sport. Constant stretching is required, particularly of the joints, muscles, and ligaments of the hips, groin, knees, and ankles, in order to achieve and maintain the optimal physical condition in which the necessary movements are possible. The back and stomach muscles must also be strengthened in order to be capable of generating the force which is to be transmitted through the leg to the striking foot, and of maintaining adequate balance, in an unnatural posture, to withstand the shock of impact. For these purposes, the stretching and strengthening exercises described in the earlier chapter on calisthenics are to be practiced as a matter of course before each session of kicking practice.

The following points are basic to all the kicking methods described in this chapter, and in fact to all the kicking techniques of Tae Kwon Do:

1. All kicking motions begin with the hip. It is as if the striking foot were the end of a long and supple whip, having, in itself, comparatively little weight or strength, but transmitting all the energy of the one who wields the whip augmented many times into tremendous force.

2. The supporting foot, which bears the whole weight of the body in standing kicks, must be securely placed, and in flying kicks must be curved up in the direction of the kick, to make available all possible force and maintain adequate balance.

3. Balance must be such as will not nullify movement, but will rather give impetus to movement, without leading to instability. Examples:

a. Movement is nullified by leaning backward while kicking to the front, which distributes the weight evenly along the length of the body, but in so doing weakens the kick and slows recovery.

b. Balance gives impetus to movement when one stands erect (leaning forward slightly) while kicking to the front, which permits the force of the body's weight to be transmitted forward to the point of impact.

c. Leaning too far forward while kicking to the front leads to instability, for one's balance is overcommitted to the action, making recovery difficult.

4. After kicking, one must recover quickly. The kicking foot must be withdrawn: to prevent its being grabbed by the opponent, to be ready for the next technique, and to have the knee of the raised leg available, if necessary, to block the opponent's counterattack to the groin or abdomen.

5. Hand position while kicking is very important to maintain balance and to protect you against a possible counterattack by the opponent. The following hand positions should be used (except when otherwise indicated) when practicing any of the kicks described in this chapter, according to whether you are kicking in Front Stance, Back Stance, or Horseback Stance.

Note: Variations in these hand positions are employed only for special purposes, for which see the later chapters on sparring and the forms.

Hand position while kicking in Front Stance:

a. Assume Ready Stance.

b. Slide your right foot one long step backward. Simultaneously cross both forearms in front of your chest with your fists palm down.

(continued)

c. Assume Front Stance. Simultaneously sweep both forearms down and outward to your sides at about a 45° angle from the horizontal, snapping your fists palm in and locking your elbows straight.

Execute a kick with your back foot with your arms in this position, extended outward to the side. After the kick is completed, bring your kicking foot back into position near the knee of your supporting leg and, simultaneously cross your forearms, as in b, above. As you put your kicking foot down and assume Front Stance, simultaneously sweep your forearms down and outward, as in c, above.

Hand position while kicking in Back Stance:

a. Assume Ready Stance.

b. Slide your right foot one step backward. Simultaneously pull your right fist back to your hip palm down, and raise your left forearm across your chest with your left fist, palm in, near your right cheek, twisting your upper body to the right.

c. Assume Back Stance. Simultaneously, sweep your left forearm forward and down into position with your left fist, palm down, out in front of you at the level of your chin, and thrust your right fist forward into position, snapping it palm in in front of your solar plexus.

Execute a kick with either foot with your arms in this position, c. After completing the kick and as you retract your kicking foot, pull both fists back, as in b, above. As you put your kicking foot down and assume Back Stance, simultaneously bring your fists forward, as in c, above.

Hand position while kicking in Horseback Stance:

a. Assume Ready Stance.

b. Slide your right foot one step forward. Simultaneously cross your forearms in front of your chest, with your left fist palm down in front of your right hip and your right fist palm in near your left cheek.

(*continued*)

c. As your right foot completes its step forward, simultaneously sweep your right forearm downward and out and pull your left fist back, crossing your wrists.

d. Assume Horseback Stance, facing right toward the opponent. Simultaneously complete the motion of sweeping your left forearm downward and out to the side into position with elbow locked straight and fist snapped palm in, at the same time pulling left fist back to hip palm up.

Execute a kick with your arms in this position, extended down and outward to the sides. After the kick is completed, bring your kicking foot back into position near the knee of your supporting leg and simultaneously cross your forearms, as in b, above. As you put your kicking foot down again, sweep your forearms down and outward, crossing your wrists, as in c, above. As you assume Horseback Stance, simultaneously complete the motion of sweeping your forearms downward and out to the sides, locking the elbows straight, as in d, above. See Side Kick, page 164, and Back Kick, page 172, for Walking Kick illustrations.

FRONT KICK (*Ap Cha-Ki*)

Effective in strikes to the face, solar plexus, ribs, and lower abdomen. In the Front Straight Kick, the knee does not bend. But in the regular Front Kick it is important to raise the knee of the kicking leg high, pointing it toward the target, before extending the leg. When kicking, keep the body erect, facing front. These techniques may be applied from any stance, though Front or Back Stance is most common. Practice first at solar plexus level, then gradually kick up as high as possible. There are different forms of Front Kick, serving different purposes. The striking area is the ball of the foot, but the instep may be used in strikes to the groin.

1. Front Straight Kick *(Ap Cha-Ol-Li-Ki)*

Swing kicking leg forward and up, keeping the knee straight, and tense the instep down to kick with the ball of the foot, with the toes curled back. (Purpose: mainly for practice in stretching to kick high.)

2. Front Thrust Kick

(*continued*)

a. Raise knee of kicking leg forward and up, keeping leg sharply bent (with kicking foot near knee of supporting leg).

b. Thrust kicking foot forward and up to target with upper body slightly bent forward, extending the hip and locking the knee straight, with the instep tensed down to kick with the ball of the foot. (This is the basic Front Kick technique, possessing the greatest strength and power to inflict the most damage.)

Front Thrust Kick with Back Stance

3. Front Snap Kick

This is essentially the same as the Front Thrust Kick, except that the hip is not fully extended, the upper body is slightly bent forward, and the kicking foot is snapped back into position near the knee of the supporting leg as quickly as possible. (The Snap Kick is faster than the Thrust Kick, more accurate, and more controllable. The kicking foot, being snapped back quickly, is less likely to be grabbed by the opponent, and one is in position to execute another kick or follow-up technique immediately. For these reasons, the Snap Kick is more often used in sparring than the Thrust Kick.)

4. Walking Front Kick

This is a Front Kick executed in combination with a step forward, toward the opponent. As with the Front Kick, the Walking Front Kick may be executed in Front Stance or Back Stance.

Assume Front Stance (or Back Stance). Shift your weight to your front foot and raise your back foot to kick. Execute a Front Kick, then bring your kicking foot back into position near the knee of your supporting leg. (All steps, thus far, are the same as in the Front Thrust Kick or Front Snap Kick, illustrated above.) Now, bring your kicking foot down one step forward and assume Front Stance (or Back Stance) again.

5. Instep Front Kick

Applied in a manner similar to the Front Snap Kick, except that the toes are pointed down and the striking area is the instep. This is used in attacks to the groin when the angle of attack makes striking with the ball of the foot inappropriate, or in sparring when one does not wish to inflict serious injury.

SIDE KICK (*Yop Cha-Ki*)

Effective in strikes to the head, face, neck, armpit, ribs, solar plexus, lower abdomen, knees, and instep (stamping). The striking areas are the heel and the Knife Foot. When kicking, bend your torso slightly forward and turned in, so that your chest is toward the target. The Side Kick may be executed from any stance.

The Side Thrust Kick is the basic form, and it is explained below. But there is also the Side Snap Kick, in which the hip is not fully extended and the kicking foot is withdrawn, as quickly as possible, into position (near the knee of the supporting leg) to kick again. The Side Straight Kick is used mainly to practice stretching to kick high to the side.

When executing a Side Kick, simultaneously execute either a Side Punch or an outward Hammer-Fist Strike parallel to the kicking leg, using the fist on the same side as the kicking foot.

1. Side Straight Kick *(Yop Cha-Ol-Li-Ki)*

Kick with the knee locked straight as an effective stretching exercise.

2. Side Thrust Kick

(continued)

Right Side Thrust Kick

a. Raise knee of kicking leg forward and up, keeping leg sharply bent (with kicking foot near knee of supporting leg).

b. Pivoting on supporting foot, swing hip of kicking leg forward and thrust kicking foot forward to target, extending the hip and locking the knee straight, with the instep pulled back and turned down on the ankle (kicking with the Knife Foot or the heel).

Left Side Thrust Kick

3. Side Snap Kick

Though not as powerful as the Side Thrust Kick, the Snap Kick is faster and more accurate, and puts one in a better position to follow up with other techniques. Thus, it is more often used in sparring.

4. Walking Side Kick

This is a Side Kick executed in combination with a step forward, toward the opponent. As indicated above, the Side Kick may be executed in Front Stance or Back Stance, but the Walking Side Kick is usually executed in Horseback Stance, as shown in the drawing.

Assume Horseback Stance, facing left, toward the target. Shift your weight to your left foot and raise your right foot, crossing it in front of your left foot. Shift your weight to your right foot and kick with your left foot. (Walking and kicking to the right side is executed in a similar manner, i.e., the walking foot crosses in front of the kicking foot.)

Walking Right Side Kick in Horseback Stance

front view

front view

(continued)

Walking Right Side Thrust Kick

Walking Left Side Thrust Kick

ROUND KICK (*Dol-Rio Cha-Ki*)

Effective in strikes to the head, face, neck, ribs, solar plexus, and lower abdomen. The striking areas are: the ball of the foot, for breaking techniques or to inflict severe injury; and the instep, for greater extension to reach a more distant target or to avoid inflicting injury in practice sparring. When kicking, twist the hip to bring the kicking leg into range while keeping the body slightly bent down to the side and turned in, facing the target.

As with the Front and Side Kicks, the Round Kick may also be executed as a Thrust or Snap Kick. In the Snap Kick, the kicking foot is withdrawn as quickly as possible, the kicking leg unwinding and snapping back with the action of a whip. The Thrust Kick, which is more forcible for breaking or to inflict injury, is the basic form, and is described below. The Round Kick is most often applied from Front or Back Stance.

1. Round Thrust Kick

Left Round Thrust Kick

a. Raise kicking knee out and up, keeping leg sharply bent out and back.

b. Pivoting on supporting foot, swing hip of kicking leg forward and whip kicking foot out, forward, and in (describing an arc) to target, extending the leg until the knee locks straight. Kick with instep pulled back and the toes curled away, striking with the ball of the foot.

Right Round Thrust Kick

2. Round Snap Kick

Applied in a manner similar to the Round Thrust Kick, except that immediately after kicking, the knee is sharply bent and the kicking foot is snapped back with a whip-like effect. This technique is less strong but faster than the Round Thrust Kick and is therefore more often used in sparring.

3. Round Kick Variation

This technique is applicable in free sparring to extend the reach of your leg to kick at a longer distance. It is also especially useful as a deceptive tactic to fake a Front Kick and, then, in a single motion, execute a Round Kick Variation. The striking surface is the instep of the foot, and the kick is usually directed to face level and executed in Back Stance.

a. Raise the knee of your kicking foot straight forward and up, as if you were preparing for a Front Kick. Hold your toes pointed down and tense your instep.

b. Execute a Round Kick Variation, twisting your hip as your kicking leg swings forward in a rising arc, and strike at face level with your instep, the knee of your kicking leg locked straight and your toes pointed.

Note: See Free Sparring section for application in free sparring.

4. Walking Round Kick

This is a Round Kick executed in combination with a step forward, toward the opponent. As with the Round Kick, the Walking Round Kick may be executed in Front Stance or Back Stance.

Assume Front Stance (or Back Stance). Shift your weight to your front foot and raise your back foot to kick. Execute a Round Kick, then bring your kicking foot back, with the knee bent sharply as if ready to kick again. (All steps, thus far, are the same as in the Round Thrust Kick or Round Snap Kick, illustrated above.) Now, bring your kicking foot down one step forward and assume Front Stance (or Back Stance) again.

BACK KICK *(Dwi Cha-Ki)*

Effective in strikes to the head, face, chest, solar plexus, ribs, knee, or instep (stamping) of opponent standing behind you. The striking area is the heel of the foot. When kicking, lean upper body slightly backward, twisting hip inward to generate power, and turn your head sufficiently to see target before you strike.* The Back Kick is easily applied from Front or Back Stance or Normal Stance.

When executing a Back Kick, it is optional to execute, simultaneously, a Side Punch or an outward Hammer-Fist Strike parallel to the kicking leg, using the fist on the same side as the kicking foot.

* One may also execute the Back Kick without looking, i.e., a Blind Back Kick. But this technique should be reserved for emergency situations only, as in an actual street fight with more than one opponent, in which it would be inadvisable to take your eye off the opponent in front. The Blind Back Kick is not recommended for sparring, for it is always dangerous to turn your back to the opponent, which opens you to attack, or to execute an attacking technique without seeing the target, which may cause accidental injury to a vital point of the sparring partner.

a. Raise knee of kicking leg forward and up, keeping leg sharply bent (with kicking foot near knee of supporting leg).

b. Thrust kicking foot straight back to target, extending the hip, until knee locks straight. Kick with the heel, keeping the instep pulled up.

Walking Back Kick

This is a Back Kick executed in combination with a step forward, toward the opponent.

With your eyes focused on the target, shift your weight to your front foot, and step toward the target with your back foot, crossing it behind your kicking foot. As you shift your weight to your walking foot, pivot and execute a Back Kick with your other foot. (In walking and kicking to either side, be sure to cross the walking foot behind the kicking foot.)

Walking Right Back Kick in Horseback Stance

front view

front view

HOOK KICK (*Dwi-Dol-Rio Cha-Ki*)

Effective in strikes to the face, head, solar plexus, ribs, and lower abdomen. It is a surprising maneuver, in that the leg is extended in one direction—like a Side Kick or Back Kick—and suddenly hooked back, to strike in another place. For breaking techniques or to inflict injury, strike with the heel. In practice sparring, in order to avoid inflicting injury turn the instep down and point the toes, to strike with the sole of the foot, or use caution when striking with the heel.

(*continued*)

a. Raise knee of kicking leg forward and up, keeping leg sharply bent (with kicking foot near knee of supporting leg).

b. Pivoting on supporting foot, swing hip of kicking leg forward and thrust kicking foot forward and slightly to the side of target (i.e., so that target is behind your heel. Up to this point, the motion is like a Side Kick that has missed its aim).

c. At the instant the kicking leg is fully extended, bend the knee sharply—without altering the position of the thigh—pulling, or "hooking," the foot horizontally back to strike the target with the heel (or the sole).

WHEEL KICK (*Hu-Rio Cha-Ki*)

Effective in strikes to the head and face. The striking area is the heel of the foot, but in practice sparring use the outer edge of the foot (Knife Foot). When kicking, keep the body erect, and generate the motion by rotating the hip.

Without bending the knee, raise the kicking leg, describing a large circle, moving the foot forward and inward (crossing in front of the supporting foot), up to head level, then swing the kicking foot outward and forward to strike the target with the heel or the Knife Foot, and down again to the floor.

Note: The muscles of the stomach, back, and hip are incorporated to move the kicking leg, with the knee locked straight, through the described circle, or "wheel." This kick is very difficult, and must be practiced diligently, for it can only be used, in actual sparring, when it can be executed with great speed. The outward and downward part of the circular motion (striking and returning to place) must be very strong.

TURNING KICK (*Dol-Myo Cha-Ki*)

When perfected and executed with speed and accuracy, the Turning Kick is an excellent surprise maneuver. The turn gives the illusion that you are moving away from the opponent, and he may not realize, until too late, that you are merely changing position rapidly to attack him from a different angle. It is especially effective as a method of ducking an attack to the head and counterattacking in a single motion. The Turning Kick is usually applied from Back Stance.

It is important, in all Turning Kicks, that the head spin faster and farther than the body, in order to keep the opponent within your sight as much as possible and to permit you to see the target before kicking.

1. Turning Back Kick *(Mom-Dol-Rio Dwi-Cha-Ki)*

a. Pivoting on front (supporting) foot, spin backward and, as you are turning, raise knee of back (kicking) leg high, keeping leg sharply bent.

b. The instant the back of your kicking hip points toward the target, thrust kicking foot straight back to strike opponent with your heel.

2. Turning Hook Kick *(Mom-Dol-Rio Dwi-Dol-Rio Cha-Ki)*

a. Pivoting on front (supporting) foot, spin backward and, as you are turning, raise knee of back (kicking) leg high, keeping leg sharply bent.

b. The instant you can see the target, thrust kicking foot out and in front of target (like a Side Kick released too soon) and immediately bend knee of kicking leg sharply, hooking foot back horizontally to strike opponent with your heel (or the sole of your foot).

3. Turning Wheel Kick *(Mom-Dol-Rio Hu-Rio-Cha-Ki)*

a. Pivoting on front (supporting) foot, spin backward—initiating the spinning motion by twisting the hip, first, in the direction of the turn—and, as you are turning, raise the back (kicking) leg straight up without bending the knee.

b. The instant you can see the target—and while your body is still spinning—swing the kicking leg, in one continuous motion, outward and down (the striking action), keeping the leg straight, and striking with the heel or Knife Foot.

4. Turning Side Kick *(Mom-Dol-Rio Yop-Cha-Ki)*

a. Pivoting on front (supporting) foot, spin backward and, as you are turning, raise knee of back (kicking) leg high, keeping leg sharply bent.

b. The instant the side of your kicking hip points toward the target (viz., when your body has turned 45° farther around toward the opponent than if you were to execute a Turning Back Kick), thrust kicking foot straight out to the side, striking target with the Knife Foot, toes pointed down.

COMPLETE TURNING KICK
(*Wan-Jon-Mom-Dol-Rio Cha-Ki*)

This is a surprise tactic similar to the Turning Kick (above), except that the body turns completely around (360°) in the process of kicking, and the kick is executed with the foot that was originally in front. The Complete Turning Kick is an advanced technique and requires much practice. It is applied from sparring stance (i.e., Back Stance), and is very effective when used in combination with other kicks following in sequence, such as Jumping Kicks, Turning Kicks, and Jumping Turning Kicks. (See pages 188–191 for jumping techniques.)

Assume Back Stance. Slide back foot forward one step and spin in one complete turn (360°), executing a Turning Wheel Kick, or Turning Hook Kick with the foot that was originally in front. For example, when standing with the left foot in back, slide the left foot forward, spin 360° to your right and execute a Turning Wheel Kick with the right foot. When standing with the right foot in back, slide the right foot forward, spin 360° to your left and execute a Back Wheel Kick with the left foot. (**Note:** while spinning, raise the kicking foot in preparation to kick when you have turned halfway, or 180°, and execute the kick as you complete the turn.)

Complete Turning Kick Variation

In this variation, a Round Kick is executed with the foot that was originally in back. Assume Back Stance. Slide back foot forward one step and spin in one complete turn (360°), executing a Round Kick with the same foot used to take the first step forward (the foot originally in back). For example, when standing with the left foot in back, slide the left foot forward, spin 360° to your right and execute a Round Kick with the left foot. When standing with the right foot in back, slide the right foot forward, spin 360° to your left and execute a Round Kick with the right foot.

CRESCENT KICK *(Pyo-Jok Cha-Ki)*

Effective in strikes to the ribs, in blocking arm and leg attacks, and in sweeping opponent's front leg out from under him. The striking areas are the arch of the foot for the Inward Crescent Kick, and the Knife Foot for the Outward Crescent Kick.

1. Inward Crescent Kick *(An-Pyo-Jok Cha-Ki)*

Raise kicking knee high in front and swing foot out, up, and in, in a smooth arc (with the foot pulled back on the ankle and toes pointing up), to block an attack to your own solar plexus (striking the punching arm, or kicking leg, with the arch of your foot), or to attack face.

Note: In this kick, the leg is not extended straight out, but the knee stays bent, so that the kicking leg itself is curved, or crescent-shaped.

This kick may be practiced by extending the opposite hand forward, thumb uppermost, and kicking the palm (viz., executing a Crescent Kick with the arch of the right foot to the palm of the left hand, and with the arch of the left foot to the palm of the right hand).

2. Outward Crescent Kick *(Ba-Kat-Pyo-Jok Cha-Ki)*

Raise kicking knee high in front and swing foot in, up, and out, in a smooth arc (with the foot pulled back on the ankle and the toes pointing up), to block an attack to your own solar plexus (striking the attacking arm or leg outward with the Knife Foot), or to attack the face.

HALF-MOON KICK (*Ban-Dal Cha-Ki*)

Essentially, the Half-Moon Kick is a blend of the Front Kick and the Round Kick. Its advantage is that it is a fast action which confuses the opponent, who does not know whether to defend against a Front Kick or a Round Kick—until it is too late. The striking area is the ball of the foot, and the kick is usually directed to the chest or stomach. It may be applied from Front or Back Stance. When kicking, keep the body erect, facing front.

a. Raise kicking knee forward and up, keeping leg sharply bent (as for a Front Kick).

b. Pivoting on supporting foot, swing hip of kicking leg forward and whip kicking foot out, forward, and in (describing an arc, similar to that in a Round Kick), extending the leg until the knee locks straight, and keeping the instep tensed down to strike with the ball of the foot.

GRAB KICK (*Job-Ko Cha-Ki*)

This is a combination technique, involving grabbing and kicking at the same time. It may be used against one opponent, or against two, by grabbing one and kicking the other simultaneously. In this technique, any kick may be used which is appropriate to the situation.

HOP KICK (*Gool-Lo Cha-Ki*)

The purpose of the hop is to move quickly and smoothly into range of an opponent standing just out of reach of your normal kick. When properly executed, the two actions, hopping and kicking, have the appearance of one smooth motion covering a surprising distance. The hop is very effective in preparation for any kick, particularly the Front Kick, Side Kick, Round Kick, and Hook Kick.

The hop itself is made by bringing the back foot quickly forward, into position next to the front foot—which is, simultaneously, raised for the kick. The Hop Kick is used in Back Stance or Horseback Stance. The Hop Side Kick is illustrated below, as an example of this technique.

1. Hop Side Kick *(Gool-Lo Yop Cha-Ki)*

a. Bring back foot quickly forward, into position next to front foot.

b. Simultaneously raise front (kicking) knee forward and twist hip, keeping leg sharply bent, in preparation for a Side Kick. (These two motions, bringing the back foot forward and raising the front knee, occur at the same time, so that when you hop forward, there is an instant in which both feet are off the ground.)

c. The instant the back foot touches the ground, thrust kicking foot out, executing a Side Kick.

2. Step-Hop Side Kick *(Dit-Ko Gool-Lo Yop Cha-Ki)*

a. Slide front foot forward one step. (The purpose of this preliminary step is to cover additional ground toward a more distant target.)

b. Hop forward with back foot and execute a Side Kick with front foot (as above).

JUMPING KICK (*Tdwi-Yo Cha-Ki*)

The purpose of the jump is to gain height and additional momentum for a very forcible kick, usually to the opponent's head, neck, or chest. The Jumping Kick is very effective as a surprise tactic to raise you above the opponent's blocking or attacking arms, or legs, into a position to kick horizontally or downward, knocking him off balance. The jump may be used mainly with the Front Kick, Round Kick, Side Kick, and Hook Kick, and may be applied from any stance.

There are three forms of Jumping Kick, but it is important, in every case, to raise the knees of both the kicking and the non-kicking leg high, and in the direction of the kick, in order to gain maximum height and momentum. It is also essential to keep the torso fairly erect, but inclined in the direction of the kick.

1. Jumping High Kick *(Tdwi-Yo No-Pi Cha-Ki)*

Slide one foot one step forward and jump as high as possible—raising the other knee, as if pumping with it to gain additional height—and kick with the jumping foot (viz., the kicking foot is the same as was used to step forward and jump).

Example: Jumping Front Kick (*Tdwi-Yo Ap-Cha-Ki*) (As stated above this technique may also be used for Jumping Side Kick, Jumping Hook Kick, and Jumping Round Kick).

2. One-Step Jumping Kick *(Tdwi-Yo Doo-Bal Cha-Ki)*

Slide one foot one step forward and jump as high as possible—executing a kick with the other foot.

Example: One-Step Jumping Side Kick (*Tdwi-Yo Doo-Bal Yop-Cha-Ki*) (This technique may also be applied to One-Step Jumping Front Kick, One-Step Jumping Hook Kick, or One-Step Jumping Round Kick).

3. Standing Jumping Kick *(Tdwi-Yo Han-Bal Cha-Ki)*

Jump as high as possible—with both feet leaving the ground at the same time, as in a broad jump—and execute a kick with either foot.

Example: Standing-Jumping Round Kick (*Tdwi-Yo Han-Bal Dol-Rio Cha-Ki*) (This technique may also be applied to Standing-Jumping Front Kick, Standing-Jumping Hook Kick, or Standing-Jumping Side Kick).

FLYING KICK (*Nal-La Cha-Ki*)

The Flying Kick is essentially the same as the Jumping Kick, except that it has more forward motion. It is used to reach more distant targets, as, for example, an opponent who is withdrawing out of your normal reach. It is also used in leaping over obstacles in order to kick at a target beyond them. For this purpose, it is often combined with a preparatory run toward the target. All the kicks used in jumping may be applied with the flying technique.

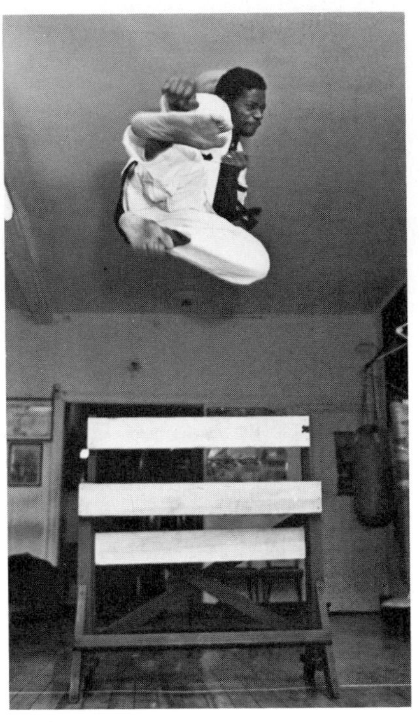

Flying Side Kick

Note that the foot used to take off is the same foot used to kick. Refer to the drawing—the right foot, used to spring into the jump, is the same foot used in kicking.

JUMPING TURNING KICK
(Tdwi-Yo Dol-Myo Cha-Ki)

Jumping may be used with any Turning Kick. In all combinations, it is important to raise both the kicking and the non-kicking legs high, in order to gain maximum height and momentum in jumping and turning.

There are two forms of Jumping Turning Kick:

1. Jumping Turning Kick *(Tdwi-Yo Mom-Dol-Rio Cha-Ki)*

a. Slide one foot forward one step and jump as high as possible.

b. As you jump, spin backward in the air (turning in the direction of the stepping and jumping foot) and kick with the same foot. (For example, when stepping forward and jumping with the right foot, spin backward to the right and kick with the right foot; when stepping forward and jumping with the left foot, spin backward to the left and kick with the left foot.)

(This technique may be combined with any of several kicks, as Jumping Turning Back Kick, Jumping Turning Hook Kick, Jumping Turning Side Kick, or Jumping Turning Wheel Kick.)

2. Standing-Jump Turning Kick *(Sun Che Tdwi-Yo Mom-Dol-Rio Cha-Ki)*

Jump as high as possible—with both feet leaving the ground at the same time—and spinning backward in the air, kick with the back foot (i.e., the foot that, on completing the turn, moves first toward the opponent, as in the regular Turning Kick).

(This technique may also be combined with any of several kicks, as Standing-Jump Turning Back Kick, Standing-Jump Turning Hook Kick, Standing-Jump Turning Side Kick, or Standing-Jump Turning Wheel Kick.)

JUMPING TWO-FOOT (Rapid Sequence) KICKS (*Doo-Bal Dang-Sang*)

This advanced technique is designed to attack two different targets in rapid sequence. It is very difficult, and requires perfect control over balance and well-stretched leg muscles and hip joints. Any of several kicks may be used in this combination, as the following examples illustrate.

1. Jumping Front Kicks (Rapid Sequence)

Jumping and executing two Front Kicks in rapid sequence to two different targets.

2. Jumping Front and Round Kicks (Rapid Sequence)

Jumping and executing a Front Kick to one target and a Round Kick to another target in rapid sequence.

3. Jumping Scissors Kicks

Jumping and catching the opponent in a scissors motion of both legs, swinging your back leg behind the opponent and your front leg, in a manner similar to a Hook Kick or Wheel Kick, in front of him. This technique may be applied at a low, middle, or high level, viz., with your back leg striking behind the opponent's ankle and your front leg striking his solar plexus, or with your back leg striking behind the opponent's knee and your front leg striking his throat, or with your back leg striking behind his thigh and your front leg striking his face. The Jumping Scissors Kick is mainly used as a combination technique to kick the opponent and simultaneously sweep him to the ground.

JUMPING DOUBLE-FOOT KICK
(Tdwi-Yo Mo-Dum-Bal Cha-Ki)

This is another advanced technique, in which both feet are employed to strike the same target simultaneously and with maximum force.

1. Jumping Double Front Kick

Jumping and executing two Front Kicks, using both feet simultaneously, to a single target.

2. Jumping Double Side Kick

Jumping and executing a Side Kick with one foot supported by a kick with the other foot simultaneously to a single target.

JUMPING ONE-FOOT DOUBLE KICK (*Tdwi-Yo Han-Bal Doo-Bon Cha-Ki)*

This technique requires maximum speed as well as agility, and only the very advanced practitioner can be expected to master it. It involves jumping as high as possible and executing two kicks in rapid sequence with the same foot.

1. Jumping One-Foot Double Front Kick

Jumping and executing two Front Kicks in rapid sequence with the same foot.

2. Jumping One-Foot Double Side Kick

Jumping and executing two Side Kicks in rapid sequence with the same foot.

KNEE KICK *(Moo-Roop Cha-Ki)*

When in close combat, and too close to the opponent to kick easily with your foot, the Knee Kick is very effective to the groin, solar plexus, and, in combination with hand techniques, in kicking to the face.

1. Front Knee Kick to the Groin or to the Solar Plexus

Raise kicking knee sharply forward and up, striking opponent in the groin.

2. Front Knee Kick to the Face

Grasp opponent's head in both hands and pull it down toward you—simultaneously raising your knee sharply forward and up, striking him in the face.

3. Round Knee Kick to the Solar Plexus

When facing opponent whose body is turned slightly away from you, raise kicking knee up and out (as in the standard Round Kick), and then swing it sharply forward and in, striking opponent's solar plexus.

HEEL KICK (*Dwi-Chook Cha-Ki*)

Downward kick with heel (stamping). Effective as a finishing technique directed against a floored opponent.

HANDSTAND DOUBLE-FOOT KICK
(*Ko-Ku-Lo Cha-Ki*)

Stoop down and raise your legs in a handstand in one swift motion, kicking opponent in the face with both feet simultaneously, or hooking both feet around his neck in a scissors hold, and pulling him forward and down, over your back, as you bring your feet down again to the floor.

FALLING KICK (*O-Po Cha-Ki*)

This kick may be executed from the floor when an opponent approaches to attack while you are down. It is also very effective when executed *as you are falling* to dodge an opponent's rushing attack.

Note: When falling to dodge an attack, one must fall to the side away from the opponent, not across him; e.g., if he attacks with a right punch, fall to his right (your left), behind the punch.

1. Falling Hook Kick (Sweep)

Fall to one side (avoiding opponent's attack) and hook uppermost leg behind opponent's front knee. Pull his knee forward and simultaneously sweep his foot back from under him with your other leg, throwing him face down or backward.

2. Falling Round Kick

Fall to one side and simultaneously execute a Round Kick with uppermost foot to opponent's face, solar plexus, or abdomen.

3. Falling Side Kick

Fall to one side and simultaneously execute a Side Kick with uppermost foot to opponent's ribs.

4. Falling Wheel Kick

Fall to one side and immediately roll forward, and as the lower leg turns uppermost, swing that foot up and back in a wide arc, striking opponent's face, solar plexus, or abdomen with your heel.

STOOPING TURNING KICK
(*Na-Chu-O Mom-Dol-Rio Cha-Ki*)*

These techniques are effective as kicks or leg sweeps. They must, however, be executed with great speed to be effective, and one should be prepared to follow up with another defending or attacking technique immediately, for if the sweep is not successful in throwing the opponent down, one will be left at a disadvantage, being on the floor himself.

1. Stooping Turning Kick—On One Knee

a. Begin from a standing position with one foot forward.

b. Bend front knee forward and inward and drop to the floor.

c. Using a twisting motion of the upper torso, turn backward, pivoting on front knee, and swing the back leg out and around, placing hands on the floor to assist in the turn.

d. Execute a Stooping Turning Kick to opponent's ankle or knee with your heel, or a sweep with the back of your ankle. (One may also kick higher, striking opponent's ribs or abdomen with the heel.)

* See page 241 for illustration of Stooping Turning Kick.

2. Stooping Turning Kick—On Ball of Foot

a. Begin from a standing position with one foot forward.

b. Bend front knee forward and inward and drop to the floor, placing weight on ball of front foot and touching hands to floor.

c. Using a twisting motion of the upper torso, turn backward, pivoting on ball of front foot, and swing back leg out and around—

d. Executing a Stooping Turning Kick, or a sweep, to opponent's ankle or knee.

Note: Turning on the ball of the foot is faster than turning on the knee, and is therefore preferable as a sweeping technique. And it has the added advantage of leaving the practitioner in a better position (i.e., squatting on the ball of the foot) to regain a standing posture at the end.

Turning on the knee places the practitioner in a more stable position on the floor, and it is therefore a stronger maneuver for kicking, rather than merely sweeping.

10

Advanced Positions and Combinations

ROCK PUSHING

Used in Blocking or Attacking

THRUST CONCENTRATION

Thrusting or Pushing Forward with Open Hands

YOKE STRIKE

Simultaneous Outward Elbow Strikes

FOREARM STRIKE

Striking (the Palm) with the Back of the Forearm

BULL BLOCK

Simultaneous High Blocks

OPEN WING CONCENTRATION

Pushing or Attacking to the Side

11

Sparring Techniques

Individual practice of the hand and foot techniques and the formal exercises is preparatory to the main training activity of Tae Kwon Do, which is sparring, or practice fighting. In sparring, the student engages with an opponent to practice applications of the basic techniques in a dynamic situation in order to quicken his perception and develop speed and coordination. Constant practice in sparring, in conjunction with the individual practice of the basic techniques, is necessary to the development of the student's practical effectiveness and self-confidence in confrontation with others.

For training purposes, there are four forms of practice fighting: Three-Step Sparring, One-Step Sparring, Arranged Free Sparring, and Free Sparring. There are many and diverse possibilities and applications within each of these categories, but due to the spatial limits of this book, they cannot all be included. Nonetheless, if the examples in each of the categories illustrated in this chapter are studied and practiced thoroughly, the student will have a solid foundation in the fundamentals of practice fighting, and indications toward more advanced techniques and combinations which he may explore.

When sparring, as at all other times, the Tae Kwon Do practitioner must be mindful of the respect due to others, and so, at the beginning of each sparring session, each partner should bow to the other, as a sign of mutual courtesy.

THREE-STEP SPARRING (*Se-Bon Kyo-Lu-Ki*)

This is the elementary form of sparring, in which the student learns basic methods of defense and counterattack, and develops speed in his reflexes. However, the emphasis in Three-Step Sparring is on speed and effectiveness in defensive techniques, and so, when performing this exercise, special attention should be paid to blocking. The examples given below should be practiced hundreds of times, until they are perfected.

Three-Step Sparring is performed as follows: One student assumes the role of attacker, and one that of defender. After each exercise, the roles are reversed. The term "Three-Step" refers to the fact that the attacker advances three long steps, executing the same attacking technique each time, and the defender responds by moving backward three long steps, executing the same blocking technique with each step. Immediately after blocking the third time, the defender executes a counterattack.

Each exercise begins, in actual practice, with these three motions:

- Attacker and defender bow and stand at attention, facing each other, about two long steps apart.

- Attacker slides his right foot back (or slides his left foot forward) one long step, assuming Front Stance, and simultaneously executes a Low Block with left forearm and yells, indicating that he is ready to attack.
- Defender, waiting at attention, yells to indicate that he is ready to defend himself.

1. High Punch Attack

a. Attacker slides right foot forward one long step, assumes Front Stance, and simultaneously executes a High Punch toward the face of defender with right fist.

b. Defender simultaneously (in response to attack) slides right foot back one long step, assumes Front Stance, and executes a High Block with left forearm, blocking the punch.

(*continued*)

c. Attacker immediately slides left foot forward and executes a High Punch with left fist.

d. Defender simultaneously slides left foot back and executes a High Block with right forearm.

e. Attacker immediately slides right foot forward and executes a High Punch with right fist.

f. Defender simultaneously slides right foot back and executes a High Block with left forearm.

g. Defender then immediately counterattacks with a High Punch to the face of attacker—

h. and a Middle Punch to his solar plexus, in rapid sequence with a yell.

2. High Punch Attack

a. Attacker advances with High Punch (three times, as before, alternating right, left, and right).

b. Defender moves back with High Block simultaneously (three times, also, as before).

(continued)

c. When defender has parried the third High Punch, he immediately steps forward with right foot and executes an Elbow Strike with right elbow to attacker's solar plexus—

d. and to his chin, in rapid sequence with a yell.

3. High Punch Attack

a. Attacker advances with High Punch (three times, as previously, alternating right, left, and right fists).

b. Defender moves back with High Block simultaneously (three times, as before).

(*continued*)

c. When defender has parried the third punch, he immediately leaps one step to his left (under the attacker's arm, which is still extended) and, assuming Horseback Stance (facing opponent's right side),

d. executes Middle Punches to his ribs with right—

e. and left fists, in rapid sequence with a yell.

4. High Punch Attack

a. Attacker advances with High Punch (three times).

b. Defender moves back with High Block (three times, as before).

(*continued*)

c. When defender has parried the third High Punch, he immediately executes a Front Snap Kick with right foot to attacker's solar plexus or groin with a yell.

Note: At the intermediate level, Three-Step Sparring may be practiced using different attacking and blocking techniques, employing the hands (in punches or strikes) the feet (kicking attacks and kicking blocks), or any combination of these.

For example, in a single Three-Step Sparring exercise:

• The attacker may use two or three different attacking techniques (punching, kicking, etc.), and the defender may use two or three different defending techniques, or

• The attacker may use the same attacking technique three times, and the defender use two or three different defending techniques against it.

ONE-STEP SPARRING (*Han-Bon Kyo-Lu-Ki*)

This is the second stage of sparring practice, similar to Three-Step Sparring except that it involves more advanced techniques, especially in counterattack. One-Step Sparring practice is an essential preliminary to Free Sparring in that it gives the student an opportunity to learn more varied blocking and dodging tactics and, more importantly, emphasizes effective counterattacking techniques and combinations. Because the defending student is required to counterattack immediately upon avoiding the first attack, One-Step Sparring serves to sharpen the speed and accuracy of reflex action far beyond the levels attained in Three-Step Sparring practice.

In practice, one student assumes the role of attacker, and one that of defender (as in Three-Step Sparring). The term "One-Step" refers to the fact that the attacker advances only one step to execute his attack against the defender, who counterattacks immediately after executing the necessary defense.

Each exercise begins with these three actions:

- Attacker and defender stand at attention, facing each other, about two long steps apart.

- Attacker slides his left foot forward one long step, assuming Front Stance, and simultaneously executes a Low Block with left forearm and yells, indicating that he is ready to attack.

- Defender, waiting at attention, yells to indicate that he is ready to defend himself.

1. High Punch Attack
(with right fist, attacker advancing one step)

a. Defender slides right foot one step back, assumes Front Stance, simultaneously parrying punch with high block, using left forearm—

(*continued*)

b. then, with or without grabbing the sleeve or wrist of the punching arm, defender immediately steps forward with right foot (outside and behind attacker's right foot) and executes an elbow strike, with right elbow, to solar plexus—

c. and to chin, in rapid sequence,

d. then immediately throws attacker down (by simultaneously sweeping with right foot and striking attacker's neck with right Tiger-Mouth Hand)—

e. and, still holding on to attacker's offending arm, delivers a downward punch to the face with right fist with a yell.

(*continued*)

2. High Punch Attack (with right fist)

a. Defender leaps one step to the right and forward (avoiding the punch), bringing weight down on right foot, and—

b. immediately executes a Side Kick with left foot to attacker's solar plexus or face.

3. High Punch Attack (with right fist)

a. Defender leaps one step to the right and forward (avoiding the punch), bringing weight down on right foot, and—

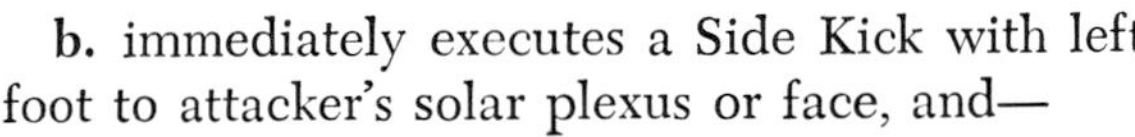

b. immediately executes a Side Kick with left foot to attacker's solar plexus or face, and—

(*continued*)

c. immediately (pulling left foot back without lowering it to the ground) executes a Jumping Round Kick with right foot to attacker's face or ribs.

4. Middle Punch Attack (with right fist)

a. Defender lunges one long step forward and to the right with right foot (assuming Horseback Stance) and simultaneously parries the punch with left forearm (swinging left forearm out to the left, up, down, and out again, in a circular motion, blocking with the outer edge of the lower forearm)—

b. and immediately executes a High Punch to attacker's face with right fist and—

(*continued*)

c. Middle Punch with same (right) fist in rapid sequence with a yell.

5. High Punch Attack (with right fist)

a. Defender leaps one step to the left and forward (avoiding the punch), bringing weight down on left foot, and—

b. immediately executes a Side Kick with right foot to attacker's ribs and—

c. immediately steps forward with right foot (assuming Back Stance) and executes a right Knife-Hand Strike to attacker's elbow and—

d. stepping forward again, follows immediately with another right Knife-Hand Strike to the neck or temple with a yell.

6. High Punch Attack

a. Defender steps forward into Horseback Stance, simultaneously striking attacker's wrist outward with a Side Block.

b. Switching hands, defender grabs wrist or sleeve and executes Outward Elbow Strike to the face.

7. High Punch Attack

a. Defender side-steps (away from attacker) and blocks punch with Knife Hand,

b. immediately grabs attacker's wrist and executes Front Kick to solar plexus, or

(*continued*)

c. immediately grabs wrist and steps forward, behind opponent, pulling him forward (in the direction of his own punch) off balance,

d. and, releasing opponent's wrist, executes inner forearm strike to the neck (with same arm),

e. and sweeps opponent's leg from under him, throwing him over backward.

8. High Punch Attack

a. Defender assumes Front Stance and simultaneously executes High Block,

b. then quickly, shifting into Horseback Stance, scoops up attacker's front leg (from the outside) with one hand and simultaneously executes Knife-Hand Strike to the throat (with the same hand, palm down, as was used in blocking), throwing attacker down backward.

9. High Punch Attack

a. Defender blocks with High Block,

b. grabs attacker's wrist with the same hand used in blocking, and grabs attacker's lapel with other hand, simultaneously thrusting back foot forward and up into attacker's abdomen and, dropping hips to the floor,

c. pulls attacker forward and down overhead, using the foot in the abdomen as a fulcrum.

10. High Punch Attack

a. Defender wards off punch with Knife-Hand High Block,

b. grabs wrist and swings attacker's arm outward and down, to grab attacker's wrist—under his own knee—with the other hand,

c. and pulls up sharply, lifting attacker's leg from under him and throwing him down backward.

11. Middle Punch Attack

a. Defender steps forward into Horseback (or Back) Stance, simultaneously striking attacker's punch outward with a Side Block,

b. grabs attacker's wrist (with same, blocking hand) and, pivoting on front foot, turns backward, lifting back leg in preparation for a kick,

c. and executes a Turning Back Kick to attacker's solar plexus.

12. Middle Punch Attack

a. Defender blocks attacker's punch with a Crescent Kick, striking attacker's wrist outward with the sole of the foot,

b. and immediately executes a Side Kick to attacker's throat with same foot (foot does not touch the ground between kicks).

13. Middle Punch Attack

a. Defender slides one foot back and drops to that knee, simultaneously warding off attacker's punch with Knife-Hand Block.

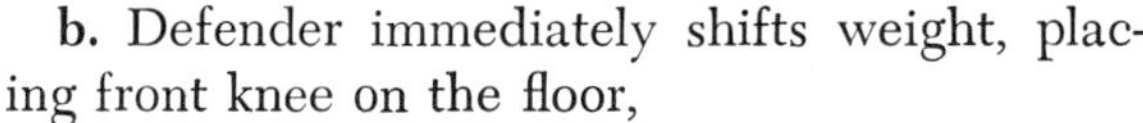

b. Defender immediately shifts weight, placing front knee on the floor,

c. and, using a twisting motion of the upper torso, turns rapidly backward, swinging back leg out and around,

d. executing a Stooping Turning Kick to attacker's ankle, sweeping him down.

e. Defender keeps kicking foot raised and, when attacker has fallen on his back,

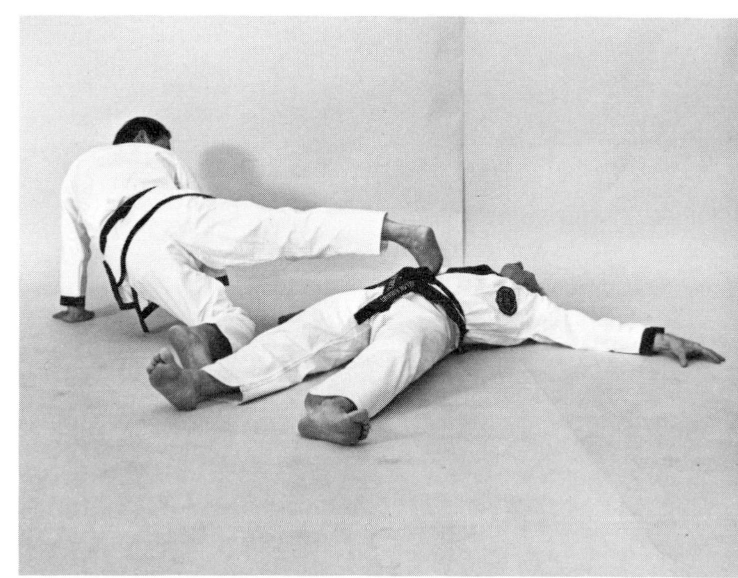

f. defender executes a Round Kick, striking downward with the ball of the foot to attacker's solar plexus or abdomen.

14. Middle Punch Attack

a. Defender falls to the side (away from attacker), dodging the punch.

b. While falling, defender raises knee of uppermost leg—

c. and executes a Falling Round Kick to attacker's solar plexus.

d. Defender then immediately hooks kicking leg behind attacker's knee and sweeps attacker's foot back with the other leg,

e. throwing attacker face down; and crossing ankles around attacker's leg, defender reaches for his foot,

f. and twists the foot in both hands, breaking the ankle.

15. Middle Punch Attack

a. Defender falls to the side (away from attacker), dodging the punch.

b. While falling, defender raises knee of uppermost leg—

c. and executes a Falling Side Kick to attacker's ribs.

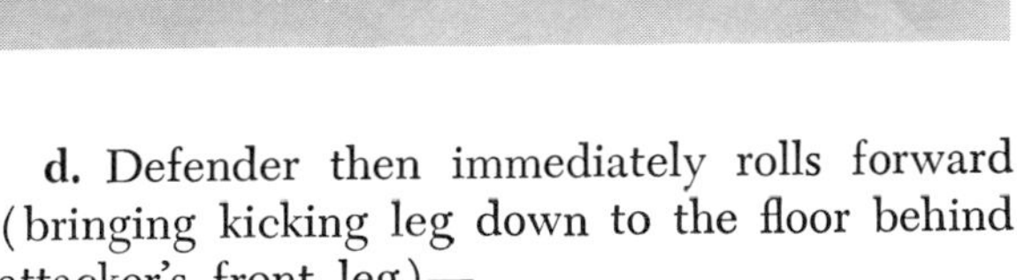

d. Defender then immediately rolls forward (bringing kicking leg down to the floor behind attacker's front leg)—

e. and swings other leg upward and back,

f. executing a Falling Wheel Kick, striking attacker's chest or solar plexus with the heel of the foot, and simultaneously (using the other leg, as he continues the rolling motion) sweeps attacker's foot from under him,

g. throwing attacker down backward;

(*continued*)

h. then immediately, as attacker has fallen, defender grabs attacker's (swept) foot and twists up and inward, breaking the shin or knee.

ARRANGED FREE SPARRING
(*Ma-Chu-O Kyo-Lu-Ki*)

In this third stage of sparring practice, all the techniques of attack and defense learned previously are applied in continuous sequence, in combinations prescribed by the instructor. The purpose is to train the student to use what he has learned, in the more or less fixed positions of One- and Three-Step Sparring, in a dynamic situation simulating actual combat. In addition to speed and accuracy, Arranged Free Sparring develops balance, coordination, reflexes, and endurance.

In practice, Arranged Free Sparring may take two forms:

- One student may assume the role of attacker, and the other that of defender. Following the rules of the instructor, the attacker will advance toward the defender using a prescribed combination of techniques in continuous sequence, until the defender, using a prescribed combination of defensive techniques, has retreated to the limits of the designated floor space. At this point, the roles of the students are reversed, and the exercise is repeated in the opposite direction.

- Another form is that in which both partners participate on an equal basis, attacking and defending at will, as they would in actual Free Sparring—except that the techniques employed are limited to those prescribed by the instructor—e.g., using hand techniques only, or kicking techniques only, or perhaps only certain punches or kicks.

Arranged Free Sparring Illustrations

1. Attack and Defense

a. One student defends, the other attacks with a Round Kick, using the back foot,

b. and pivots, keeping the same leg raised,

c. to execute a Side Kick.

2. Attack and Counterattack

a. One student advances, crossing the back foot in front;

b. raises the front foot in preparation for a Side Kick;

c. executes Side Kick, as other student counters —too late—with Reverse Punch.

FREE SPARRING (*Kyo-Lu-Ki*)

This is the fourth, most advanced stage of sparring practice. It is the form most nearly simulating actual combat, and calls upon all the resources of the practitioner in speed, reflexes, accuracy, balance, coordination, endurance, and, most important, quickness and accuracy of perception in anticipating the opponent's moves. All previously learned techniques of attack and defense are employed, and the practitioner is called upon to apply them in combinations, both new and previously learned, using his judgment as to which should be most effective at the given moment. This is the stage of sparring practice which keeps the practitioner most mindful of his own progress in training, for he must rely on those techniques which he feels he has mastered sufficiently to execute to advantage.

Free Sparring generally takes place within a limited area of floor space, and each match is normally restricted in time—e.g., thirty seconds, one minute, or perhaps up to three or four minutes, or even longer. Certain rules are generally applied, such as limiting all techniques to very light contact when sparring without padded protectors, and avoiding injurious strikes to the more vital areas of the head and body, as, for example, the eyes, temples, top of the head, neck, back, and groin.*

Weight Distribution

When sparring, one normally assumes Back Stance, that is, with 70 percent of one's weight on the back foot. In actual practice, however, one is in a dynamic situation, in which the weight may be shifted slightly forward at certain moments. The following are guidelines, to be applied generally—but not rigidly.

* Rules for Free Sparring in tournaments are in some ways different from those used in class practice. If the student wishes to participate in Tae Kwon Do sports competition, he should acquaint himself with tournament rules and practice accordingly. See Chapter 15, "Tae Kwon Do as a Sport," for a discussion of tournament rules.

1. Defensive position: 70 percent of weight on back foot.

2. Offensive position: 60–70 percent of weight on front foot (without necessarily assuming Front Stance).

3. When weight is evenly distributed on both legs, one may shift readily into offensive (forward) or defending (back) position, as the situation demands.

Faking

One may fool the opponent and catch him off guard by reversing weight distribution in relation to one's intent. For example, assuming a defensive position, weight on back foot, and attacking with a kick using the front foot.

Attacking

The difficulty in attacking effectively is that as one initiates an attack, the opponent has the opportunity to perceive the starting action, anticipate the intent, and respond accordingly. Therefore, the following points should be observed:

1. An attacking technique should be executed with great speed, and with attention to position and balance, so that should the opponent respond with a counterattack, one is immediately ready to defend himself against it.

2. One must be able to judge the opponent's likely reactions to an attack; this calls for some insight into the opponent's character, attitude, concentration, speed, agility, and a knowledge of his best or favorite techniques. If one knows the opponent in this manner, one is better able to fake and execute effective attacks focusing on the opponent's weak points.

3. One should use imagination, varying his attacking methods, thus sustaining an element of surprise and keeping the opponent in a state of uncertainty so that he cannot anticipate the attack and prepare a devastating response.

4. One must judge the distance between himself and his target on the opponent accurately, and take into account the opponent's height, weight, and strength, then apply his techniques accordingly.

5. One should determine the target—the exact point for an effective strike—before launching an attack.

6. One should have a clear determination of his own intent, so that the attack will be executed with perfect focus—i.e., great speed, accuracy, and strength.

7. One should use time wisely:

a. One should be aware of his own best fighting rhythms and those of his opponent, and attempt to take the best advantage of the tempo of the match by applying his techniques in the most effective sequence at a given moment.

b. One should be aware of the time allotted to the sparring match and pace himself accordingly, using the first part of the time to acquaint himself with the opponent's character, speed, and favorite techniques, and applying one's own techniques in such a manner as not to become exhausted too soon.

8. Thus, it is wiser to be defensive in the beginning, in order to learn the opponent's habits.

9. Do not "telegraph" an attack. The attacking motion should be as swift and economical as possible, so that preparatory shifts in balance cannot be detected. For example:

a. When in Back Stance, with knees bent, one should be as low as necessary to enable one to leap instantly forward or straight up to execute a punching or kicking attack, without having, first, to stoop lower to pump for the leap.

b. When stepping forward or backward or when merely shifting weight from one leg to the other, one's head should not move up or down, but should remain on a level, parallel to the floor, so that the shift in position is barely perceptible.

c. Avoid false starts, or "priming," that is, shifting the weight forward and backward or rocking on the legs, preparatory to launching an attack. If one has a habit of priming, the opponent may recognize it quickly and take advantage of it by executing an attack himself, while one's weight is being shifted, thus catching one off balance.

10. Feint to advantage. Feinting is different from priming, for in priming no technique is thrown. The purposes of feinting are to test the opponent's reactions, or to prompt him to defend one target and thereby expose another. Thus, in feinting, one must have at least two targets in mind—the faked and the real—and one must be ready to execute at least two attacking techniques in rapid succession. For example, one may feint a Front Kick to the solar plexus, and when the opponent moves his hands down to cover that target, one may execute—immediately, with the same leg, as if the two motions were one motion—a Round Kick to the face. Also, the feint should be executed in such a manner that, if the opponent does not respond with an adequate defense against it, the feinted technique can be fully extended as a scoring attack.

11. Attack using combinations in rapid sequence. One should not execute one technique at a time, but should develop the habit, in attacking, of executing two, three, four, or more techniques in rapid succession (e.g., Front Kick and Round Kick with the same leg; or Front Kick and Jumping Round Kick with alternate legs; or Front Kick, Side Kick, Wheel Kick, Turning Back Kick, and Reverse Punch or Double High or Middle Punch). One should also be able to execute two techniques simultaneously (e.g., Reverse Punch and sweeping with the foot or straight Side Punch and Side Kick; or Turning Back Kick and Outward Hammer Fist Strike). By attacking with combinations in rapid sequence, one keeps the opponent under pressure, on the defensive, and off balance.

Defending

An effective defense is essential in sparring, for if one is not able to ward off the opponent's attack, one may never get the chance to launch his own attacking techniques.

There are many possible methods of defense, which may be used separately or in combination. Examples are:

1. Basic blocking techniques, using the hands, arms, legs, and feet (see Chapter 8).

2. Dodging: One may evade an attack by leaning or stepping back; dodging to the side or side-stepping; ducking under a high attack; or jumping above a low attack. Dodging requires greater speed and agility than blocking, and misjudgment could lead to injury. The manner in which one blocks or dodges an attack depends, in part, on one's intended follow-up. This is tactical fighting. If one possesses sufficient speed, agility, and judgment, one may dodge the opponent continually, and in a variety of ways, in order to confuse, frustrate, and tire him.

3. One may block or stop the opponent's attacking advance by executing a sudden, unexpected Front, Side, or Back Kick. This is especially effective when the opponent advances with a rush, and is a good surprising maneuver when used after a series of more passive responses to attack, such as dodging or rapid retreats.

4. Sweeping and throwing: One may forestall an attack perceived as imminent, or block or dodge the attack itself, and sweep the opponent off balance with a Standing Crescent Kick or Hook Kick, or a Stooping Turning Kick used in a sweeping motion to the opponent's leg. One may also dodge or block an attack, grab the offending arm or leg, and use it to throw the opponent to the ground.

5. Avoid repetition: One should use as much variety in defending methods as possible, keeping the opponent uncertain of one's responses and thus depriving him of the confidence necessary to plan an effective attacking sequence.

6. Develop counterattacking methods: One should not stop after evading an attack and merely await the next; one should be ready immediately to launch a counterattack—in any of a variety of ways—in order to take instant advantage of any possible opening in the opponent's defenses, or weakness in his balance or position, resulting from his own method of attack. (See Counterattacking, below.)

Counterattacking

By definition, a counterattack is an attack executed *after defending* against an opponent's attack, or *in response* to his initiating an attack. Therefore, a counterattack is normally launched from a defensive position (weight on the back foot).

Effective counterattack technique requires experience, imagination, and very fast reflexes. One must learn, within the time allotted to the sparring match, the opponent's habits of attack, his attitude, speed, favorite techniques, strengths, and weaknesses. And one must be able to do several things simultaneously, in the split second between the time the opponent starts his attacking motion and the time he completes it:

- Determine, from the briefest initiating motion, the opponent's intended attack.
- Decide upon and execute the best defense against it.
- Perceive an opening, present or imminent, resulting from the opponent's attacking technique.
- Choose a counterattack appropriate to take advantage of that opening.
- Execute the counterattack swiftly enough to score effectively before the opponent can perceive one's own intent and defend against it.

Examples:

1. Assume defensive position, and as opponent rushes in to attack with a punch, execute a Front, Side, Round, or Wheel Kick, or a Back Kick (in each case, a strong thrust kick to stop opponent's advance), kicking with the front foot and keeping weight on the back foot.

2. Assume offensive position, and as opponent rushes into attack, block or dodge his attack and counter with a Reverse Punch.

3. Assume defensive position, and as opponent rushes in to attack, jump back one step (sliding both feet backward), shift weight to front foot, and pivot immediately, executing a Turning Back Kick or Turning Wheel Kick (with the back foot).

4. Assume defensive position, and as opponent rushes in to attack, side-step to the left or right (with or without blocking, as situation demands), and immediately counter with a Reverse Punch or a kick.

5. Assume defensive position, and as opponent rushes in to attack, jump as high as possible and execute a Jumping Kick or Jumping Turning Kick.

6. Assume defensive position, and as opponent rushes in to attack, quickly stoop to the floor and execute a Stooping Turning Sweep or Kick. (This technique is very difficult, and must be executed with great speed and in such a manner as to permit one to follow up immediately with another technique, defensive or offensive. Should the technique not be effective in sweeping the opponent to the floor, one will be left at a disadvantage, being on the floor himself, and in danger of another attack.)

Note: One should practice until he has mastered the basic techniques of attack and defense (covered in the earlier chapters on blocking, hand and arm attacks, and kicking techniques). Nonetheless, Free Sparring is a dynamic situation, in which one is called upon to respond to the behavior of an opponent, and therefore one must be able to use initiative and imagination to adapt the basic techniques in a variety of ways to suit the opportunities of the given moment.

Certain of the basic techniques will undergo necessary changes when applied in Free Sparring. The Round Kick is one example. In executing the basic Round Kick, the kicking knee is raised up and out to the side, before the foot is swung around to strike a target directly in front. This action, in basic practice, serves the purpose of stretching the muscles of the hip and leg, and accustoming the student to the motion, necessary to the Round Kick, of turning the hip over. But this manner of execution is not good for sparring because, when the knee is raised outward, time is lost in the outward motion, the solar plexus and abdomen are open to attack, and the kick itself is "telegraphed," for the opponent will know that only a Round Kick is likely from that position. Therefore, it is better, in sparring, to begin a Round Kick by bringing the knee straight up in front—protecting the abdomen, and presenting the opponent with the problem of having to defend against a possible Front Kick, Side Kick, or Round Kick—the Round Kick itself being executed, then, by merely turning the hip over and simultaneously swinging the foot out, up, and around to strike the target in a smooth, swift, barely perceptible arc. Also, in the basic Round Kick, the ball of the foot is used as the striking surface. But in sparring, the instep is more often used, (a) because it is less likely to cause injury, and (b) because it extends the foot to reach a more distant, or a retreating, target in the same motion.

Positions and Techniques of Free Sparring

1. Reverse Punch and Counterattack

a. High Reverse Punch blocked with Knife Hand.

b. Defender grabs sleeve of attacker.

c. Counters with Reverse Punch.

2. Reverse Punch and Counterattack

a. Defender simultaneously blocks Reverse Punch with Palm Heel and forestalls opponent's advance for kicking attack with Side Kick to knee.

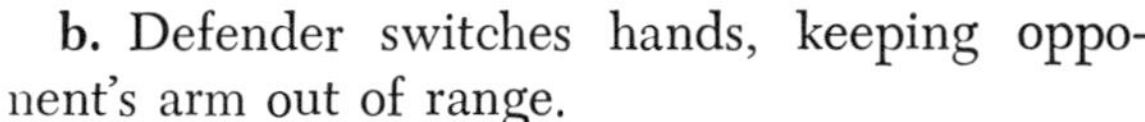

b. Defender switches hands, keeping opponent's arm out of range.

c. Holding opponent's fist in one hand, defender executes outward Knife-Hand Strike to neck.

3. Front Kick and Counterattack

a. Defender wards off attacker's Front Kick with a Low Block.

b. Brings back blocking arm in preparation for a counterattack.

c. Counters with outward Knife-Hand Strike to temple.

4. Front Kick and Counterattack

a. Defender blocks attacker's Front Kick with Low Block.

(continued)

b. Counters with Reverse Punch.

5. Simultaneous Hand-and-Foot Attack

a. Attacker raises leading Knife Hand and front foot simultaneously.

b. Executes outward Knife-Hand Strike to neck and Side Kick to knee at the same time.

6. Simultaneous Hand-and-Foot Attack

Attacker executes Ripping-Hand Strike to face and, simultaneously, an Outward Crescent Kick to abdomen.

Note: The Ripping-Hand Strike is not usually permitted in sparring because it is difficult to control and may cause injury.

7. Simultaneous Hand-and-Foot Attack and Counter-attack

a. Defender shifts weight to front foot and stands in Crane Stance, blocking attacker's Front Kick with Low Block.

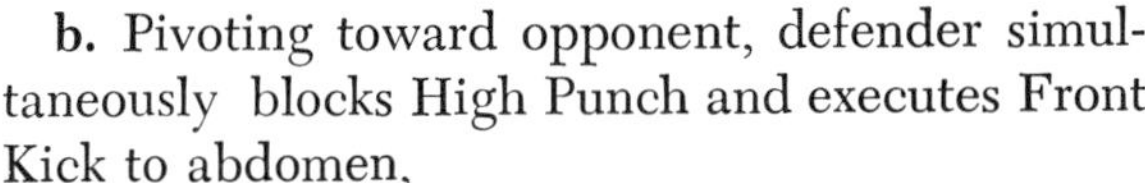

b. Pivoting toward opponent, defender simultaneously blocks High Punch and executes Front Kick to abdomen,

c. then grabs sleeve, pulling opponent forward and down, off balance, and executes Downward Knife-Hand Strike to neck.

8. Round Kick and Counterattack

a. Defender blocks attacker's Round Kick with High Block,

b. and counters with Front Kick to solar plexus.

9. Double-Kicking Attack

a. Attacker strikes and blocks opponent's knee with Front Kick,

b. and pivots immediately to execute a Side Kick to the neck with same foot.

10. Front Kick and Throwing Counterattack

a. Defender blocks attacker's Front Kick with Double-Fist X Block,

b. slips one hand under attacker's ankle and the other over his thigh,

c. and pushes attacker's thigh outward and down, forcing attacker to the ground,

(*continued*)

d. and, twisting opponent's foot in both hands, executes a Heel Kick downward to the face.

11. Triple-Kicking Attack Sequence

a. Attacker executes Front Kick to opponent's abdomen,

b. immediately brings foot back in preparation for another attack,

c. executes a Round Kick to the head with same foot,

d. immediately brings foot back and pivots for another attack,

e. executes a Side Kick to the chest.

Note: All three kicks are performed with the same foot in rapid sequence, and without that foot touching the ground between kicks.

12. Front Kick and Double-Kicking Counterattack

a. Defender wards off attacker's Front Kick with Low Block,

b. immediately counters with a Round Kick to the head,

c. and follows immediately with a Wheel Kick to the face with same foot.

13. Front Kick and Hand-and-Foot Counterattack Combination

a. Defender wards off opponent's Front Kick attack with Low Block,

b. counters with Reverse Punch,

(*continued*)

c. and immediately follows with a Crescent Kick to the face (or a Front Kick, depending on the distance to be covered),

d. and a Side Kick to the face with same foot.

14. Reverse Punch and Jumping Turning Kick Counterattack

a. Attacker advances with a High Reverse Punch, and defender leaps into the air to block punch with a Crescent Kick (using the back foot).

b. Defender, still in the air, spins around in one continuous motion,

c. and executes a Jumping Turning Back Kick with alternate foot.

15. Front Kick and Four-Kick Counterattacking Sequence

a. Defender blocks attacker's Front Kick with Side Kick to the shin,

(*continued*)

b. and immediately executes another Side Kick to solar plexus with same foot;

c. then shifts weight to front foot,

d. pivots and spins backward, raising back foot in preparation for a kick,

e. and executes a Turning Wheel Kick to the face.

f. The Wheel Kick may be intended as a fake, to draw opponent in for an apparent opening;

g. thus, defender keeps arms raised to block the possible attack—

h. and follows immediately with a Round Kick to the neck (with same foot as was used in the Wheel Kick).

16. Others

12

Self-Defense Techniques

The techniques illustrated in this section are designed to enable the defender to ward off an assault by an opponent—in many cases without necessarily executing a counterattack. The techniques involve twists, throws, strikes, bone breaking, and counter-holds, and they are effective against grabs, pickpocketing, assaults with weapons, and other threatening attacks. Generally, the purpose of these defensive techniques is to discourage the assailant by using his own initiative against him, the defender employing as little force as possible and overcoming his assailant without regard to the latter's possibly greater physical strength or weight.

These techniques should be practiced until they become second nature, so that one will not be overcome by surprise.

BASIC SELF-DEFENSE

1. Shaking Hands

a. Step forward and across (e.g., when shaking with right hands, step in with right foot toward opponent's right foot).

b. Pivot on the stepping foot and turn toward your own held hand until your back is to opponent. Simultaneously bend your free arm around opponent's held arm.

c. Twist and press his held hand downward, breaking his elbow. (Be sure to have the point of his elbow accurately on your forearm.)

2. Shaking Hands

(*continued*)

a. Step forward and across, turning your back to opponent (as above). Simultaneously grab opponent's held hand with your free hand.

b. Twisting outward, raise opponent's hand over your shoulder.

c. Bring his elbow down directly on your shoulder.

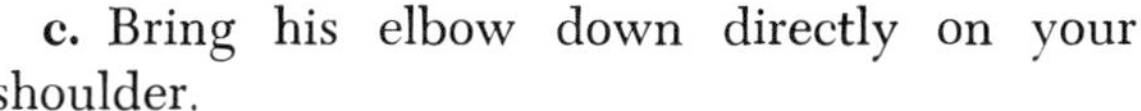

d. Press downward sharply, breaking his elbow.

3. Shaking Hands

a. Step forward and across, turning your back to opponent. Simultaneously grab opponent's held hand with your free hand (as above).

b. Raise opponent's hand over your head, twisting his wrist outward, and bring his elbow down on your shoulder (viz., his right elbow on your right shoulder).

c. Press downward sharply, breaking his elbow.

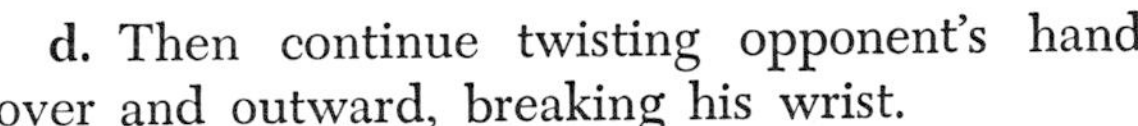

d. Then continue twisting opponent's hand over and outward, breaking his wrist.

4. Wrist Grabbed by Opponent's Opposite Hand

a. Grab his hand with your free hand.

b. Close-up.

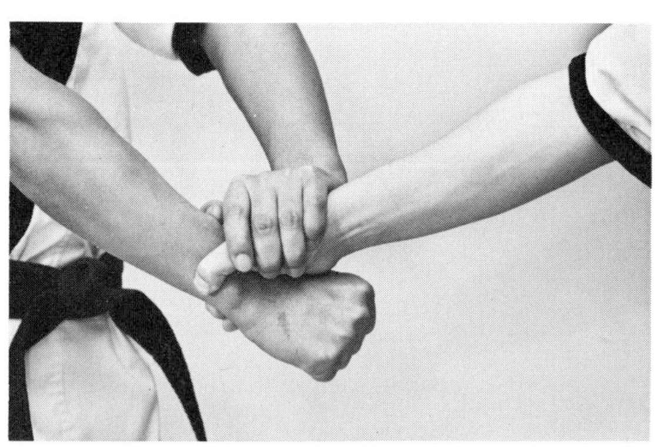

c. Swing your arms in, up, and overhead, simultaneously twisting your captured hand over his wrist.

d. Close-up.

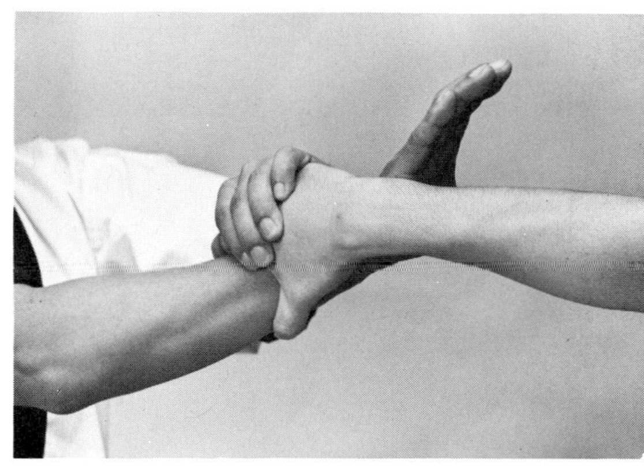

e. Slide back the foot that is on the same side as your captured hand and, using both hands, bear straight downward, breaking his wrist.

f. Close-up: Outer edge (pinkie side) of opponent's forearm should be turned straight up; if twisted too far over, the wrist will bend and not break.

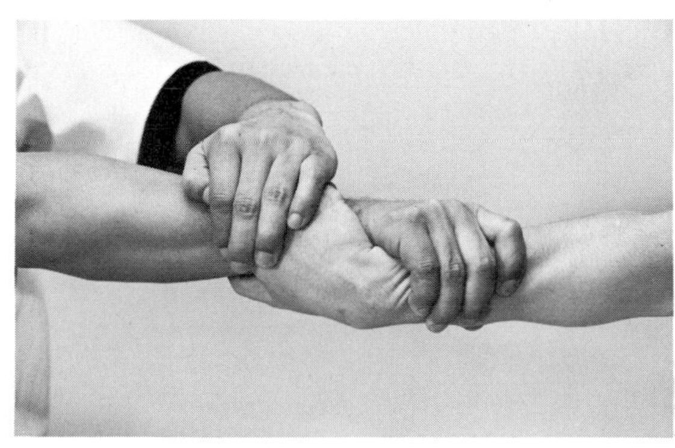

5. Wrist Grabbed by Opponent's Hand on Same Side

a. Grab his hand with your free hand.

b. Close-up.

c. Swing your arms out, up, and overhead.

d. Twist your captured wrist, palm in, and press it straight forward and down against opponent's thumb, breaking his hold. Keep a firm hold on his hand with your other hand. (See close-up.)

e. Grab his held hand with the hand you have just freed.

f. Close-up: Using both your hands, hold his hand bent up at the wrist.

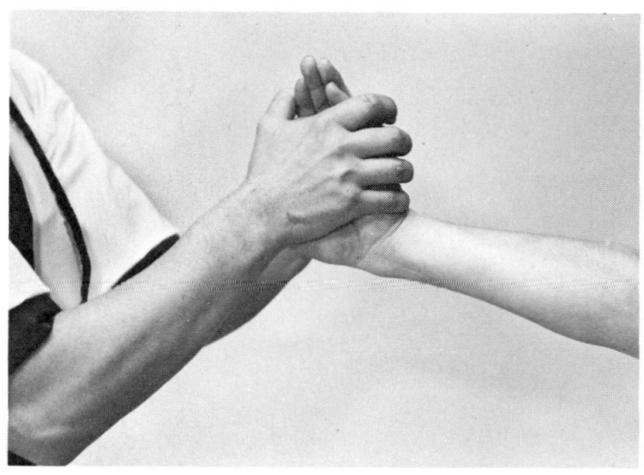

g. Slide back the foot that is on the same side as opponent's held hand, and bear straight down with both hands, breaking his wrist.

6. Wrist Grabbed by Two Hands

a. Step forward with the foot that is on the same side as the held wrist and simultaneously grab your own captured fist with your free hand.

b. Pull your arm free, using the power of both arms—pulling the freed hand up and inward across your chest at shoulder level.

c. Open the freed hand, palm in.

d. Execute a Knife-Hand Strike to opponent's neck or temple, snapping Knife Hand palm down.

7. Lapel Grabbed by One Hand

a. Step forward and across, turning toward the offending hand, and simultaneously grab the offending hand with your own opposite hand, fingers downward (covering back of opponent's hand with your palm).

b. Turn your body back to original position, simultaneously twisting opponent's hand over (turning your own fingers upward, thus twisting his hand thumb down). Simultaneously grab opponent's twisting hand with your free hand.

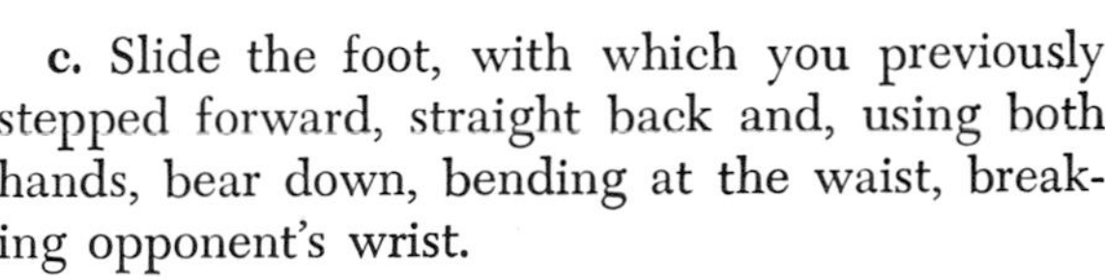

c. Slide the foot, with which you previously stepped forward, straight back and, using both hands, bear down, bending at the waist, breaking opponent's wrist.

8. Lapel Grabbed by One Hand

a. Grab offending hand with your own, using the hand on the same side as the offender's, with your fingers downward (covering opponent's palm with your own palm).

b. Step forward and across (shifting the foot on your free side across and behind opponent's opposite foot) and sweep his foot from under him. Simultaneously strike opponent's throat with Tiger-Mouth attack, using your free hand.

c. As opponent falls, follow downward motion, twisting his hand outward—extending his arm straight out from his side—so that the point of his elbow is uppermost, and strike his elbow with your knee (the knee of the same leg used to sweep him down), breaking his elbow.

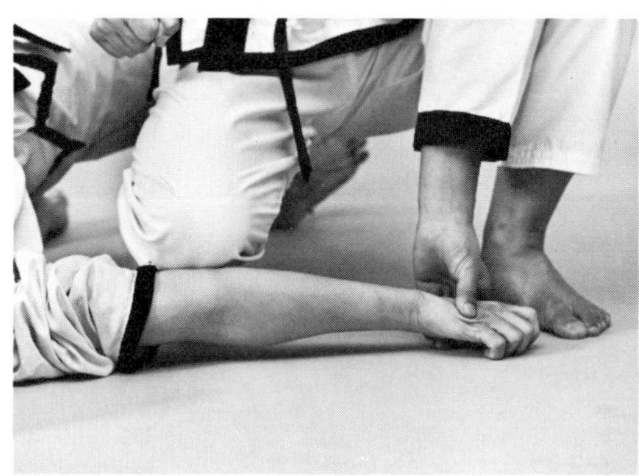

d. Close-up.

e. Still holding his captured hand, use your free hand to execute a Spear-Hand attack to opponent's eyes.

9. Hair Grabbed by One Hand

a. Clasp both hands over the offending hand in such a manner that both your thumbs are pressed against his palm.

b. Immediately drop down, bending opponent's hand backward, breaking his wrist.

10. Pickpocket

a. Grab offending hand with your own hand on the same side.

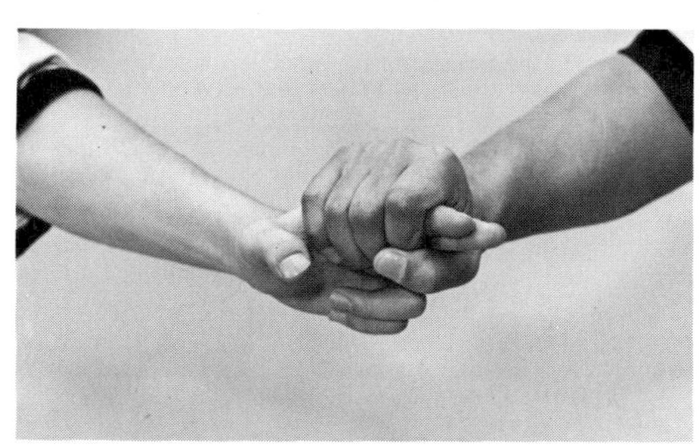

b. Close-up: Hold offender's hand tightly with your palm against the backs of his fingers.

c. Twist offender's hand upward behind his back, and simultaneously grasp his throat in a Tiger-Mouth attack with your free hand, palm up. As you thrust offender's jaw away from you with a straight arm, twist and pull his captured hand upward and toward you. If this is done with sufficient pressure, you will choke off offender's air supply, break his wrist, and dislocate his shoulder at the same time.

d. Close-up: Proper method of twisting offender's hand upward behind his back.

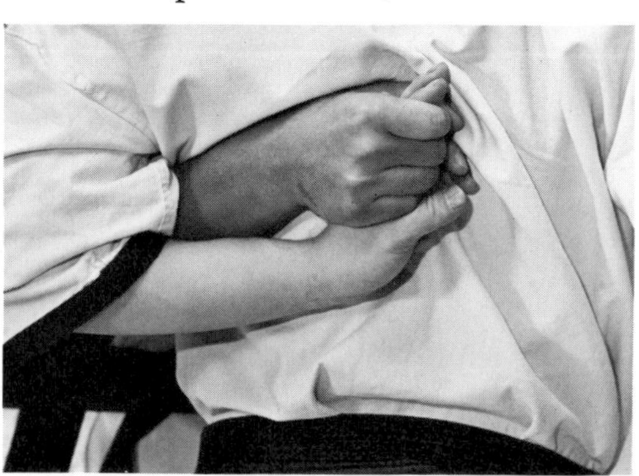

11. Wrist Grabbed by Opponent's Opposite Hand

a. Grab opponent's wrist firmly with your own captured hand.

b. Step forward and across with the foot on your free side, and simultaneously thrust your free hand under opponent's elbow and grab his opposite shoulder or lapel.

c. Twist his captured hand outward and press down, breaking his elbow on your forearm.

12. Belt Grabbed by One Hand in Front

a. Bend forward and hook opponent's offending arm, close to the wrist, in the crook of your elbow (using the elbow opposite opponent's offending arm—e.g., if he grabs your belt with his right hand, hook his right wrist in your right elbow). Simultaneously slide back the foot on the same side as your hooking elbow.

b. Locking opponent's arm firmly in the crook of your elbow, twist quickly up and away (turning back, past your original position). As you turn backward, place your free hand palm down on the point of the elbow of opponent's captured arm and bear down hard, breaking his elbow and pressing him to the ground.

13. Lapels Grabbed by Two Hands

a. Thrust both Knife Hands forcibly upward and outward between opponent's forearms, breaking his hold with a Spread Knife-Hand Block, palms out. Simultaneously slide right foot straight back.

b. Immediately swing both Knife Hands downward and in.

c. Execute a double Knife-Hand Strike forward and inward, snapping both wrists palm up and striking just under opponent's ribs on both sides simultaneously, sliding front foot forward.

14. Overhand Wrist Hold by One Hand on the Same Side

a. When opponent grabs your wrist with one hand, palm down, grasp his offending hand firmly with your free hand. Simultaneously shift the foot on your free side back.

b. Pull straight inward, across your abdomen, bending your captured arm sharply to strike downward with the point of your elbow against opponent's elbow, breaking it.

15. Shoulder Sleeve Grabbed by One Hand in Front

a. Swing the arm in the held sleeve in a wide circle, in, up, and around.

b. Finish swinging motion by hooking opponent's offending arm firmly in the crook of your elbow and lift upward, threatening to break the arm.

c. Immediately step forward and across (shifting the foot on your free side across and behind opponent's opposite foot). Simultaneously execute a Palm-Heel Strike to opponent's chin with your free hand.

d. Immediately, as you strike with the Palm Heel, sweep opponent's leg out from under him, throwing him down. (Keep a firm hold on his arm in the crook of your elbow.) Following the downward motion, complete an arm lock on opponent's captured arm (hooking your free elbow under your other hand and placing your free hand down on opponent's upper arm). Press downward on opponent's upper arm, breaking his elbow against the fulcrum of your forearm.

Note: If opponent's elbow does not break immediately, step over him—with the foot used to sweep him down—and shift your body forward. This will certainly break the arm. Two points should be observed: (1) the point of opponent's elbow must be accurately placed against your own hooked forearm; (2) in holding the fallen opponent in an arm lock, your knees should be bent, but the elbow-breaking action is in lifting your torso erect at the waist.

BASIC FALLING PRACTICE

When encountering an opponent, one may himself be the victim of a throw or a fall. In which case, one should know how to fall without suffering injury. The following exercises should be practiced toward this end.

1. Falling to the Side from a Squatting Position

Falling to the right:

a. Squat with right hand extended straight out in front, left hand on left knee.

b. Thrust right foot forward and to the left, simultaneously bending right arm so that right hand, palm down, is in front of left shoulder; fall backward and to the right, landing on right hip first.

c. Continuing the falling motion, the instant right shoulder touches the floor, slap right palm on floor as hard as possible, elbow locked, with right arm extended out at 45° angle from side. (Note: Head should not touch floor.) Finish with legs raised as much as the movement requires.

d. Repeat this exercise, landing—without using the hip—on right shoulder and right palm.

Falling to the left:

a. Squat with left hand extended, as above.

b. Thrust left foot forward and to the right, simultaneously bending left arm so that left hand is in front of right shoulder; fall backward and to the left, landing on left hip first.

c. Continuing falling motion, slap left palm on floor as hard as possible, elbow locked, the instant left shoulder touches the floor. Finish with legs raised.

d. Repeat this exercise, landing—without using the hip—on left shoulder and left palm.

2. Falling Backward from a Squatting Position

a. Squat with both hands extended straight out in front.

b. Thrusting both feet forward, roll backward, crossing both hands in front of forehead, landing on hips first.

c. Continuing falling motion, slap both palms as hard as possible on the floor with elbows locked (arms out 45° from your sides), and finish fall on your shoulders, both feet in the air. (Note: Head should not touch the floor.)

d. Repeat this exercise, landing—without using your hips—on your palms first and then your shoulders.

3. Falling Forward from a Squatting Position

a. Squat with both hands extended straight out in front.

b. Fall forward, landing on knees first.

c. Continuing falling motion, touch both palms to the floor, then both elbows, ending with body fully extended, legs straight back.

d. Repeat this exercise, landing—without using your knees—on both palms first and then both elbows.

4. Falling to the Side from a Standing Position

Falling to the right:

a. Stand straight, with right hand held straight out in front.

b. Raise right foot forward and to the left, simultaneously bending right arm so that right hand is palm down in front of left shoulder; push off with left foot to raise body slightly into the air, and fall backward and to the right.

c. The instant before right shoulder touches the ground, slap right palm on floor as hard as possible, elbow locked, with arm extended at 45° angle out from side. Finish with legs straight out on floor.

Falling to the left:

a. Stand straight, with left hand held straight out in front.

b. Raise left foot forward and to the right, simultaneously bending left arm so that left hand is palm down in front of right shoulder; push off with right foot to raise body slightly into the air, and fall backward and to the left.

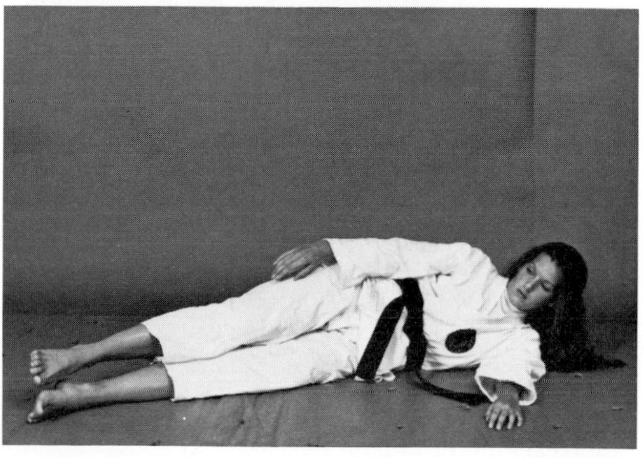

c. The instant before left shoulder touches the ground, slap left palm on floor as hard as possible, elbow locked, with arm extended at 45° angle out from side. Finish with legs straight out.

5. Rolling Forward from a Stooping Position

a. Stoop forward and place right hand (or the hand on the side you intend to land on first) on floor, palm down, fingers pointing in, and place other hand, palm down, on floor with fingers pointing forward.

b. Roll forward, landing on right (left) elbow first, then (left) right shoulder.

Note: Do not collapse right (left) arm so that elbow hits floor with shock force.

c. Continue rolling motion, touching back to floor, then crossing, as you roll, to touch opposite hip and leg, finishing with legs straight out on floor.

d. Repeat this exercise, beginning with a running start.

e. Repeat, with a running start, executing the "roll" rapidly in midair—that is, touching the hand on the floor first, then flipping over in midair, without touching shoulder or back to the floor, and landing on the hand again before legs touch the ground.

BASIC THROWING PRACTICE

Note: The following throws are illustrated to one side, but should be practiced to both sides.

1. Foot Sweep

a. Stand naturally, and grasp opponent's right sleeve above the elbow with your left hand, and with your right hand grasp his lapel.

b. Place the sole of your left foot on his right foot, below the ankle.

c. Sweep his right foot out from under him (to his left), simultaneously pulling him over (to your left).

d. Opponent falls, slapping his left hand on the floor.

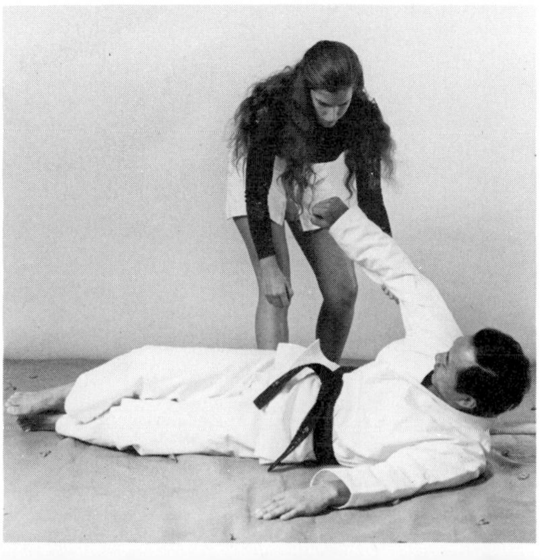

Note: The foot sweep may also be applied by using the sole of your foot to sweep opponent's knee, following through in the same manner.

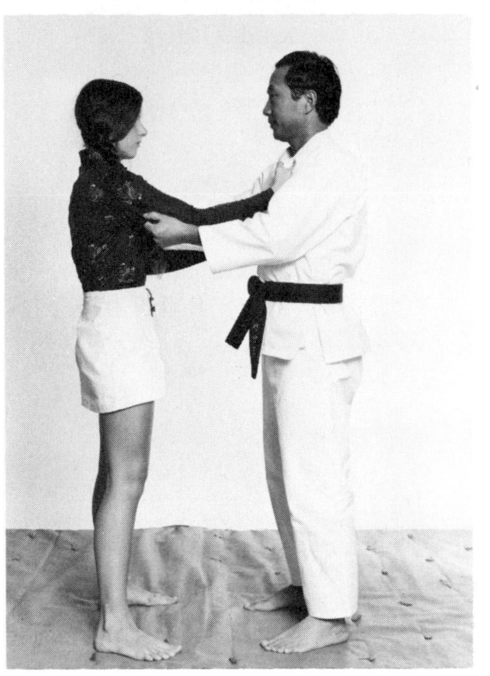

2. Leg Throw—Crossing Behind

a. Stand naturally, grasping opponent's right sleeve above the elbow with your left hand.

b. Shift right leg across, going outside and behind opponent's right leg, and simultaneously slip your right arm around opponent's body.

c. Sweep opponent's right leg out from under him with your right leg, and simultaneously pull him over (to his right).

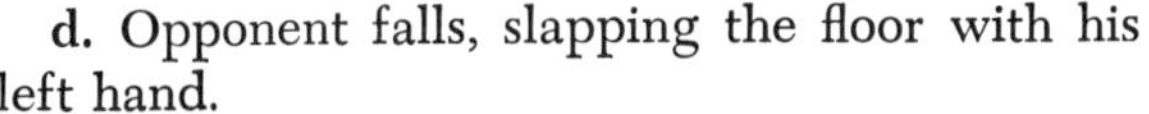

d. Opponent falls, slapping the floor with his left hand.

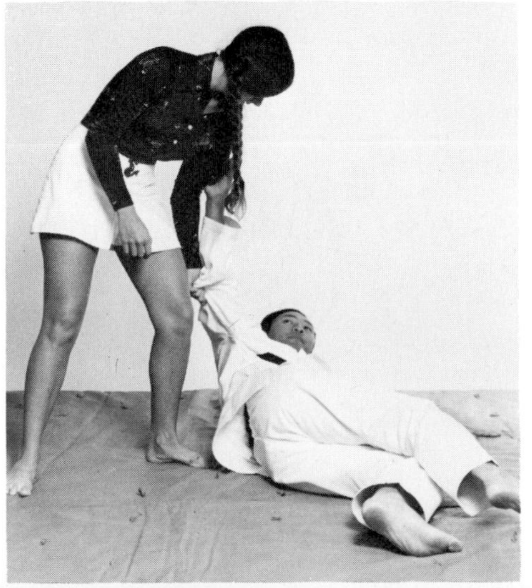

3. Leg Throw—Stepping Between

a. Stand naturally, grasping opponent's right sleeve above the elbow in your left hand, and his lapel in your right hand.

b. Step forward, putting your right leg between opponent's legs.

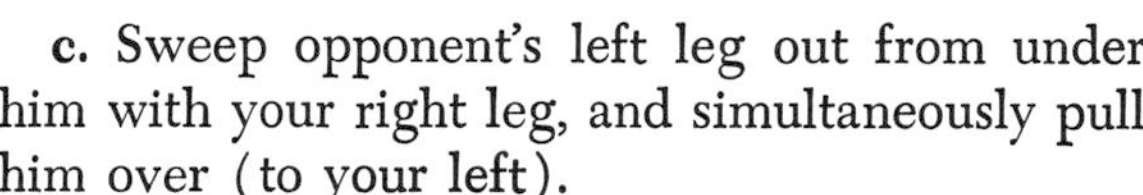

c. Sweep opponent's left leg out from under him with your right leg, and simultaneously pull him over (to your left).

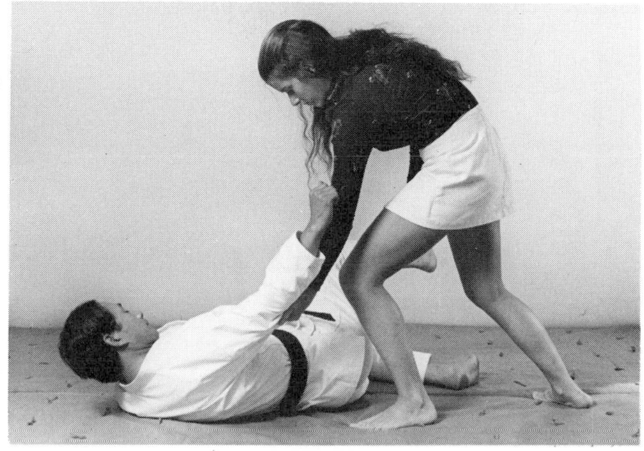

d. Opponent falls, slapping floor with his left hand.

4. Hip Throw

a. Grasp opponent's right sleeve above the elbow in your left hand and his lapel in your right hand.

b. Step forward and across with your right foot, pivoting so that your right heel is in front of his right toe, and turn your back to him—maintaining your hold on his sleeve and his lapel.

c. Push back with your hips and pull opponent forward, throwing him over your right hip.

d. Opponent's hips and legs are raised into the air as his head is pulled down.

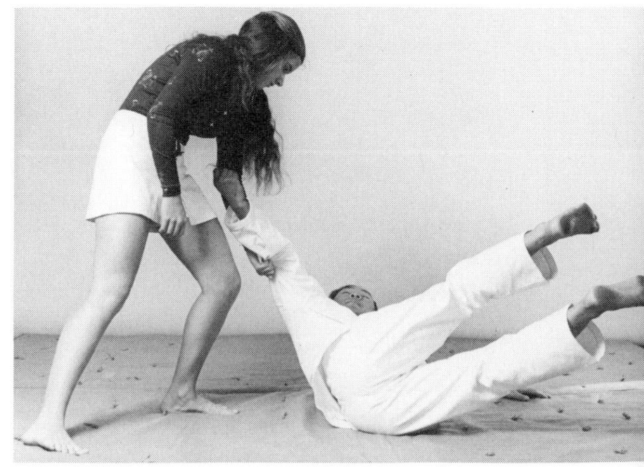

e. Opponent falls, slapping the floor with his left hand.

5. Shoulder Throw

a. Grasp opponent's right sleeve above the elbow in your left hand and his lapel in your right hand, and step forward and across with your right foot.

b. Pivoting on your right foot, turn around (to the left), simultaneously pulling his right arm around in front of you, as you stand with your back to him.

c. Bend forward sharply, thrusting opponent's hips into the air.

d. Pull opponent forward over your shoulder.

e. Opponent falls, slapping the floor with his left hand.

6. Rolling Over Backward

a. Standing with your left hand grasping opponent's right sleeve above the elbow and your right hand holding his left lapel, push forward strongly, prompting him to keep his balance by pushing back, shifting his weight forward to the toes of both his feet.

b. When opponent has pushed his weight forward, move your left hand from his right sleeve to his right lapel, shift your left foot forward, bending it sharply at the knee, and as you drop your hips to sit down on the floor, place the ball of your right foot on opponent's abdomen.

c. Roll backward, pulling opponent forward and pushing up with your right foot.

d. Opponent falls over your head, landing on his back and slapping the floor with both hands.

DEFENSES IN LYING-DOWN POSITIONS

1. Choked from Front

a. Grasp opponent's wrists in both hands.

b. Raise both legs and kick his ribs on both sides with your heels, thrusting forward and up.

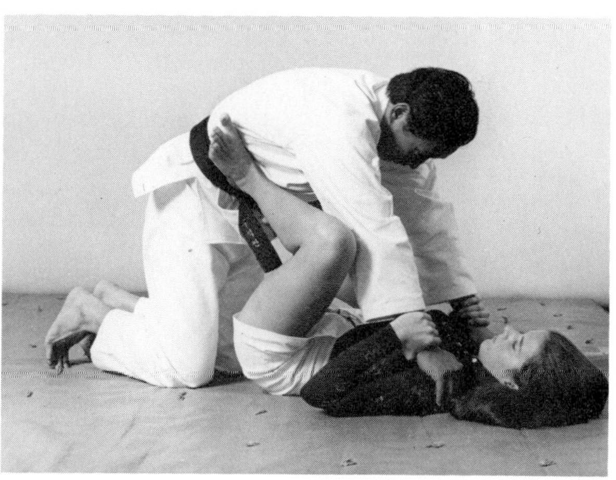

c. Push forward with both legs, thrusting opponent away.

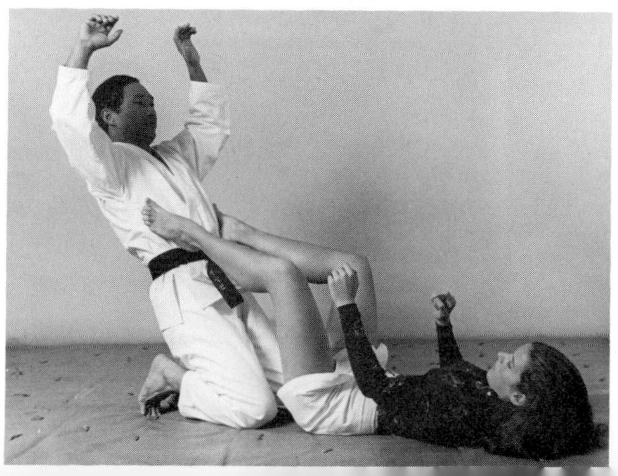

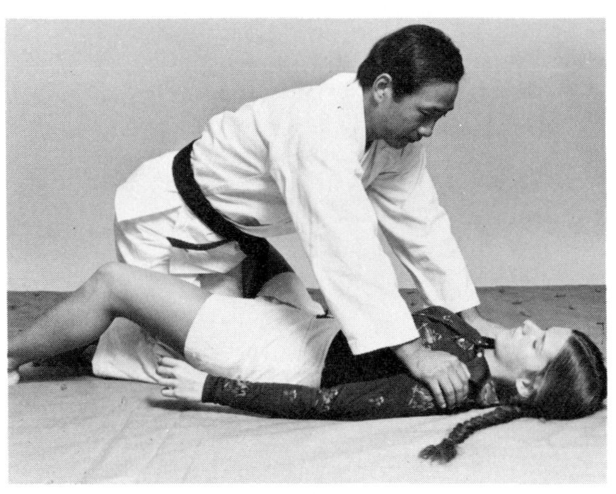

2. Shoulders Pinned

a. Grasp opponent's wrists in both hands.

b. Raise both legs, and hook feet together behind his back, squeezing his ribs between your knees in a scissors hold.

c. Pull his hands outward, off your shoulders, and thrust both hands up, attacking his throat with Tiger Mouth Hands.

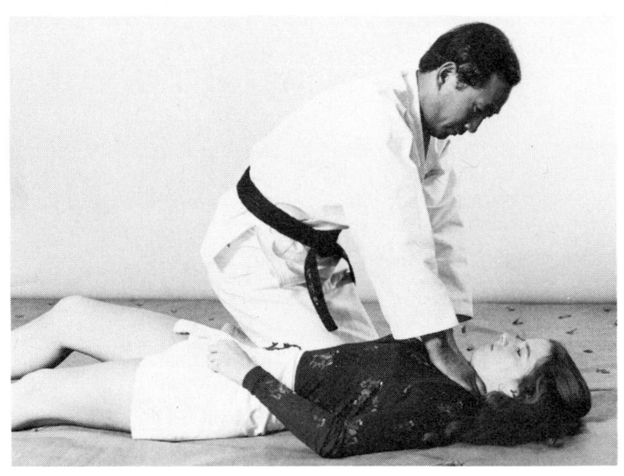

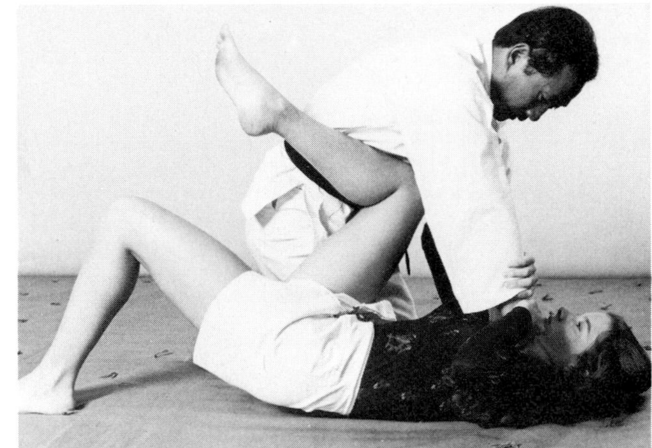

3. Choked from Side

a. If opponent chokes you from your right side, grasp his right wrist in both hands and raise your right knee to his chest.

b. Raise left leg across, into position against the left side of his neck.

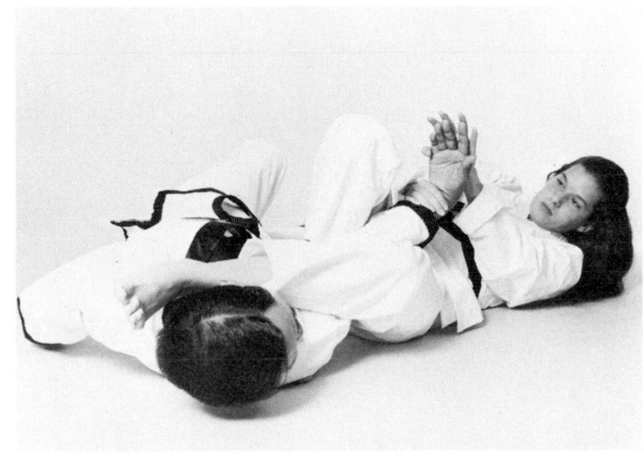

c. Pull down with left leg, throwing him over to your left, and simultaneously bend his held hand inward (palm to forearm), breaking his wrist.

4. Choked from Back

a. Grasp both of opponent's wrists, and raise both legs, catching his neck between your ankles.

b. Bring both legs down, pulling opponent forward and throwing him over you, on his back.

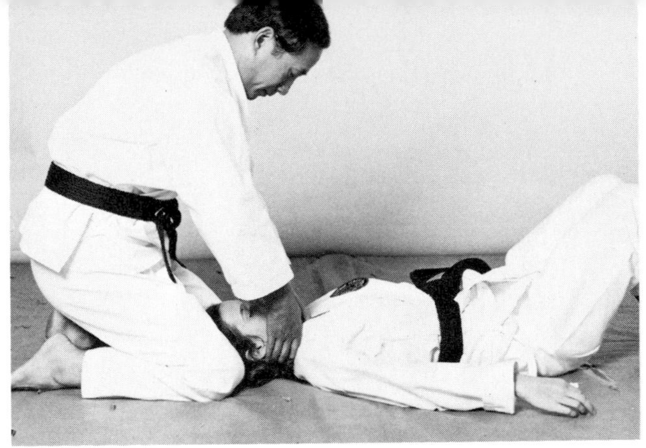

5. Choked from Back

a. Grasp both of opponent's wrists, and raise both legs, kicking him in the face or chest with one foot.

b. Opponent is thrust away.

6. Shoulders Pinned

a. Grab one of opponent's wrists in both hands, and raise your leg (on the same side as his held hand), hooking your knee over his elbow.

b. Push your leg down, throwing him over, and simultaneously bend the held hand inward (palm to forearm), breaking his wrist.

7. Choked from Side

a. If choked from your right side, grasp opponent's right wrist in both hands, and raise both your legs.

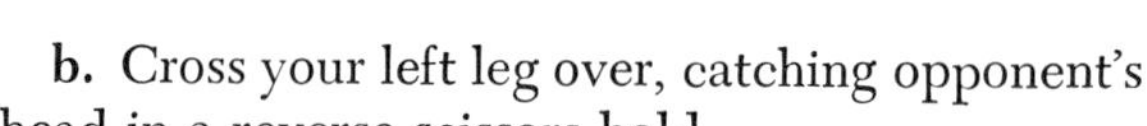

b. Cross your left leg over, catching opponent's head in a reverse scissors hold.

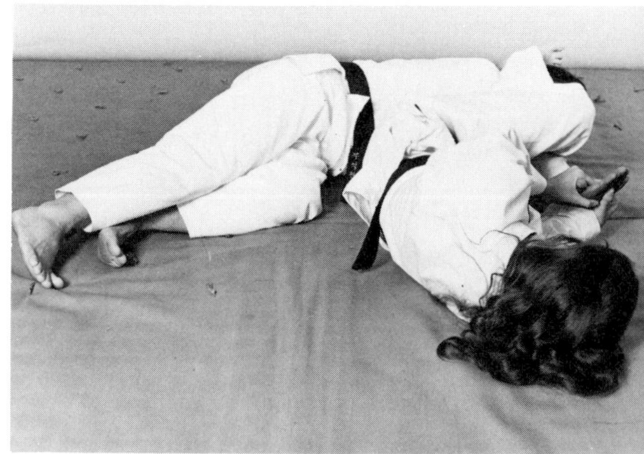

c. Continuing the motion of your legs and hips to your right, push opponent over to the right, throwing him to the floor, and simultaneously bend the held hand inward (palm to forearm), breaking his wrist.

OTHER SELF-DEFENSE TECHNIQUES AGAINST MISCELLANEOUS GRABS AND HOLDS

Other Self-Defense Techniques Against Miscellaneous Grabs and Holds (continued)

Other Self-Defense Techniques Against Miscellaneous Grabs and Holds (continued)

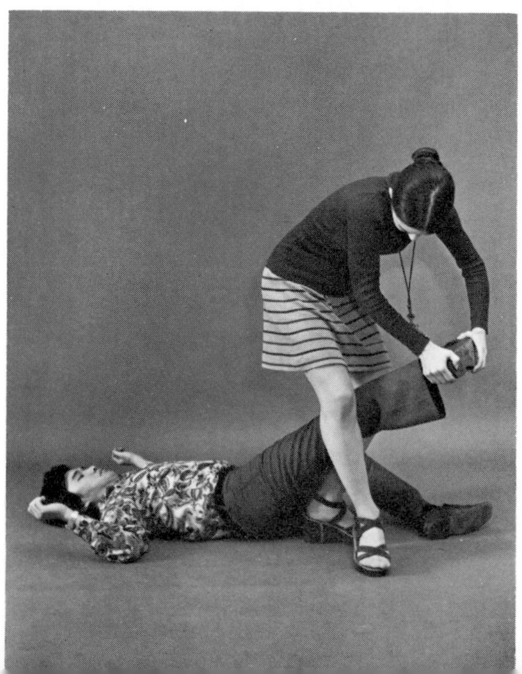

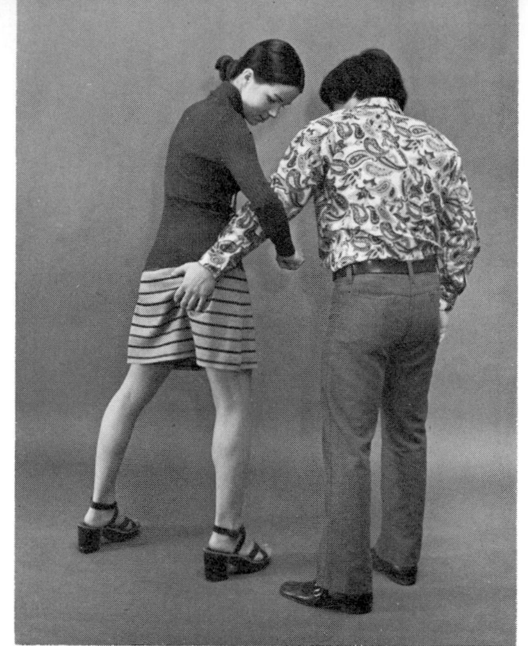

Other Self-Defense Techniques Against Miscellaneous Grabs and Holds (continued)

Other Self-Defense Techniques Against Miscellaneous Grabs and Holds (continued)

DEFENSES AGAINST ASSAULTS WITH WEAPONS

1. Defenses Against Assaults with a Stick

Attacker swings stick overhead:

a. Step forward, simultaneously executing High Knife-Hand X Block.

b. Grab stick and twist outward and down, simultaneously bringing back knee forward and up in preparation for a Side Kick.

c. Execute Side Kick to attacker's solar plexus, simultaneously pulling stick out of his hands.

d. Thrust point of stick forward, striking attacker's philtrum.

Attacker swings stick overhead:

a. Execute Knife-Hand High Block.

b. Grab stick, with blocking hand palm down and other hand palm up.

c. Turn high end of stick down.

d. Pull stick free of attacker's grasp.

e. Thrust low end of stick forward and up, striking attacker's chin.

2. Defenses Against Underhand Knife Attack

When carrying a coat or jacket, and opponent advances with underhand knife attack:

a. Wrap coat around your forearm.

b. Block knife thrust with protected forearm (blocking outward).

c. Grasp attacker's wrist with other hand, palm down.

d. Twist attacker's wrist palm up, simultaneously executing Front Kick to his solar plexus.

If wearing a belt, draw it out when opponent advances with underhand knife attack:

a. Swing the buckle end (heavy end) of belt over opponent's attacking hand so that it winds around, grabbing tightly.

b. Pull attacker's hand toward you with the belt until you can grab his wrist in both hands and twist it (breaking it). Simultaneously execute a Front Kick to his solar plexus.

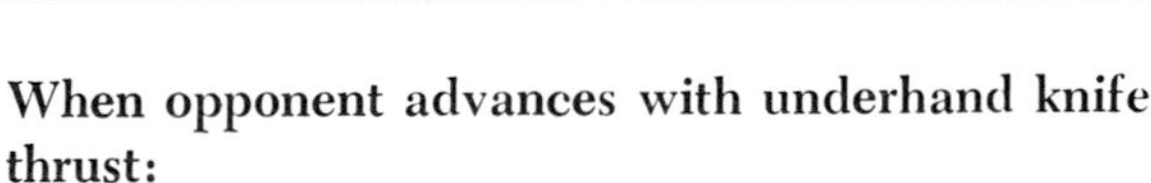

When opponent advances with underhand knife thrust:

a. Execute a Crescent Kick, blocking the thrust and striking his wrist outward with the arch or sole of your foot.

b. Using the same (kicking) foot before it touches the ground, immediately execute a Side Kick to the solar plexus, simultaneously grabbing opponent's wrist.

3. Defenses Against Overhead Knife Attack

Drop to the floor (toward the outside of attacking arm):

a. Place sole of lower foot along outside of attacker's front foot, simultaneously raising other foot for a kick.

b. Execute Side Kick to attacker's solar plexus, simultaneously grabbing his wrist as knife descends.

c. Sweep him to the floor (thrusting his front foot out from under him), simultaneously twisting his wrist with both hands outward and down, breaking it.

Step forward, simultaneously executing Double-Fist High X Block:

a. Open hands, grabbing attacker's wrist.

b. Twist his wrist outward and down.

c. Holding his wrist firmly in your outside hand, execute a Knife-Hand Strike to attacker's neck with other hand, then grab back of neck with striking hand and, pulling his head forward and down, execute Knee Kick to solar plexus, then to face.

4. Defenses Against Assaults with a Pistol

Assault from front:

a. Swing both hands forward simultaneously, striking back of attacker's wrist with palm of one hand, and striking pistol in opposite direction with palm of other hand (hooking thumb under barrel).

b. Twist pistol out of attacker's hand (grasping it by the barrel), simultaneously twisting attacker's wrist palm up with other hand.

c. Thrust pistol forward and up, striking attacker's temple with the butt.

Assault from front:

a. Swing both hands forward simultaneonsly, grasping back of attacker's wrist with one hand and barrel of pistol with the other—thrusting barrel upward, out of range.

b. Holding attacker's wrist firmly, thrust pistol straight forward and up, striking him on the philtrum with the butt.

Assault from front:

a. Swing one hand forward, grabbing back of attacker's wrist and thrusting pistol to the side, out of range. Simultaneously pull other fist back to hip and step forward.

b. Keeping firm hold on attacker's wrist, execute a Reverse Punch to solar plexus.

c. Follow immediately with a Front Kick to solar plexus and simultaneously twist his wrist upward and back with both hands, breaking it.

When pistol is held at temple:

a. Pivot toward attacker, simultaneously striking pistol out of range with Knife-Hand High Block.

b. Grab back of attacker's wrist in your palm and twist outward and down.

c. Using both hands, twist attacker's wrist around and forward, turning pistol toward him.

When pistol is held at back of head:

a. Turn toward attacker, simultaneously striking pistol out of range to the side with elbow.

b. Grabbing his wrist with blocking hand, execute Knife-Hand Strike to temple with other hand.

c. Maintaining hold on attacker's wrist, bend striking arm down over his elbow, bending his arm upward.

d. Continue motion, bending attacker's arm backward and down in an arm lock.

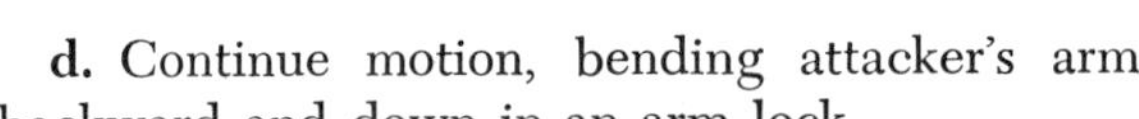

When pistol is held at your back:

a. Turn toward attacker, simultaneously striking pistol out of range to the side with your forearm.

b. Grab attacker's wrist (holding pistol out of range) and execute a Side Kick to solar plexus.

c. Using both hands, twist attacker's wrist over, back, and down, breaking it.

DEFENSES IN SITTING POSITIONS

1. Facing Opponent Across a Table

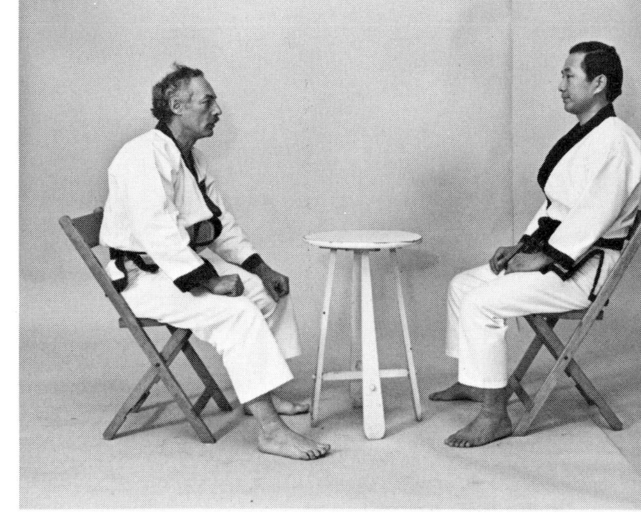

a. Ward off opponent's punching attack to the face with a Knife-Hand Block.

b. Immediately grabbing opponent's wrist or sleeve, counter with a Round Kick to the head.

2. Grabbing or Choking Attack from an Opponent Standing in Front

a. Ward off opponent's attack with a Spread Knife-Hand Block.

b. Immediately grabbing opponent's forearms or sleeves with both hands, execute a Front Kick to solar plexus or groin.

c. Follow immediately with a Side Kick, breaking opponent's knee.

d. When opponent falls backward, finish with a downward Heel Kick to his face.

3. Lapel Grabbed by Opponent Sitting to the Side

a. Grab offending hand using the hand from your opposite, free side, and simultaneously break opponent's elbow with a forward Elbow Strike using the arm closest to him, with your fist pressed against your hip for support.

b. Twisting opponent's offending hand over and out, finish with a downward Elbow Strike to the back of the head or neck.

DEFENSES AGAINST TWO ASSAILANTS

One assailant holds your neck and wrist from behind, and the other advances with a High Punch in front:

a. Block the punch with your free forearm and, grabbing attacker's arm or sleeve, execute a Front Kick to solar plexus or abdomen.

b. Pivot and execute an over-the-shoulder Pincers-Hand Strike (or Spear-Hand Thrust) to the eyes of assailant behind you.

c. Grab the hand opponent has around your neck, twist out of neck hold, and, still holding that hand, execute an elbow attack outward and back to opponent's face.

One assailant holds your neck and wrist from behind, and the other threatens to attack in front:

a. Twist and execute an over-the-shoulder punch to the face of assailant in back with your free fist.

b. Immediately pivot and ward off punch from assailant in front with a Knife-Hand Block.

c. Grab attacker's wrist or sleeve and counter with a Round Kick to the head.

d. Immediately pivot and, using the same foot, execute a Back Kick or Side Kick to the face of opponent in back.

Wrists grabbed by one assailant on each side:

a. Twist to one side and execute a Front Kick with your back foot to one assailant's solar plexus or abdomen.

b. Pivot immediately and execute a Back Kick or Side Kick to other opponent's throat or face, using the same foot.

c. Follow with an outward Knife-Hand Strike to same opponent's neck,

d. and a reverse punch to his solar plexus.

e. Pivot and finish other assailant with a Downward Forefist Punch to the back of the head.

13

Breaking and

The ability to break through hard surfaces with the bare hands and feet is not the aim of Tae Kwon Do, but merely the natural outcome of years of training in the basic principles and techniques of the art. Constant practice in the fundamentals of Tae Kwon Do develops the coordination of strength, speed, and accuracy to an extraordinary degree, and these features constitute the basis of breaking techniques.

Accuracy is essential. One must judge correctly the distance between himself and the target, in order to strike at the range of maximum force. If one is too close, there will not be room for the striking movement to develop enough speed to break through the target. If one is too far away, his force will have been spent before he reaches the target. Accuracy in coordination is also necessary in order to be sure of striking the point of weakness in the target material with the point of greatest force in the striking area of the hand, foot, etc., so that one will shatter the target stone or board—and not injure his own limb. Strength, though very important, is not sufficient unto itself. Strength in breaking techniques is the product of accuracy and speed. It is speed which provides the shock force necessary to break through hard materials. So it is that the point of a straw, borne in a hurricane wind, can penetrate the trunk of a tree. Focus, i.e., the concentration of strength, speed, and accuracy, is the effective principle that achieves tasks which seem impossible to the uninitiated.

In breaking, there are certain points to remember: (1) Select materials that have a perceptible grain running throughout, so that it is possible for them to split in a fairly straight line along that grain. (2) The piece selected should be rectangular, longer in the direction perpendicular to the grain than it is wide in the direction parallel to the grain; it should not be too thick in proportion to its length and width; it should be fairly flat, at least at the striking point. (3) The piece to be broken should be firmly held, by a constructed frame or several assistants, as close to the edges of its length—perpendicular to the grain—as possible. (This is especially important when one is first learning breaking techniques. Later, when the practitioner has developed the ability to execute his techniques with great speed, it may be possible for him to break wooden boards, for example, which are loosely held by the fingertips of an assistant at one edge, or which are floating in a tub of water, or which are even thrown into midair.) (4) One must strike the target material along the line of the grain, and as close to the center of the piece as possible.

In the beginning, one should select materials that are fairly easy to break, in order to practice the technique without fear of injury, and to build confidence toward more ambitious ventures. One should not attempt to break a piece unless he is convinced, beforehand, that he can do it. If an attempt at breaking fails, the student's confidence may be shattered, and his training set back many months. Clear pine boards are best at the beginning, for the wood is fairly soft, the grain is straight and easily perceived, and there are no knots in the wood to resist splitting. The board to be broken is normally three-quarters of an inch thick, ten inches wide (along the grain), and twelve inches long (perpendicular to the grain). When the student has been able to break one such board successfully, with one stroke, many times, and using a variety of striking techniques, such as the Forefist Punch, Knife-Hand Strike, Palm-Heel Thrust, Front Kick, Side Kick, and others (many of which are illustrated in this section), he may go on to break two such boards—held firmly together, with the grain running in the same direction—then three, four, and possibly even five. Afterward, he may go on to break harder woods, such as birch and oak, and increasingly thicker boards, up to three or four inches. Eventually he may proceed to break cinder blocks, bricks, certain stones, and even blocks of ice.

BREAKING WITH THE HAND AND ARM

1. Forefist

2. Hammer Fist

3. Spear Hand

4. Knife Hand

5. **Elbow Strike**

6. **Palm Heel**

BREAKING WITH THE HEAD

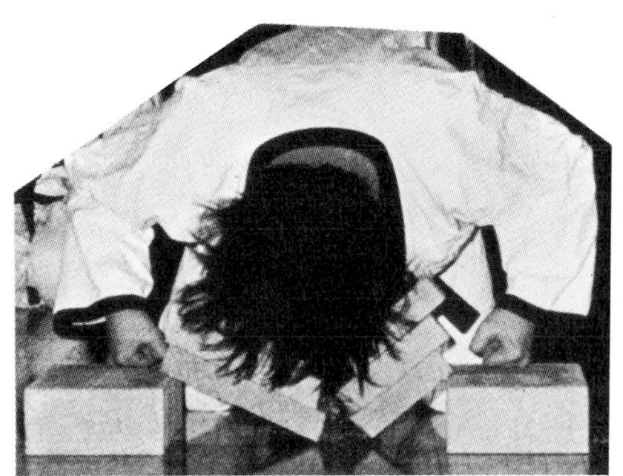

BREAKING WITH THE FEET (*Kicking*)

1. Front Kick

2. Round Kick

3. Side Kick

4. Turning Wheel Kick

5. Jumping Front Kick

6. Jumping Round Kick

7. Jumping Side Kick

8. Heel Kick (Stamping)

9. **Jumping Double Front Kick**

SPEED BREAKING

Speed Breaking is a special technique that should be attempted by the advanced student only, after he has mastered the more basic breaking methods.

In order to execute this technique effectively, the practitioner depends less on strength and concentrates more on developing great speed and accuracy. The board or other material to be broken is not held firmly in place in this case, and so the object is to strike through with such tremendous speed that the board itself will not have the split second necessary to be thrust out of the way on contact. And extraordinary accuracy is equally necessary, in order that the practitioner strike the board exactly at its weak point, or again it may not break but simply be thrust away.

Speed Breaking may be done in many ways: for example, the board to be broken may be held loosely at one edge by the fingertips of an assistant, or suspended at the edges by slips of paper, or thrown up to be struck in midair.

14

Using Equipment for Training

In order to develop the strength, speed, and accuracy essential to Tae Kwon Do, many forms of equipment may be used to supplement the basic stretching and strengthening exercises, which are illustrated in the earlier chapter on calisthenics. One should practice before a mirror, for example, to check that one's posture is correct when assuming any of the basic or advanced positions or when executing a blocking or attacking technique. Weights may be attached to the feet or ankles to strengthen the legs in kicking practice. Weights may also be held in the hands when practicing thrusts, punches, and strikes in order to strengthen the arms. In working with weights, however, it is very important to bear in mind that the purpose is to develop strength *as well as suppleness for speed.* The weights used should be in proportion to one's own body weight and strength to avoid straining oneself to the point of injury, and to avoid building up massive tissue, which will only result in becoming musclebound, thereby inhibiting the suppleness and elasticity necessary to effective movement.

This chapter illustrates various forms of equipment which are used to advantage in sound training practice.

OVERHEAD PULLEY

a. By pulling down on the rope with both hands, the foot is raised straight up in front in a leather loop, stretching the leg for a high Front Kick.

b. By turning the hip over, the pulley may be used to stretch the leg for a high Side Kick.

SKIPPING ROPE

This develops strength and endurance in the legs and good coordination.

IRON HORSE

Hook the feet under the front rung and rest the thighs over the pad: lower the head backward to the floor and do sit-ups. This stretches and strengthens the back and stomach.

BARBELL (*Long Weighted Bar for Two Hands*)

1. Jerk and Press

a. Ready position: squat to grip the bar, with body weight stable and feet firmly planted on the floor. Be sure weights are adjusted and your hands, palm down, placed at even distances from both ends of the bar.

b. Jerk the bar up to your shoulders, simultaneously rising to a standing position, and press the bar to arms' length overhead. This strengthens the legs, back, chest, arms, and shoulders.

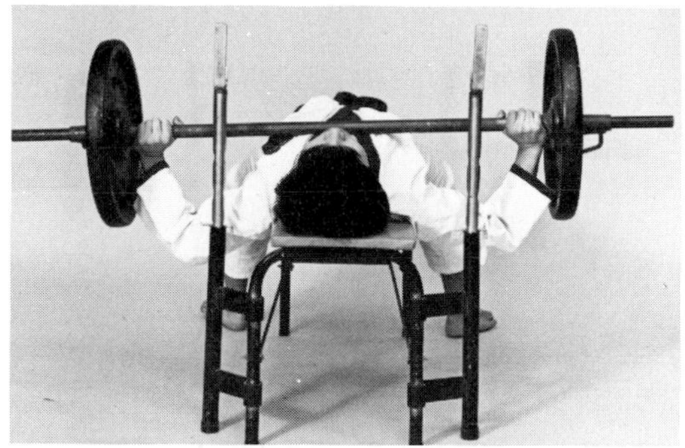

2. Bench Press

a. Lie back on the bench with your feet braced on the floor, grip the bar with both hands at an even distance from the ends and lower it to your chest.

b. Press the bar straight up to arms' length. This strengthens arms, shoulders, and chest.

3. Curling

a. Ready position: hold the bar with your hands, palm up, down at your sides.

b. Pull the bar up to your shoulders, employing equal force in both arms. This strengthens forearms, biceps, and shoulders.

4. Rolling Barbell on Forearms

Rest the bar on both forearms with fists palm up and roll the bar back and forth from wrists to elbows. This strengthens and toughens forearm muscles.

5. Squats

Hold the barbell between the legs with one hand in front and one in back, and do squat repetitions, bending the knees until the weights touch the floor and straightening the knees again to rise to standing position. This strengthens the legs.

DUMBBELLS (*Individual Hand Weights*)

1. Raising Arms to the Side

a. Standing erect, raise both arms simultaneously outward and up to shoulder level (or overhead), holding equal weights in both hands, palm down, then repeat with hands palm up.

b. Stand with torso bent forward at the waist into position parallel to floor, and raise arms outward and up, holding equal weights in both hands, palm down.

These exercises strengthen the shoulders.

2. One-Arm Curls

Holding equal weights in both hands, palm up, raise and lower each weight alternately, strengthening the biceps and forearms.

SANDBAG

a. The sandbag may be used to practice punches, thrusts, and strikes with the hands. The photo shows practice with the Forefist Punch.

b. The sandbag is also useful in practicing all kicking techniques. Photo shows Round Kick practice.

c. Ideal as a target for practicing Jumping Kicks and Jumping Turning Kicks.

HAND-HELD TARGET PADS

One student holds up a padded target, and the other executes a Jumping Front Kick. This method may be used in the practice of high Front Kicks, Side Kicks, and Round Kicks, and for Jumping Kicks.

ROPE-WOUND STRIKING BOARD

This is very effective as a means of toughening the striking surfaces of the hands, feet, and even forearms.

1. Striking with Forefist Punch

2. Striking with Ball of Foot in Round Kick

WOODEN HORSE

The Wooden Horse is very useful as an aid in kicking practice to stretch the legs, strengthen the muscles used in jumping, and develop accuracy.

1. High Side Kick (kicking over the wooden horse)

2. High Hook Kick

Note: The High Side Kick and High Hook Kick may be practiced separately, or together in one exercise by executing the Side Kick and then immediately hooking the foot back while it is still in position high above the horse.

3. One-Foot Double Kick

a. High Side Kick, over the horse,

b. immediately followed by knee-level Side Kick through the gap in the wooden horse—both kicks executed in rapid succession with the same foot while that foot is still in the air.

Note: This exercise may be used in One-Foot Double Kicks, kicking first high, then low—as illustrated—or first low, then high, and the method may be used with combinations consisting of double Front Kicks, Front Kick–Side Kick, or low Front Kick—high Round Kick. It is a very effective exercise to develop accuracy as well as speed.

4. Flying Kick

The wooden horse, especially when its height is adjustable, is very helpful as an aid in practicing Flying Kicks, particularly Front Kicks and Side Kicks.

a. Flying Side Kick, side view.

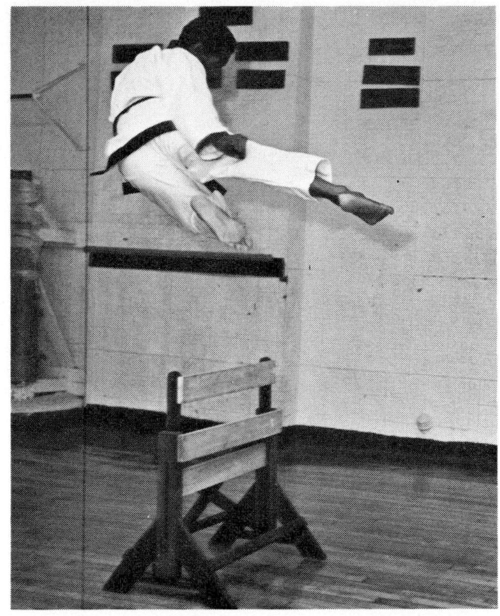

b. Flying Side Kick, front view.

제1회 세계 태권도 선수권대회
THE 1ST WORLD TAE KWON DO CHAMPIONSHIPS
A코-트 COURT
B코-트 COURT

제2회 세계 태권도 선수권대회
THE 2nd WORLD TAEKWONDO CHAMPIONSHIPS

In recent years, Tae Kwon Do has become increasingly popular as a sport throughout the world. Local and nationwide competitive events provide more and more opportunities for the Tae Kwon Do practitioner to prove his excellence in the field. In May 1973 and again in August 1975 more than fifty countries participated in each of the first and second worldwide championship events to be held in this sport, at the invitation of the Tae Kwon Do Association, in Seoul, Korea.

The rules and scoring system vary among the different localities and sponsors of the events, though certain conditions are standard. In the United States, for example, sparring competition is generally restricted to no-contact scoring; that is, the competitor is given a score for techniques executed as close to the vulnerable points of his opponent as possible, without actually touching him. Actual contact is given no score, or a negative score. In Korea, on the other hand, full-contact competition is normal, and for this purpose a cushioned pad is worn by the participants, protecting chest, ribs, and abdomen. Therefore, practitioners in the United States who plan to compete in sparring matches in Korea should practice full-contact sparring—with a chest protector—beforehand. Scoring methods are fairly standardized according to a point system, in which the competitors

receive a point for every attacking technique, such as a punch, kick, knife-hand strike, etc., which is executed accurately to its mark and is not blocked by an arm or leg interposed in defense. Injurious strikes to certain vital points are generally not permitted, such as spear-hand attacks to the eyes, choking attacks to the throat, and punches or kicks to the back or to the groin. A knockdown is scored as a point, but more than one technique of attack directed against the fallen participant, while he is down, is normally forbidden. The participants are required to control their tempers, as well as their techniques. Violent or vicious attacks executed in rage are not permitted and may result in disqualification. Negative scores are given to infractions of the rules, such as stepping outside the prescribed area of combat, executing attacks after the time limit is called, or executing illegal attacks. The time limit set for sparring matches also varies. Three minutes is common. If the competitors do not score, or their scores are tied at the end of the initial time limit, a sudden-death match is usually called, in which they are enjoined to spar until either party scores the first point, and is proclaimed the winner.

In addition to sparring, tournaments sometimes provide competition in the performance of the formal exercises, in which the most perfect demonstration of technique is given full recognition.

In any case, the levels of competition are fixed to correspond with the levels of achievement of the participants, where, for example, beginners compete within their own class, intermediates within theirs, and the more advanced, such as brown belt and black belt holders, within their respective categories. Sometimes, categories are further divided according to body weight.

In the First World Tae Kwon Do Championship, in May 1973, Korea won first place, the United States won second place, and the Republic of China and Mexico tied for third place. The winners in the Second World Tae Kwon Do Championship, in August 1975, were Korea, first place; Republic of China, second place; and Mexico, third place.

The General Assembly of the World Tae Kwon Do Federation has selected Manila, Philippines, for the Third World Championship in 1977, and the United States for the Fourth World Championship in 1979.

Richard Chun, Head Coach (*far left*), and the U.S.A. Tae Kwon Do Team at the First World Tae Kwon Do Championship, Seoul, Korea, 1973.

The Second World Tae Kwon Do Championship, Seoul, Korea, 1975.

Richard Chun, Technical Advisor to the Second World Tae Kwon Do Championship, Seoul, Korea, 1975.

RULES AND POINT SYSTEM OF THE SECOND WORLD TAE KWON DO CHAMPIONSHIP

As an example of the organization of a large-scale competitive event in the field, a portion of the program of the Second World Tae Kwon Do Championship, held in 1975, is reprinted below.

Scope of Participation

Each participating nation may send a total of eight contestants, one representative contestant in each of the eight weight classes.

Qualification of Participant

Grade of the contestant shall be the First Dan black belt through the Third Dan black belt authorized by the Kuk Ki Won.

Methods of Competition

(1) Both individual and team contests will be performed in individual tournament style by weight class between competing nations. There are loser's consolation contests.

(2) The rules and regulations of the World Taekwondo Federation will be applied.

Time Limit of Match

Each match will have three rounds, two minutes each, with 30-second intervals between rounds.

Participating Contestants

In accordance with article 2, paragraph 4, regulations of the competition committee, one from each weight class in general division may participate in the competition. The general division weight classifications are as follows:

Class	Weight
fin weight	48 kg –below
fly weight	48 kg –53 kg
bantam weight	53 kg –58 kg
feather weight	58 kg –63 kg
light weight	63 kg –68 kg
welter weight	68 kg –74 kg
middle weight	74 kg –80 kg
heavy weight	80 kg –up

Methods of Scoring

(1) Final ranking of each nation is determined by the number of medals won by individual contestants from each of the eight weight classes who participated in the team contest. We apply the principle that one gold medal scores more points than several silver medals combined and that one silver medal scores more points than several bronze medals combined.

(2) Final ranking of a team which did not win any medals is determined by the total number of points scored by individual contestants from each of the eight weight classes who participated in the team contest.

(3) To understand how the scoring system works, see the sample* shown below.

(4) In the event that a contestant concedes a game or fails to show up for the contest, he will score zero point.

*Sample for Scoring

a) In case of participation by 5 teams.

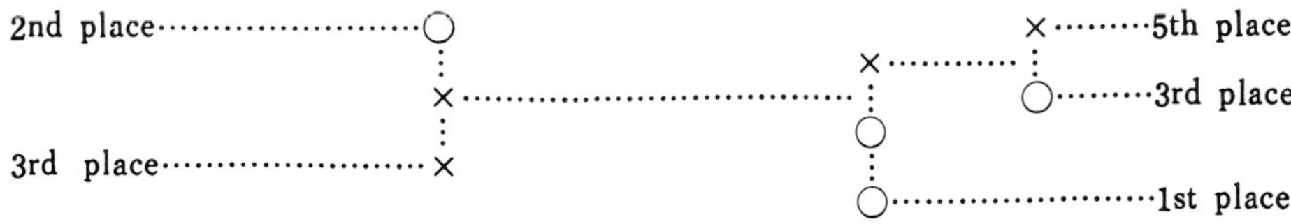

place	1st place	2nd place	3rd place	5th place
score	5 points	4 points	2.5 points	1 point

The Order of Valid Scores

(1) Single attack by fist in perfect posture will be scored.

(a) Successful attack on solar plexus, flanks, or belly by fist scores one point.

(2) Single attack by foot (the instep, axis, heel or foot-knife) in perfect posture will be scored.

(a) Successful attack on solar plexus, flanks or belly by foot scores one point.

(b) Successful attack on the face by foot scores two points when the opponent is staggered by the hit.

(c) Successful attack on the face by foot scores one point when the opponent does not stagger in spite of the hit.

(3) Successful attack on any part of the opponent except the private parts scores one point if the opponent falls by the hit.

(4) The following attacks will not be scored:

(a) Holding the opponent or falling down after the effective attack by fist or foot.

(b) Continued clinching.

Deduction of point

(1) Attacking a contestant who fell down.

(2) Hurting a contestant's face by attacking with fist.

(3) Butting.

(4) Intentional attack after declaration of "Galyeo" (break).

Warning

(1) Holding an opponent.
(2) Escaping from fighting by turning his back to his opponent.
(3) Stepping out of boundary line.
(4) Throwing the opponent down.
(5) Attacking with knee.
(6) Pretending pain.
(7) Moving around the line.
(8) Attacking the private parts.
(9) Pushing the opponent with shoulder or body or pushing the opponent by his hand.
(10) Falling down intentionally.
(11) Falling down in the path of the opponent's sweeping foot.
(12) Attacking the opponent's face with fist.

Chief referee will warn the contestant when he commits any of fouls mentioned above. Deduction of one point shall be declared if the contestant gets the same warning twice in a round.

Other Matters

(1) Warnings shall not be counted in grand total but in each round.

(2) Contestants shall obey unconditionally the instructions of chief referee.

(3) Competitors shall not leave their position until the announcement of the decision by chief referee.

(4) Even an effective attack becomes void when executed after the announcement of "Kelyeo" (Break) order.

(5) If a contestant quits during a competition, he shall forfeit the match.

(6) A contestant who gets three deductions of points shall be defeated by penalty.

(7) In case chief referee or assistant referee is guilty of misjudgment or failure in duty the jury can report him to the council for the following disciplinary action: (a) warning; (b) suspension of qualification; (c) deprivation of qualification.

(8) In case of dissents over decision after the declaration of end of the competition, the coach and manager shall submit a formal written complaint to the council. Oral complaints will not be accepted.

16

The Forms [Poom-Se]
—Formal Exercises

Out of their training and experience in the basic techniques which constitute Tae Kwon Do, the masters of the past designed the formal exercises as archetypal patterns of fighting practice. Their object was to provide a means of training their students to perform the basic techniques in continuous sequence, so that they should be able to defend themselves against more than one opponent, and in any direction, for as long as was necessary without tiring. Practice in the formal exercises develops balance, accuracy, concentration, coordination, and endurance. These elements are essential to the performance of Tae Kwon Do, and so the formal exercises are the foundation of the art. Thus it is said, without forms there is no Tae Kwon Do.

Three categories of formal exercise fundamental to the study of Tae Kwon Do are Ki-Cho Forms, Pal-Gwe Forms, and Tae-Kook Forms. Ki-Cho 1 and all eight Pal-Gwe Forms are presented in this volume with full explanatory texts and illustrative drawings and photographs. All three Ki-Cho Forms follow the same H pattern and consist of similar, very basic movements. Due to limitations of space, however, Ki-Cho 2 and 3 and the Tae-Kook Forms have had to be omitted.

Most of the basic techniques are executed many times throughout the formal exercises, providing the student with an opportunity to review these techniques until he has perfected them. The forms should be practiced diligently before the student attempts much free sparring, in order that his techniques be as perfect and accurate in actual fighting as in solo training sessions. The forms are designed purposely so that the student should develop patience through repetition.

Each category of the forms was conceived with a particular viewpoint. The Ki-Cho Forms are the most basic, and are executed in an H pattern, to give the student practice in performing the fundamental techniques of walking, turning, blocking, and punching in continuous sequence in all four directions. They begin and end in the same place, and when performing them, the student should bear in mind that their pattern represents the fact that we all are born as we shall die, naked, bringing nothing into the world and taking nothing out of it. The Tae-Kook Forms are the basic combat forms, and constitute patterns of modern fighting sequences forward and backward, to the front and to the rear. The Pal-Gwe Forms have a deep philosophical reference. They are dynamic symbols of eternal truths, going back in Oriental thought to the ancient Chinese concepts of Yin and Yang.

The Pal-Gwe Forms refer to a philosophy of universal being, which comprehends Truth as a constant within the phenomenon of an ever-changing cosmos. Inherent in the concept of "form," in this context, is the awareness that the universe is infinite and unknowable, having no apparent ties binding it together—and yet some integrating force of cosmic cohesion keeps order: movement within perceptible patterns, energy within stillness, lines of force inscribed within circles of harmony, yielding an integral strength. By merely being so, life is sustained within it. The constancy of truth, and the truth of constant change, are both symbolized in the Pal-Gwe Forms. In Oriental thought, there are three *Dos*, or Levels of Being: Heaven (i.e., the Cosmic Universe), which is Content; Man, which is Subject; and Earth, which is the World of Objective Form. That which is true in Heaven, is mirrored in Man, and takes form on Earth. On each level, the firm or yielding (Yang or Yin) character of the entity combines with the character of the place and time, resulting in a great multiplicity of effects, the world of free possibility. On each level, therefore, conditions of equilibrium yield harmony, and conditions of disturbed equilibrium yield confusion and chaos: coinciding, cooperative forces which yield conditions of equilibrium in Heaven are reflected as harmony in Man, and take the form of good fortune on Earth; and, correspondingly, conflicting forces yielding chaos in Heaven are reflected as confusion and disharmony in Man, and take the form of misfortune and conflict on Earth. The principle of Pal-Gwe is that one who knows himself and his environment, and who understands the three *Dos*, will find the path of harmony between the changeable forces of the world in which he lives and the constant values of human ethics. Such a man will act effectively in the world, without falling into moral error. Pal-Gwe means "Law, Command," and as the Tae Kwon Do practitioner executes the Pal-Gwe Forms, he is obliged to bear in mind the reciprocal commands they represent, which may be translated as follows:

1. Know yourself, and be in harmony with the universe.
2. Be responsible for yourself, and loyal to your commitments.
3. Be respectful of your relationships; know the limits beyond which your freedom encroaches upon the freedom of another.
4. Be pure in motive, and direct in action.

Note: The following points should be observed in the performance of all formal exercises:

1. Execute each position cleanly and completely, before going on to the next: do not run any two positions together.

2. Breathe regularly throughout the form, using the diaphragm rather than the chest, and exhale simultaneously with the last action in each position.

3. Keep your fists tight and your body relaxed. Throughout the forms, your body should be relaxed, except at the instant you complete each block, punch, strike, and kick, when your whole body should be locked into tense focus on that action.

4. While standing at Attention, before beginning the form, take a deep breath, using the diaphragm, not the chest, and concentrate on what you are about to do.

KI-CHO 1
START
1
2
3
4
5
6
7
8
9←8
9
10
11
12

16
16
16→17
17
18
15
15
20
19
14
14
STOP
FRONT VIEW
13
13
1. Low Block
2. Middle Punch
3. Low Block
4. Middle Punch
5. Low Block
6. Middle Punch
7. Middle Punch
8. Middle Punch and Yell
9. Low Block
10. Middle Punch
11. Low Block
12. Middle Punch
13. Low Block
14. Middle Punch
15. Middle Punch
16. Middle Punch and Yell
17. Low Block
18. Middle Punch
19. Low Block
20. Middle Punch

Ki-Cho 1

Number of positions: 20 (excluding Ready Stance and Stop).

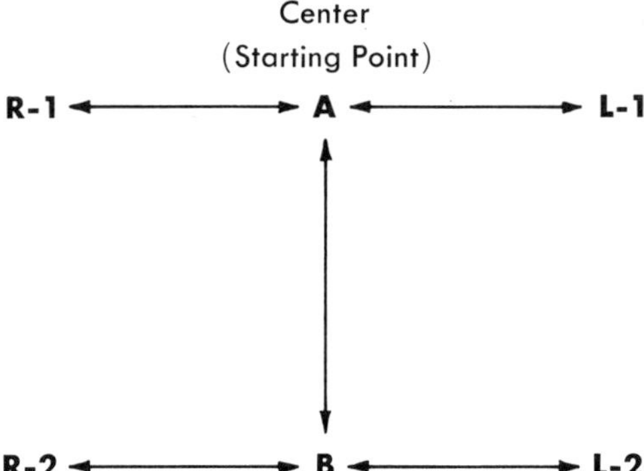

Movement proceeds in an H pattern, beginning at A:

Ready Stance

Stand at Attention at Starting Point, **A,** eyes focused straight ahead, body relaxed, fists tightly closed and held close together a little in front of abdomen, with arms slightly bent, feet parallel, one foot-length apart, with toes pointing straight ahead.

First Position: Low Block

a. Turn 90° to the left, pivoting on right foot and sliding left foot one step forward (toward **L–1**).

b. Assume Front Stance (put two-thirds of your weight on front leg, which is bent at the knee, and keep back leg locked straight).

c. Simultaneously execute a Low Block with left forearm (cross forearms in front of chest, left fist palm in near right ear and right fist palm down under left elbow; then sweep left forearm downward, across abdomen and groin, into position with left fist above left knee, and simultaneously pull right fist back to right hip. Snap both wrists around at the instant of completing the motion, so that left fist is palm down over knee and right fist is palm up at hip.* The blocking surface is the outer edge of the lower left forearm).

* In every block, punch, and strike, snap both wrists around at the last instant and—except where otherwise indicated—pull the other, "idle" fist back to the hip simultaneously with the motion of the "active" hand or forearm, thus providing more impetus to the indicated block, punch, or strike.

Second Position: Middle Punch

a. Slide right foot forward one step (to **L–1**).

b. Assume Front Stance.

c. Simultaneously execute a Middle Punch with right fist (thrust right fist to arm's length at solar plexus level, and simultaneously pull left fist back to hip.* Snap both wrists around at last instant of action so that right fist is palm down and left fist is palm up).

* Except where otherwise indicated (as in "cross forearms" or "raise forearms"), it is to be understood that each motion of the hands or forearms begins with the hands moving from the hip—that is, the hands return into position beside the hips, elbows straight back, after the completion of each motion and in the process of beginning the next.

Third Position: Low Block

a. Pivoting on left foot, slide right foot out and back in a wide arc, turning 180° (to face **R–1**).

b. Assume Front Stance.

c. Simultaneously execute a Low Block with right forearm.

Fourth Position: Middle Punch

a. Slide left foot forward one step (to **R–1**).

b. Assume Front Stance.

c. Simultaneously execute a Middle Punch with left fist.

Fifth Position: Low Block

a. Pivoting on right foot, slide left foot out, turning 90° (to face **B**).

b. Assume Front Stance.

c. Simultaneously execute a Low Block with left forearm.

Sixth Position: Middle Punch

a. Slide right foot forward one step (toward **B**).

b. Assume Front Stance.

c. Simultaneously execute a Middle Punch with right fist.

Seventh Position: Middle Punch

a. Slide left foot forward one step (toward **B**).

b. Assume Front Stance.

c. Simultaneously execute a Middle Punch with left fist.

Eighth Position: Middle Punch and Yell

a. Slide right foot forward one step (to **B**).

b. Assume Front Stance.

c. Simultaneously execute a Middle Punch with right fist and yell.

Ninth Position: Low Block

a. Pivoting on right foot, slide left foot out and back in a wide arc, turning 270° (three-quarters of a circle, to face **R–2**).

b. Assume Front Stance.

c. Simultaneously execute a Low Block with left forearm.

Tenth Position: Middle Punch

a. Slide right foot forward one step (to **R–2**).

b. Assume Front Stance.

c. Simultaneously execute a Middle Punch with right fist.

Eleventh Position: Low Block

a. Pivoting on left foot, slide right foot out and back in a wide arc, turning 180° (to face **L–2**).

b. Assume Front Stance.

c. Simultaneously execute a Low Block with right forearm.

Twelfth Position: Middle Punch

a. Slide left foot forward one step (to **L–2**).

b. Assume Front Stance.

c. Simultaneously execute a Middle Punch with left fist.

Thirteenth Position: Low Block

a. Pivoting on right foot, slide left foot out, turning 90° (to face **A**).

b. Assume Front Stance.

c. Simultaneously execute a Low Block with left forearm.

Fourteenth Position: Middle Punch

a. Slide right foot forward one step (toward **A**).

b. Assume Front Stance.

c. Simultaneously execute a Middle Punch with right fist.

Fifteenth Position: Middle Punch

a. Slide left foot forward one step (toward **A**).

b. Assume Front Stance.

c. Simultaneously execute a Middle Punch with left fist.

Sixteenth Position: Middle Punch and Yell

a. Slide right foot forward one step (to **A**).

b. Assume Front Stance.

c. Simultaneously execute a Middle Punch with right fist and yell.

Seventeenth Position: Low Block

a. Pivoting on right foot, slide left foot out and back in a wide arc, turning 270° (to face **L–1**).

b. Assume Front Stance.

c. Simultaneously execute a Low Block with left forearm.

Eighteenth Position: Middle Punch

a. Slide right foot forward one step (to **L–1**).

b. Assume Front Stance.

c. Simultaneously execute a Middle Punch with right fist.

Nineteenth Position: Low Block

a. Pivoting on left foot, slide right foot out and back, turning 180° (to face **R–1**).

b. Assume Front Stance.

c. Simultaneously execute a Low Block with right forearm.

Twentieth Position: Middle Punch

a. Slide left foot forward one step (to **R–1**).

b. Assume Front Stance.

c. Simultaneously execute a Middle Punch with left fist.

Stop

Pivoting on right foot, slide left foot out and back, turning 90° to the front (resuming Starting Point, **A**). Assume Ready Stance (Attention, eyes focused straight ahead).

PAL-GWE 1
START
1
2
3
4
5
6
7
8
9
10
11
12
13
14
15
16
17
18
STOP
19
20
9←8

16
16
16→17
17
18
15
15
20
19
14
14
FRONT VIEW
13
13
STOP
1. Low Block
2. Inside Middle Block
3. Low Block
4. Inside Middle Block
5. Low Block
6. Inside Middle Block
7. Inside Middle Block
8. Middle Punch and Yell
9. Knife-Hand Middle Block
10. Inside Middle Block
11. Knife-Hand Middle Block
12. Inside Middle Block
13. Low Block
14. Knife-Hand Strike
15. Knife-Hand Strike
16. Middle Punch and Yell
17. Low Block
18. Inside Middle Block
19. Low Block
20. Inside Middle Block

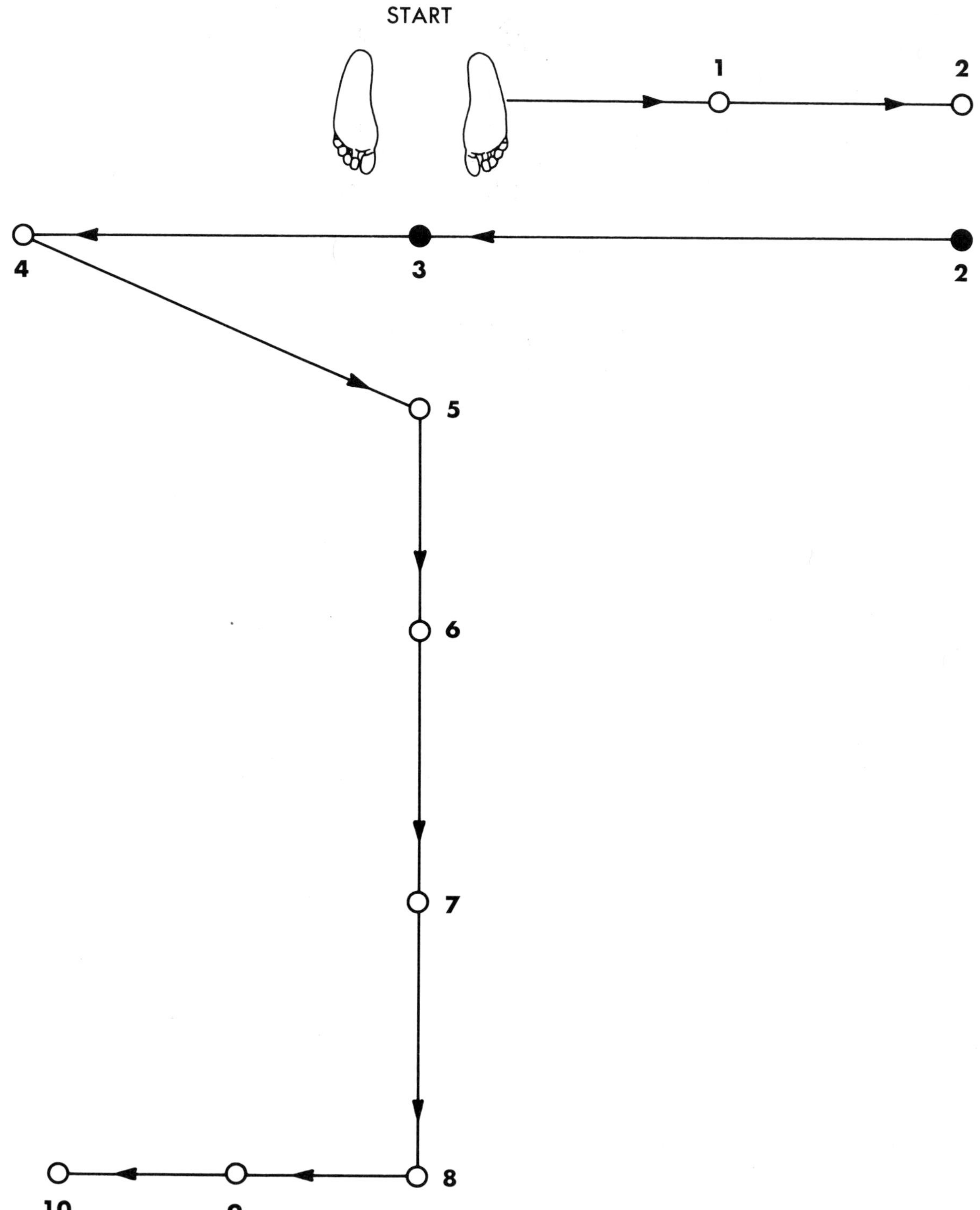
START
1
2
4
3
2
5
6
7
8
10
9

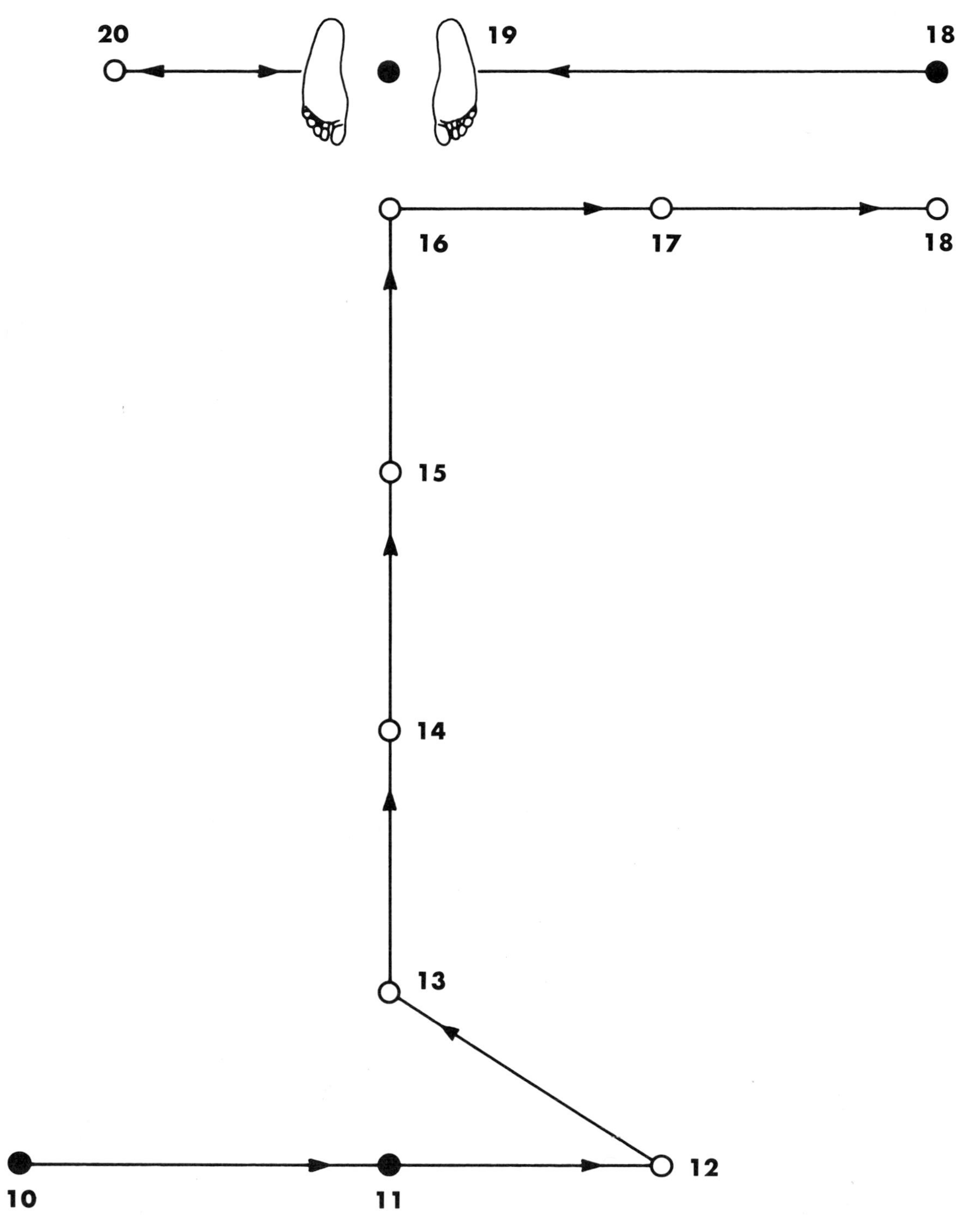
STOP
20
19
18
16
17
18
15
14
13
12
10
11

PAL-GWE 1 (*Pal-Gwe Il-Chang*)

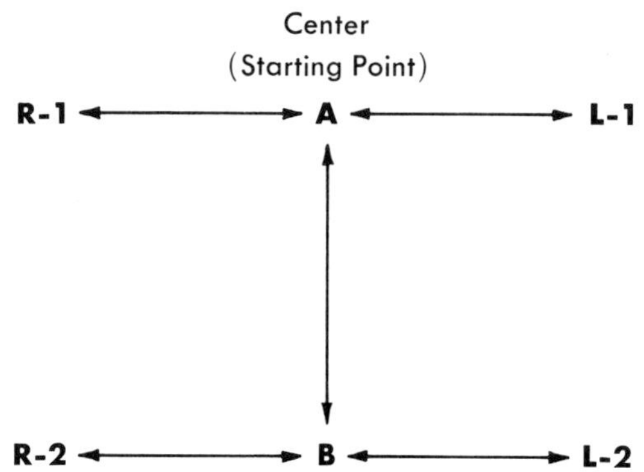

Number of positions: 20 (excluding Ready Stance and Stop).

Movement proceeds in an H pattern, beginning at A.

Ready Stance

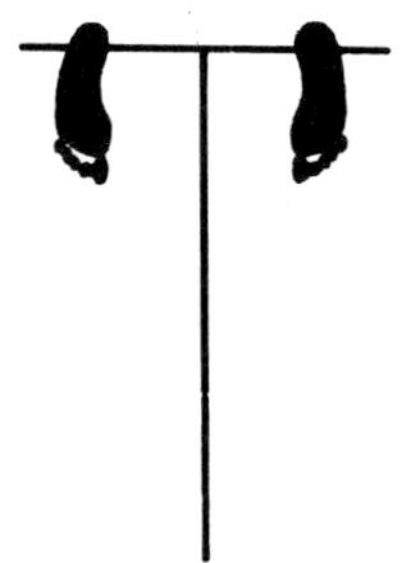

Stand at Attention at Starting Point, **A,** eyes focused straight ahead.

First Position: Low Block

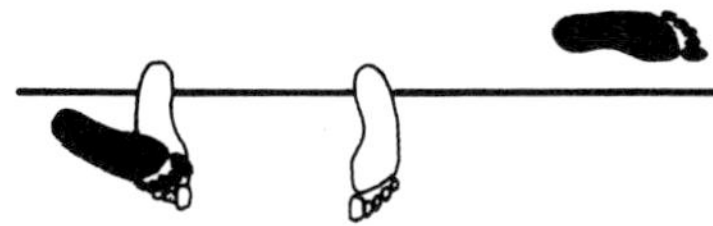

a. Turn 90° to the left, pivoting on right foot and sliding left foot one step forward (toward **L–1**).

b. Assume Front Stance (put two-thirds of your weight on front leg, which is bent at the knee, and keep back leg locked straight).

c. Simultaneously execute a Low Block with left forearm (cross forearms in front of chest, left fist palm in near right ear and right fist palm down under left elbow; then sweep left forearm downward, across abdomen and groin, into position with left fist above left knee, and simultaneously pull right fist back to right hip. Snap both wrists around at the instant of completing the motion, so that left fist is palm down and right fist is palm up.* The blocking surface is the outer edge of the lower left forearm).

* In every block, punch, and strike, snap both wrists around at the last instant and—except where otherwise indicated—pull the other, "idle" fist back to the hip simultaneously with the motion of the "active" hand or forearm, thus providing more impetus to the indicated block, punch, or strike.

Second Position: Inside Middle Block

a. Slide right foot forward one step (to **L–1**).

b. Assume Front Stance.

c. Simultaneously execute an Inside Middle Block with right forearm (swing right forearm out to the side, holding it vertically, into position with elbow sharply bent behind and below shoulder, and fist, palm out, to the side and just above shoulder; then immediately—as in one continuous motion—sweep right forearm strongly forward and down, snapping wrist palm in, into position with elbow, bent down, close beside and in front of body, and fist out in front of chest and level with shoulder—and simultaneously pull left fist back to hip, snapping wrist palm up.* The blocking surface is the outer edge, or pinkie side, of the lower right forearm).

* Except where otherwise indicated (as in "cross forearms" or "raise forearms"), it is to be understood that each motion of the hands or forearms generally begins with the hands moving from the hip—that is, the hands return into position beside the hips, elbows straight back, after the completion of each motion and in the process of beginning the next.

Third Position: Low Block

a. Pivoting on left foot, slide right foot out and back in a wide arc, turning 180° (to face **R–1**).

b. Assume Front Stance.

c. Simultaneously execute a Low Block with right forearm.

Fourth Position: Inside Middle Block

a. Slide left foot forward one step (to **R–1**).

b. Assume Front Stance.

c. Simultaneously execute an Inside Middle Block with left forearm.

Fifth Position: Low Block

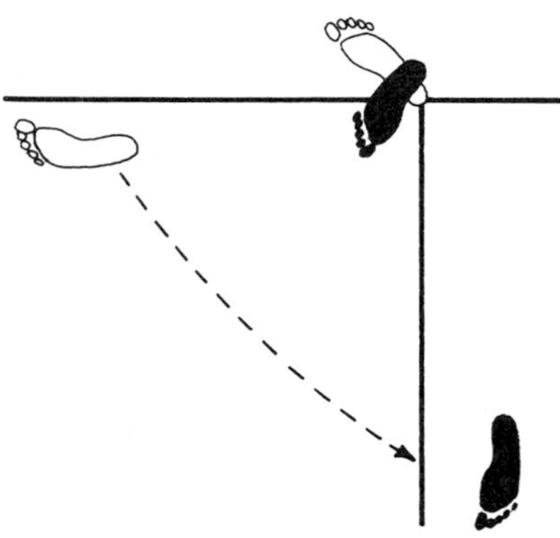

a. Pivoting on right foot, slide left foot out, turning 90° (toward **B**).

b. Assume Front Stance.

c. Simultaneously execute a Low Block with left forearm.

Sixth Position: Inside Middle Block

a. Slide right foot forward one step (toward **B**).

b. Assume Back Stance (both knees bent outward, two-thirds of your weight on back leg).

c. Simultaneously execute an Inside Middle Block with right forearm.

Seventh Position: Inside Middle Block

a. Slide left foot forward one step (toward **B**).

b. Assume Back Stance.

c. Simultaneously execute an Inside Middle Block with left forearm.

Eighth Position: Middle Punch and Yell

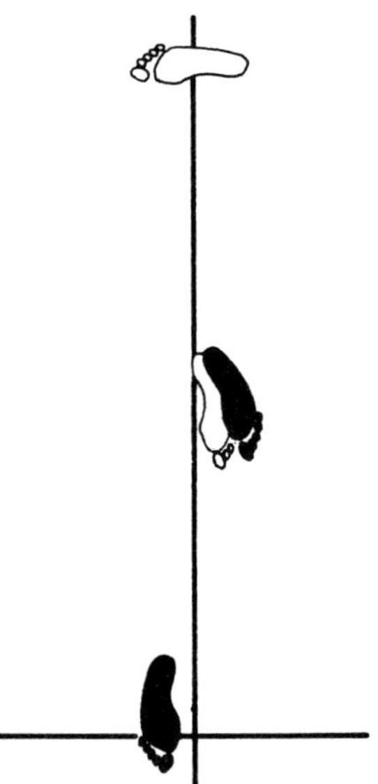

a. Slide right foot forward one step (to **B**).

b. Assume Front Stance.

c. Simultaneously execute a Middle Punch with right fist (punching at the level of your own solar plexus, and snapping wrist around so that fist is palm down on contact. Simultaneously pull left fist back to hip palm up)—and yell.

Ninth Position: Knife-Hand Middle Block

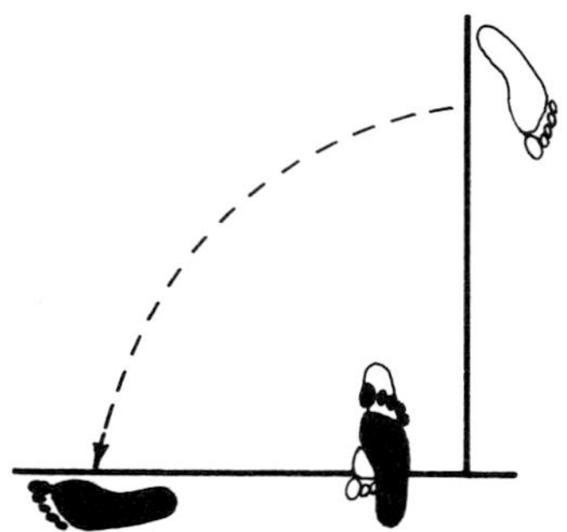

a. Pivot on right foot, slide left foot out and back in a wide arc, turning 270° (three-quarters of a circle, to face **R–2**).

b. Assume Back Stance.

c. Simultaneously execute a Knife-Hand Middle Block with left hand, right Knife Hand assisting (raise left Knife Hand to right ear, palm in, and sweep outward and down into position with left elbow bent downward and fingertips of left Knife Hand extended at shoulder level out to a point at the side of the face, focused toward **R–2**, snapping the wrist palm out. Simultaneously pull right hand back to hip, as open Knife Hand, and thrust out again into place, palm up, immediately in front of solar plexus. The blocking surface is the outer edge of the left Knife Hand, while the right Knife Hand, assisting, protects the solar plexus).

Tenth Position: Inside Middle Block

a. Slide right foot forward one step (to **R–2**).

b. Assume Back Stance.

c. Simultaneously execute an Inside Middle Block with right forearm.

Eleventh Position: Knife-Hand Middle Block

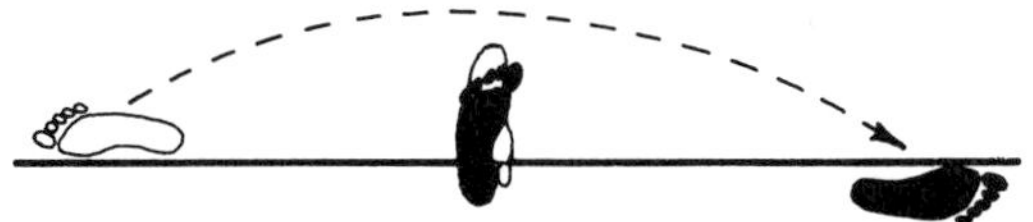

a. Pivoting on left foot, slide right foot out and back in a wide arc, turning 180° (to face **L–2**).

b. Assume Back Stance.

c. Simultaneously execute a Knife-Hand Middle Block with right hand, left Knife Hand assisting.

Twelfth Position: Inside Middle Block

a. Slide left foot forward one step (to **L–2**).

b. Assume Back Stance.

c. Simultaneously execute an Inside Middle Block with left forearm.

Thirteenth Position: Low Block

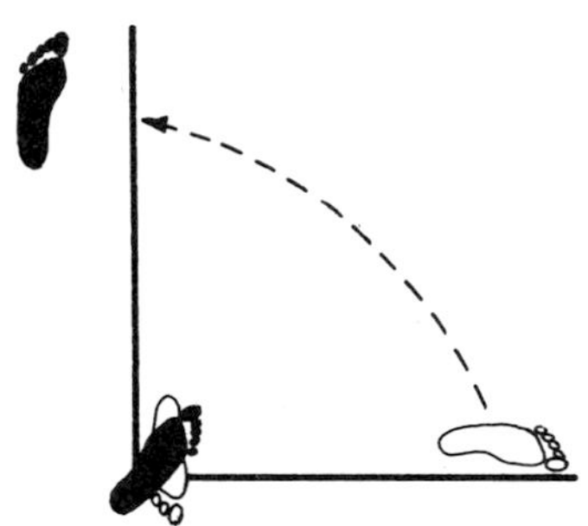

front view

a. Pivoting on right foot, slide left foot out, turning 90° (to face **A**).

b. Assume Front Stance.

c. Simultaneously execute a Low Block with left forearm.

Fourteenth Position: Right Knife-Hand Strike to the Neck

front view

a. Slide right foot forward one step (toward **A**).

b. Assume Front Stance.

c. Simultaneously execute a Knife-Hand Strike to the neck with right hand (thrusting right Knife Hand out and forward in a slight arc from right shoulder to imaginary opponent's neck, snapping wrist palm up. Striking surface is the outer edge of right Knife Hand).

Fifteenth Position: Left Knife-Hand Strike to the Neck

front view

a. Slide left foot forward one step (toward **A**).

b. Assume Front Stance.

c. Simultaneously execute a Knife-Hand Strike to the neck with left hand.

Sixteenth Position: Middle Punch and Yell

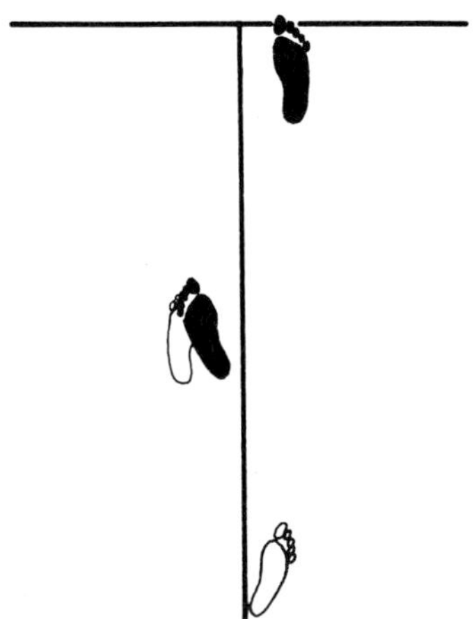

a. Slide right foot forward one step (to **A**).

b. Assume Front Stance.

c. Simultaneously execute a Middle Punch with right fist and yell.

Seventeenth Position: Low Block

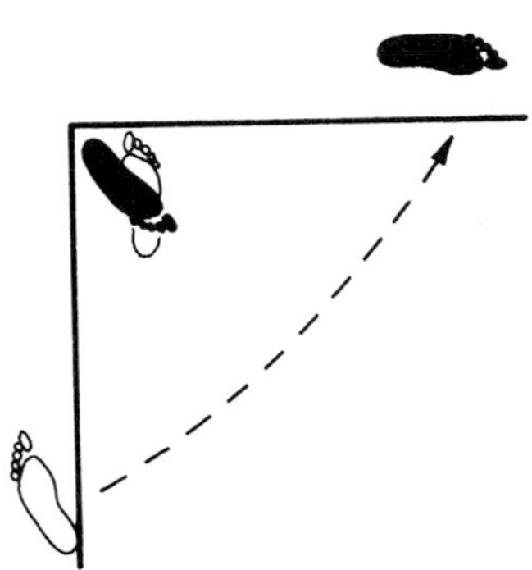

a. Pivoting on right foot, slide left foot out and back in a wide arc, turning 270° (to face **L–1**).

b. Assume Front Stance.

c. Simultaneously execute a Low Block with left forearm.

Eighteenth Position: Inside Middle Block

a. Slide right foot forward one step (to **L–1**).

b. Assume Front Stance.

c. Simultaneously execute an Inside Middle Block with right forearm.

Nineteenth Position: Low Block

a. Pivoting on left foot, slide right foot out and back, turning 180° (to face **R–1**).

b. Assume Front Stance.

c. Simultaneously execute a Low Block with right forearm.

Twentieth Position: Inside Middle Block

a. Slide left foot forward one step (to **R–1**).

b. Assume Front Stance.

c. Simultaneously execute an Inside Middle Block with left forearm.

Stop

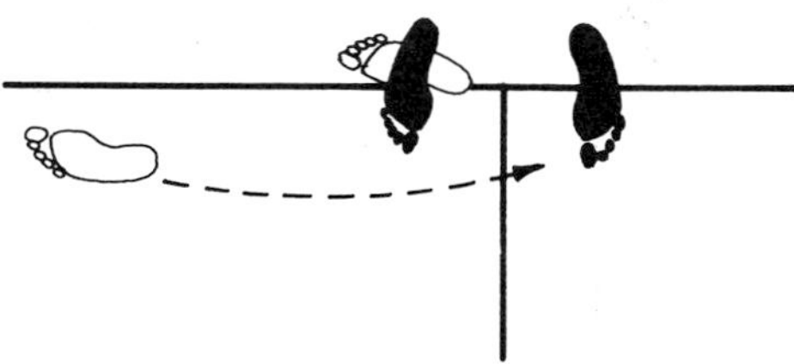

Pivoting on right foot, slide left foot out and back, turning 90° (to resume Starting Point, **A**). Assume Ready Stance (Attention, with eyes focused straight ahead).

PAL-GWE 2
START
1
2 (1)
2 (2)
3
4 (1)
4 (2)
5
6
7
8
8→9
9
10 (1)
10 (2)
11
12 (1)
12 (2)

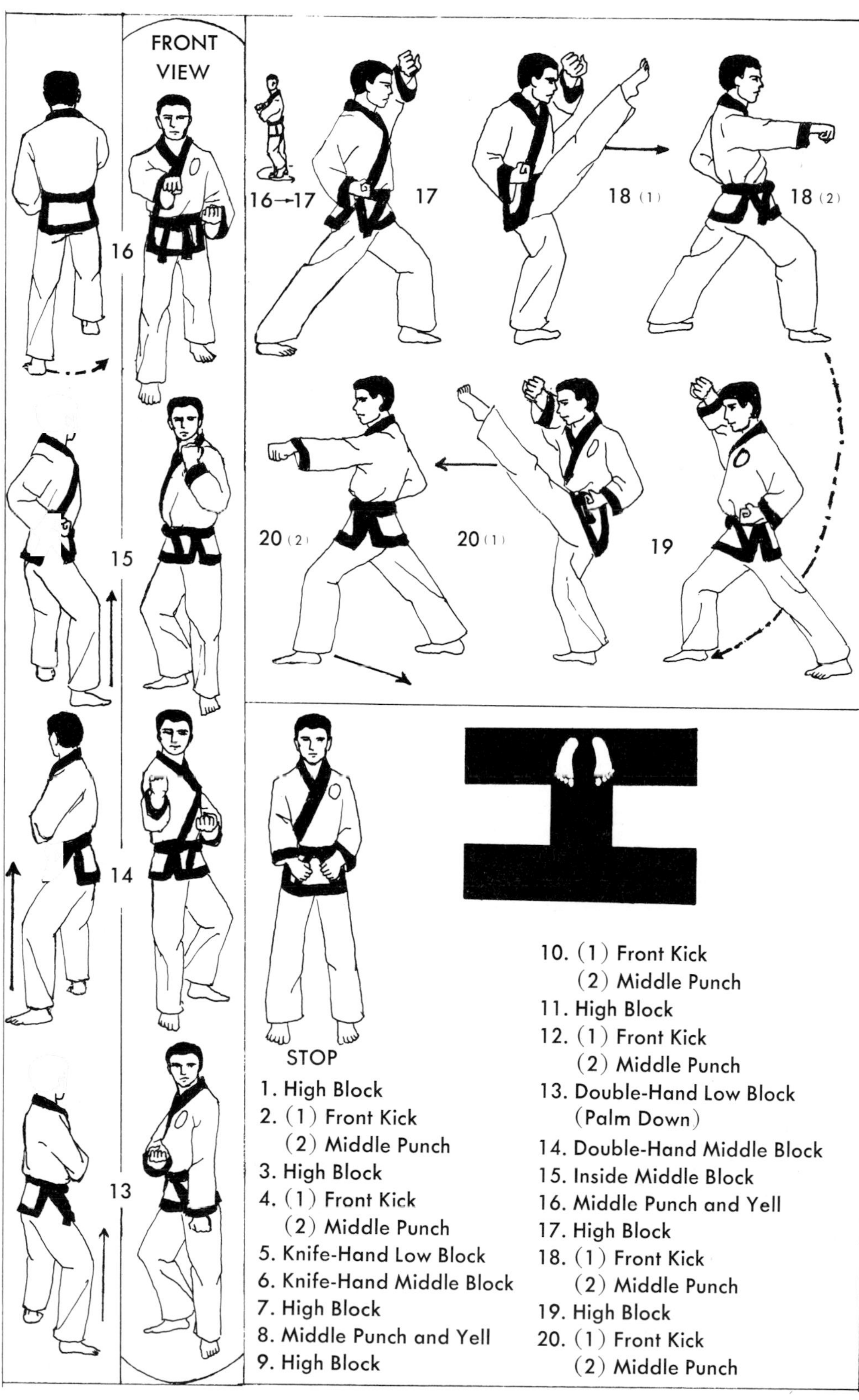
FRONT VIEW
16
15
14
13
16→17
17
18 (1)
18 (2)
20 (2)
20 (1)
19
STOP
1. High Block
2. (1) Front Kick
(2) Middle Punch
3. High Block
4. (1) Front Kick
(2) Middle Punch
5. Knife-Hand Low Block
6. Knife-Hand Middle Block
7. High Block
8. Middle Punch and Yell
9. High Block
10. (1) Front Kick
(2) Middle Punch
11. High Block
12. (1) Front Kick
(2) Middle Punch
13. Double-Hand Low Block
(Palm Down)
14. Double-Hand Middle Block
15. Inside Middle Block
16. Middle Punch and Yell
17. High Block
18. (1) Front Kick
(2) Middle Punch
19. High Block
20. (1) Front Kick
(2) Middle Punch

PAL-GWE 2 (*Pal Gwe Ee-Chang*)

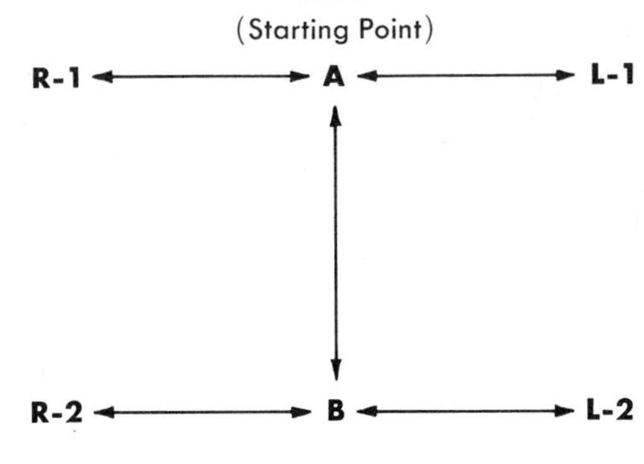

Number of positions: 20 (excluding Ready Stance and Stop)

Movement proceeds in an H pattern, beginning at A:

Ready Stance

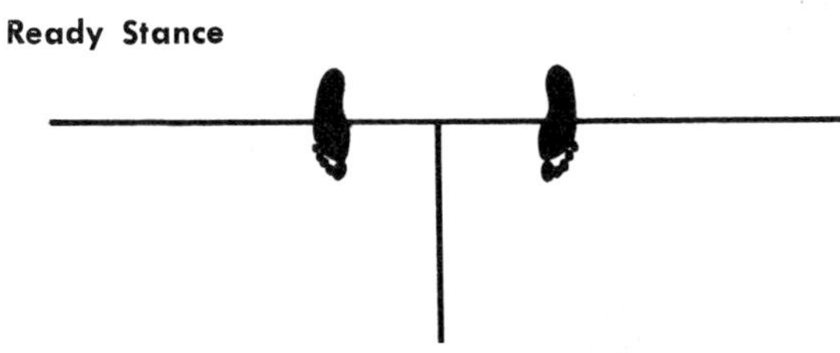

Stand at Attention at Starting Point, **A.**

First Position: High Block

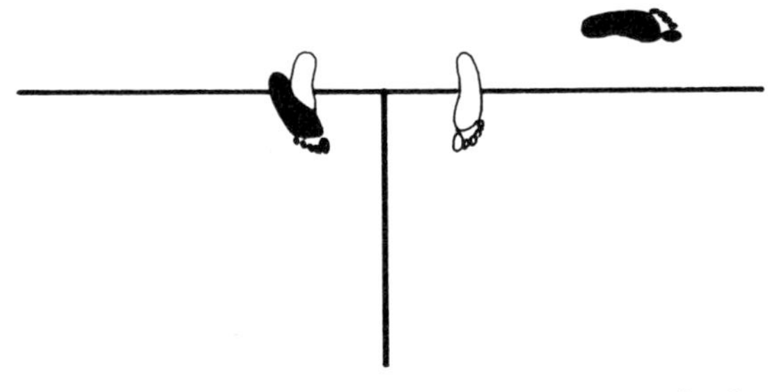

a. Turn 90° to the left, pivoting on right foot and sliding left foot one step forward (toward **L–1**).

b. Assume Front Stance.

c. Simultaneously execute a High Block with left forearm (cross forearms in front of chest, right fist palm in near left ear and left fist palm up under right elbow; then sweep left forearm up—outside right forearm—into position with left wrist palm out one fist-width above and in front of forehead and left forearm at 45° angle to floor. Simultaneously pull right fist back to right hip, palm up. The blocking surface is the outer edge of lower left forearm).

Second Position: Front Kick, Middle Punch

Note: The two motions, 1 and 2, are performed in continuous motion.

1. Front Kick

a. Execute a high Front Thrust Kick with right foot, holding left forearm in High Block position.

b. Bring right foot to rest one step forward (to **L–1**).*

2. Middle Punch

a. Assume Front Stance.

b. Simultaneously execute a Middle Punch with right fist, pulling left fist back to left hip at the same time.

* In all forms, after every kick, the kicking foot should be pulled back into position (ready to kick again) near the knee of the supporting leg—before you go on to execute the next indicated motion of the feet or legs.

Third Position: High Block

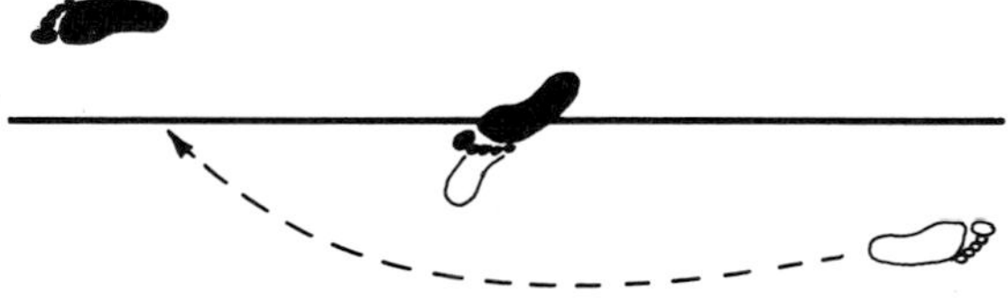

a. Pivoting on left foot, slide right foot out and back in a wide arc, turning 180° (to face **R–1**).

b. Assume Front Stance.

c. Simultaneously execute a High Block with right forearm.

Fourth Position: Front Kick, Middle Punch

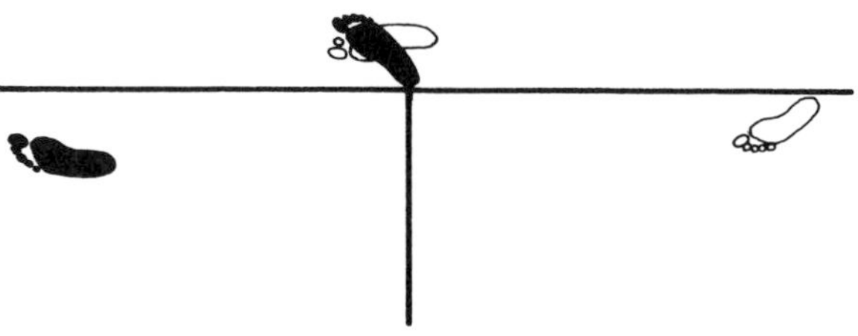

Note: The two motions, 1 and 2, are performed in continuous motion.

1. Front Kick

a. Execute a high Front Thrust Kick with left foot, holding right forearm in High Block position.

b. Bring left foot to rest one step forward (to **R–1**).

2. Middle Punch

a. Assume Front Stance.

b. Simultaneously execute a Middle Punch with left fist, pulling right fist back to right hip at the same time.

Fifth Position: Knife-Hand Low Block

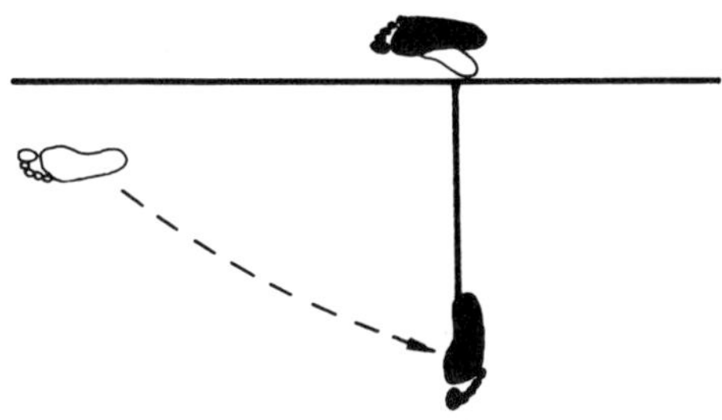

a. Pivoting on right foot, slide left foot out, turning 90° (toward **B**).

b. Assume Back Stance.

c. Simultaneously execute a Knife-Hand Low Block with left hand, right Knife Hand assisting.

Sixth Position: Knife-Hand Middle Block

a. Slide right foot forward one step (toward **B**).

b. Assume Back Stance.

c. Simultaneously execute a Knife-Hand Middle Block with right hand, left Knife Hand assisting.

Seventh Position: High Block

a. Slide left foot forward one step (toward **B**).

b. Assume Front Stance.

c. Simultaneously execute a High Block with left forearm.

Eighth Position: Middle Punch and Yell

a. Slide right foot forward one step (to **B**).

b. Assume Front Stance.

c. Simultaneously execute a Middle Punch with right fist and yell.

Ninth Position: High Block

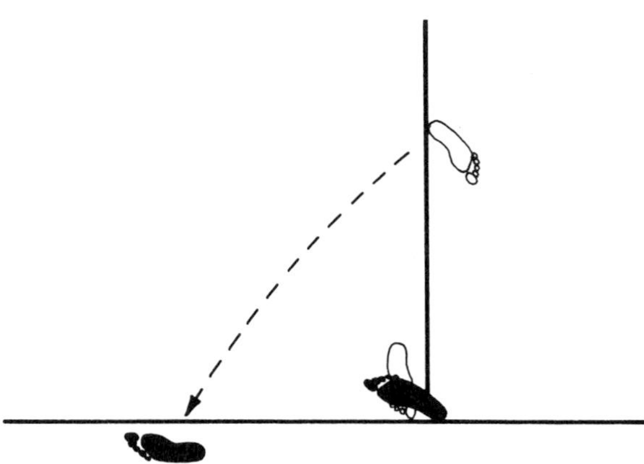

a. Pivoting on right foot, slide left foot out and back in a wide arc, turning 270° (three-quarters of a circle, to face **R–2**).

b. Assume Front Stance.

c. Simultaneously execute a High Block with left forearm.

Tenth Position: Front Kick, Middle Punch

Note: The two motions, 1 and 2, are performed in continuous motion.

1. Front Kick

a. Execute a high Front Thrust Kick with right foot, holding left forearm in High Block position.

b. Bring right foot to rest one step forward (to **R–2**).

2. Middle Punch

a. Assume Front Stance.

b. Simultaneously execute a Middle Punch with right fist, pulling left fist back to left hip at the same time.

Eleventh Position: High Block

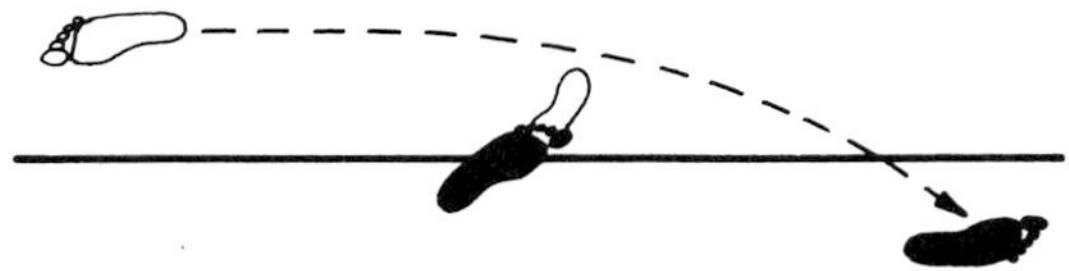

a. Pivoting on left foot, slide right foot out and back in a wide arc, turning 180° (to face **L–2**).

b. Assume Front Stance.

c. Simultaneously execute a High Block with right forearm.

Twelfth Position: Front Kick, Middle Punch

Note: The two motions, 1 and 2, are performed in continuous motion.

1. Front Kick

a. Execute a high Front Thrust Kick with left foot, holding right forearm in High Block position.

b. Bring left foot to rest one step forward (to **L–2**).

2. Middle Punch

a. Assume Front Stance.

b. Simultaneously execute a Middle Punch with left fist, pulling right fist back to right hip at the same time.

Thirteenth Position: Double-Hand Low Block (Palm Down)

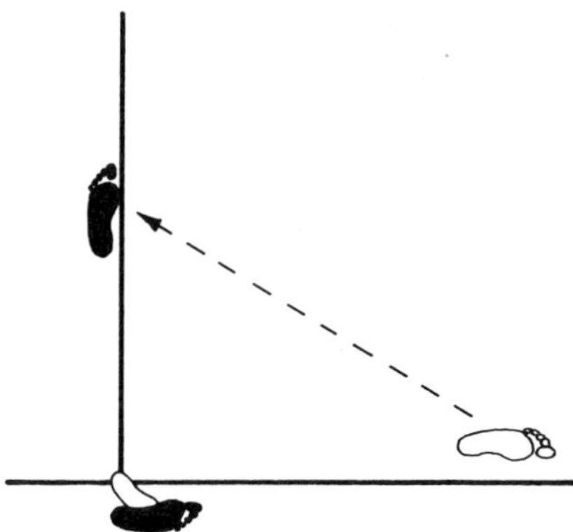

front view

a. Pivoting on right foot, slide left foot out, turning 90° (to face **A**).

b. Assume Back Stance.

c. Simultaneously execute a Low Block with left forearm, palm down, right fist assisting at solar plexus.

Fourteenth Position: Double-Hand Middle Block

front view

a. Slide right foot forward one step (toward **A**).

b. Assume Back Stance.

c. Simultaneously execute a Double-Hand Middle Block with right forearm, left forearm assisting (beginning with right forearm level with shoulders and parallel to floor, fist palm down, and left fist at left hip, palm down, sweep right forearm down and forward into position with right fist, turned palm in, level with right shoulder, and at the same time thrust left fist forward into position, palm up, in front of solar plexus. The blocking surface is the inside of the right lower forearm, the left forearm assisting).

Fifteenth Position: Inside Middle Block

front view

a. Slide left foot forward one step (toward **A**).

b. Assume Back Stance.

c. Simultaneously execute an Inside Middle Block with left forearm.

Sixteenth Position: Middle Punch and Yell

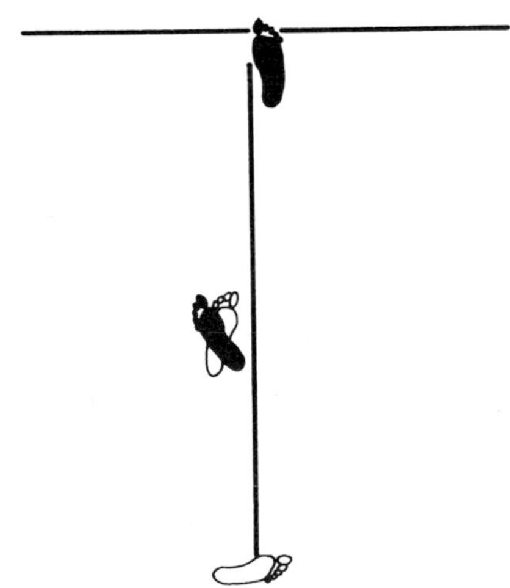

front view

a. Slide right foot forward one step (to **A**).

b. Assume Front Stance.

c. Simultaneously execute a Middle Punch with right fist and yell.

Seventeenth Position: High Block

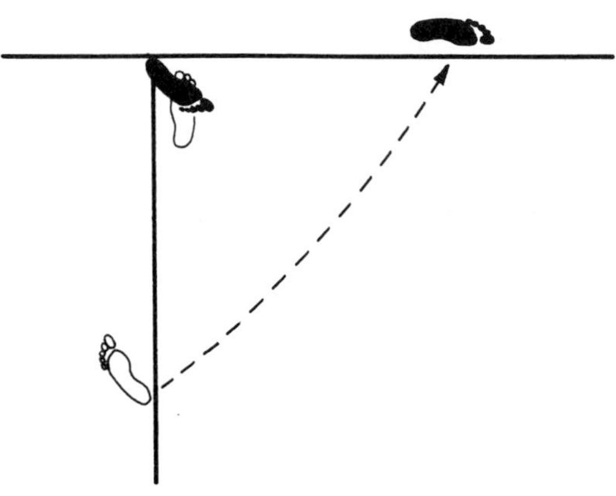

a. Pivoting on right foot, slide left foot out and back in a wide arc, turning 270° (to face **L–1**).

b. Assume Front Stance.

c. Simultaneously execute a High Block with left forearm.

Eighteenth Position: Front Kick, Middle Punch

Note: The two motions, 1 and 2, are performed in continuous motion.

1. Front Kick

a. Execute a high Front Thrust Kick with right foot, holding left forearm in High Block position.

b. Bring right foot to rest one step forward (to **L–1**).

2. Middle Punch

a. Assume Front Stance.

b. Simultaneously execute a Middle Punch with right fist, pulling left fist back to left hip at the same time.

Nineteenth Position: High Block

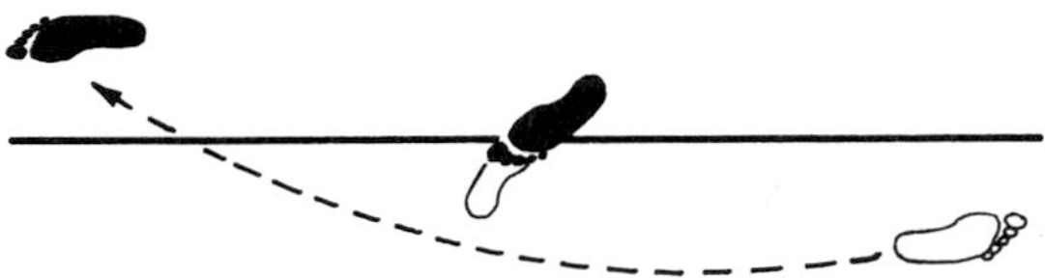

a. Pivoting on left foot, slide right foot out and back, turning 180° (to face **R–1**).

b. Assume Front Stance.

c. Simultaneously execute a High Block with right forearm.

Twentieth Position: Front Kick, Middle Punch

Note: The two motions, 1 and 2, are performed in continuous motion.

1. Front Kick

a. Execute a high Front Thrust Kick with left foot, holding right forearm in High Block position.

b. Bring left foot to rest one step forward (to **R–1**).

2. Middle Punch

a. Assume Front Stance.

b. Simultaneously execute a Middle Punch with left fist, pulling right fist back to right hip at the same time.

Stop

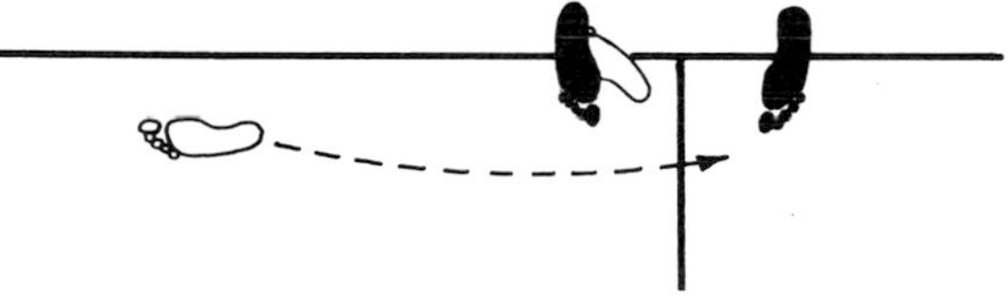

Pivoting on right foot, slide left foot out and back, turning 90° (to resume Starting Point, **A**). Assume Ready Stance (Attention, with eyes focused straight ahead).

PAL-GWE
3
READY
1
2
3
4
5
6
7
8
9
10
11
12
13
14

1. Low Block
2. Middle Punch
3. Low Block
4. Middle Punch
5. Low Block
6. High Block
7. High Block
8. High Punch and Yell
9. Knife-Hand Middle Block
10. Knife-Hand Middle Block
11. Knife-Hand Middle Block
12. Knife-Hand Middle Block
13. Outside Middle Block
14. Outside Middle Block
15. Inside Middle Block
16. Inside Middle Block
17. Inside Middle Block
18. Outside Middle Block
19. High Block
20. High Punch
21. High Block
22. High Punch and Yell

PAL-GWE 3 (*Pal-Gwe Sam-Chang*)

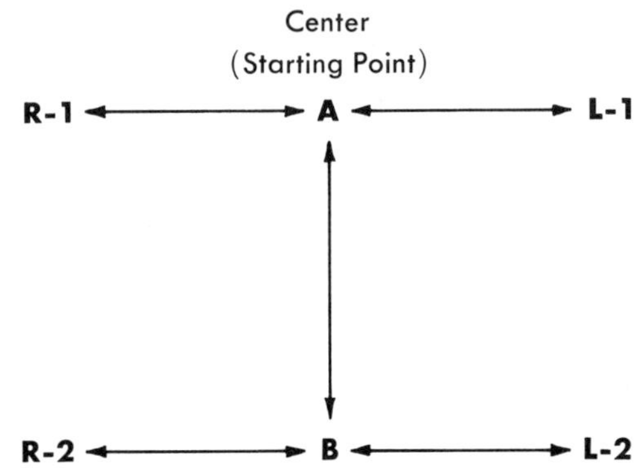

Number of positions: 22 (excluding Ready Stance and Stop)

Movement proceeds in an H pattern, beginning at A:

Ready Stance

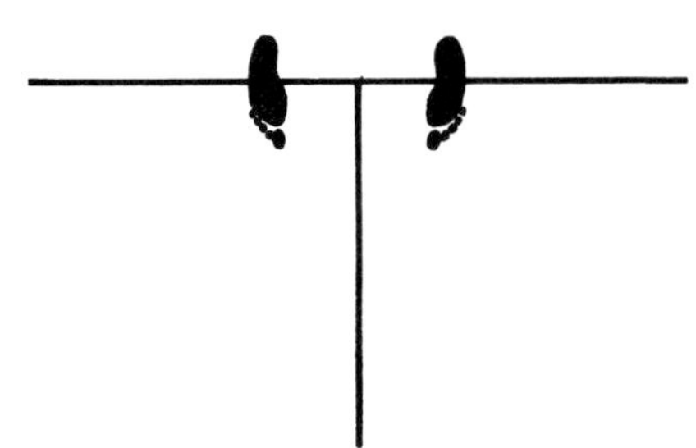

Stand at Attention at Starting Point, **A**.

First Position: Low Block

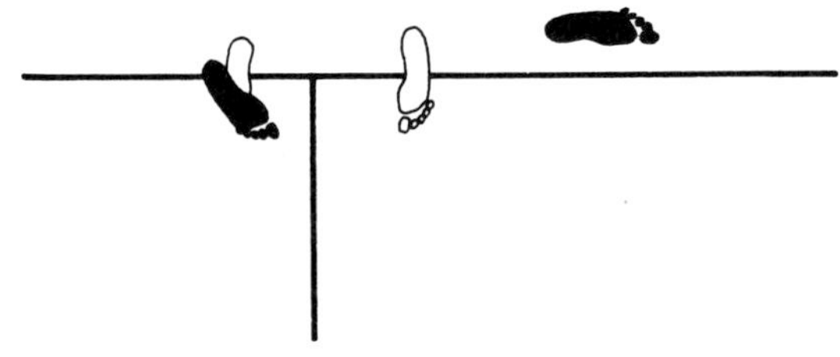

a. Turn 90° to the left, pivoting on right foot and sliding left foot one step forward (toward **L–1**).

b. Assume Front Stance.

c. Simultaneously execute a Low Block with left forearm.

Second Position: Middle Punch

a. Slide right foot forward one step (to **L–1**).

b. Assume Front Stance.

c. Simultaneously execute a Middle Punch with right fist.

Third Position: Low Block

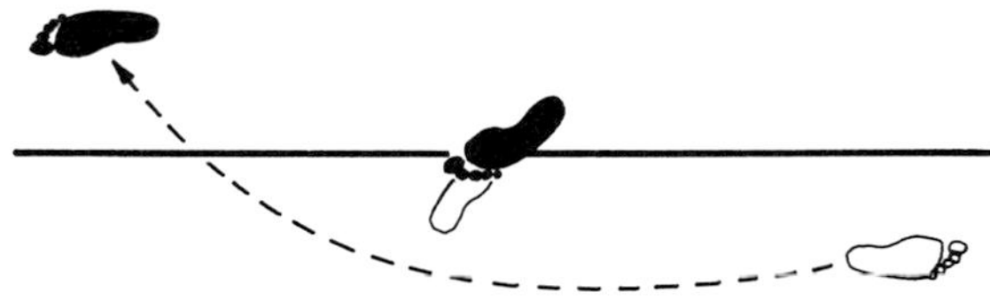

a. Pivoting on left foot, slide right foot out and back in a wide arc, turning 180° (to face **R–1**).

b. Assume Front Stance.

c. Simultaneously execute a Low Block with right forearm.

Fourth Position: Middle Punch

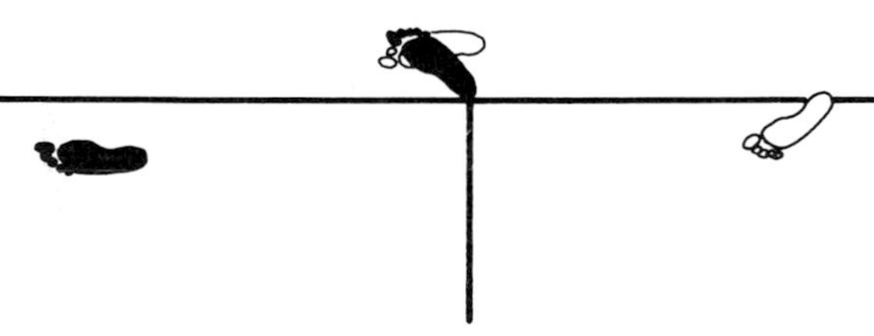

a. Slide left foot forward one step (to **R–1**).

b. Assume Front Stance.

c. Simultaneously execute a Middle Punch with left fist.

Fifth Position: Low Block

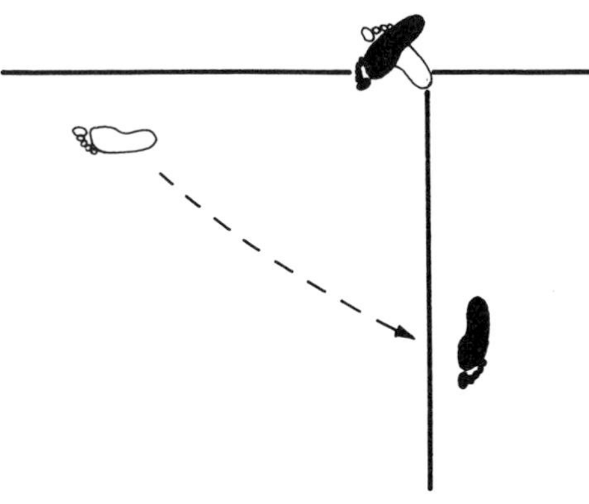

a. Pivoting on right foot, slide left foot out, turning 90° (toward **B**).

b. Assume Front Stance.

c. Simultaneously execute a Low Block with left forearm.

Sixth Position: High Block

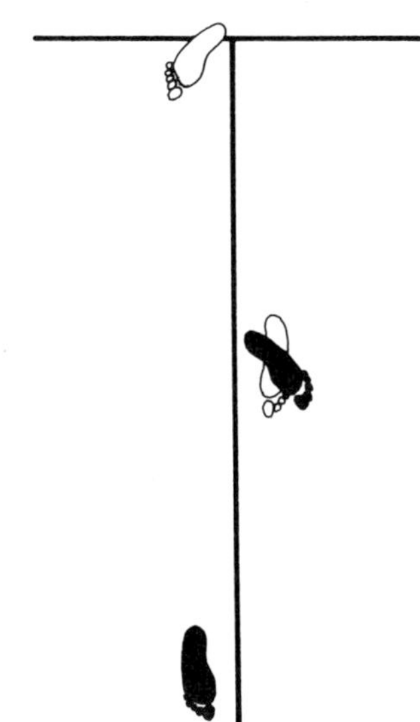

a. Slide right foot forward one step (toward **B**).

b. Assume Front Stance.

c. Simultaneously execute a High Block with right forearm.

Seventh Position: High Block

a. Slide left foot forward one step (toward **B**).

b. Assume Front Stance.

c. Simultaneously execute a High Block with left forearm.

Eighth Position: High Punch and Yell

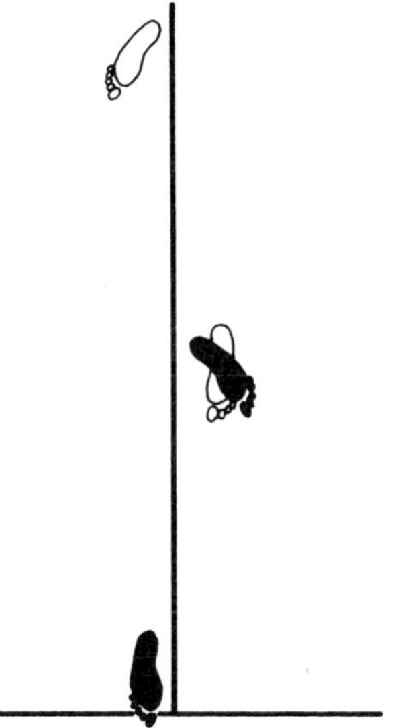

a. Slide right foot forward one step (to **B**).

b. Assume Front Stance.

c. Simultaneously execute a High Punch with right fist and yell.

Ninth Position: Knife-Hand Middle Block

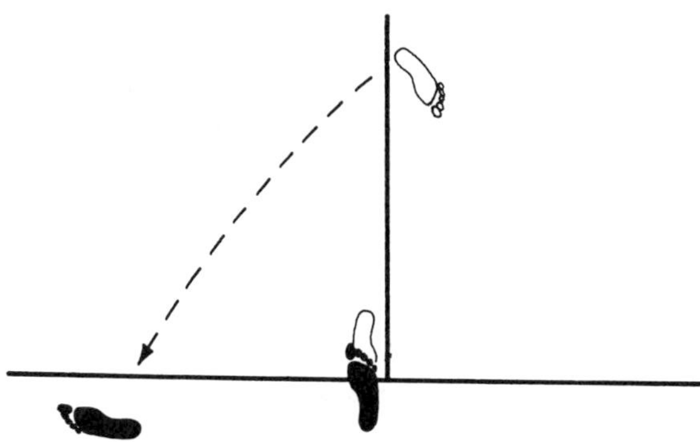

a. Pivoting on right foot, slide left foot out and back in a wide arc, turning 270° (three-quarters of a circle, to face **R–2**).

b. Assume Back Stance.

c. Simultaneously execute a Knife-Hand Middle Block with left hand, right Knife Hand assisting.

Tenth Position: Knife-Hand Middle Block

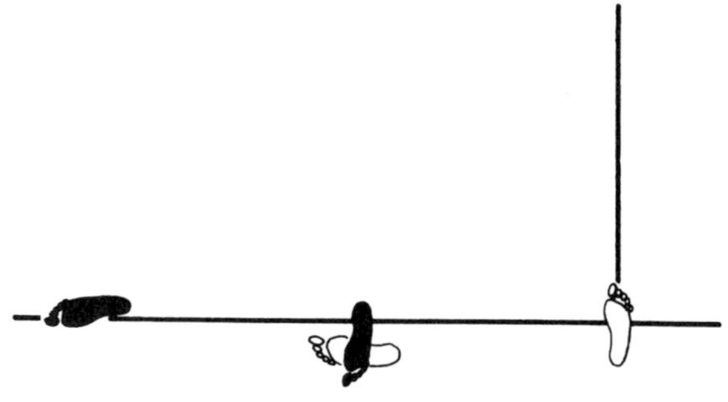

a. Slide right foot forward one step (to **R–2**).

b. Assume Back Stance.

c. Simultaneously execute a Knife-Hand Middle Block with right hand, left Knife Hand assisting.

Eleventh Position: Knife-Hand Middle Block

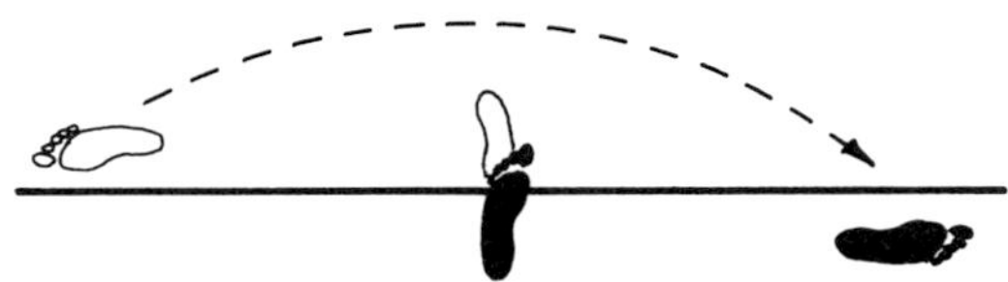

a. Pivoting on left foot, slide right foot out and back in a wide arc, turning 180° (to face **L–2**).

b. Assume Back Stance.

c. Simultaneously execute a Knife-Hand Middle Block with right hand, left Knife Hand assisting.

Twelfth Position: Knife-Hand Middle Block

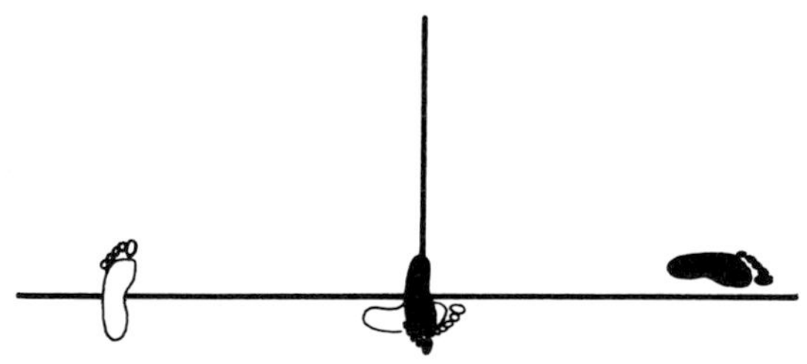

a. Slide left foot forward one step (to **L–2**).

b. Assume Back Stance.

c. Simultaneously execute a Knife-Hand Middle Block with left hand, right Knife Hand assisting.

Thirteenth Position: Outside Middle Block

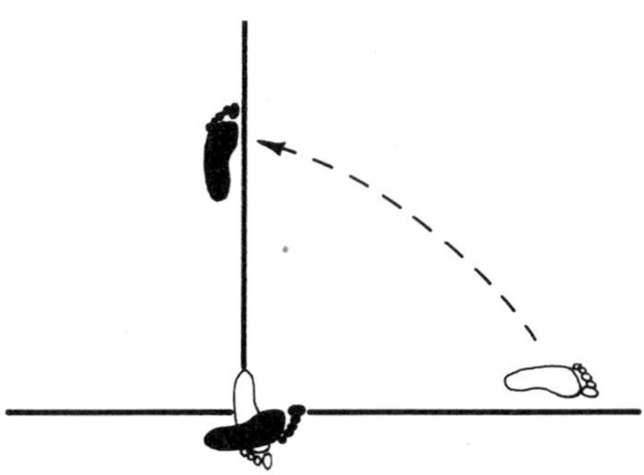

a. Pivoting on right foot, slide left foot out, turning 90° (to face **A**).

b. Assume Back Stance.

c. Simultaneously execute an Outside Middle Block with left forearm (cross forearms in front of solar plexus and parallel to floor, with both fists palm down and left forearm beneath right forearm; then swing left forearm up and outward, snapping wrist palm in, into position with fist out in front of, and on a level with, shoulder —and simultaneously pull right fist back to hip, snapping wrist palm up. The blocking surface is the inner edge, or thumb side, of the lower left forearm).

Fourteenth Position: Outside Middle Block

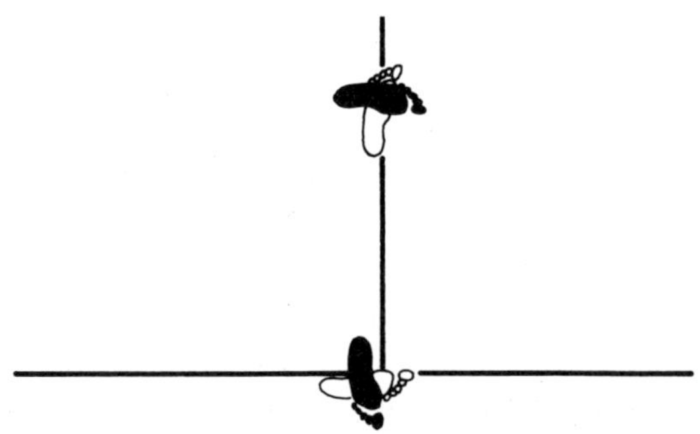

a. Pivoting on left foot, shift right foot out and back, turning about-face, to the front (remaining at point **B**).

b. Assume Back Stance (facing **B**).

c. Simultaneously execute an Outside Middle Block with right forearm.

Fifteenth Position: Inside Middle Block

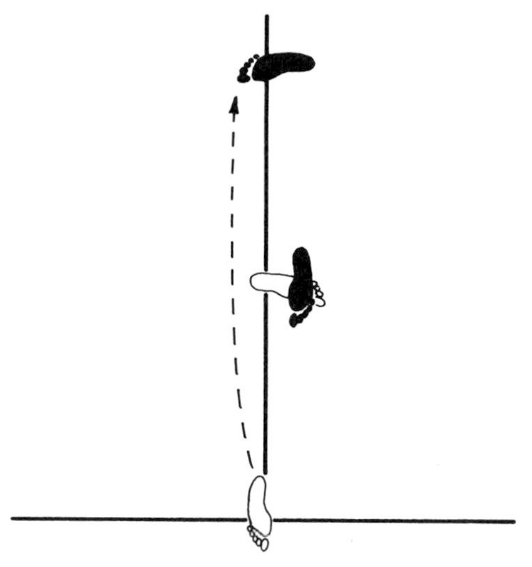

a. Pivoting on left foot, slide right foot out and backward one step (toward **A**).

b. Assume Back Stance (facing **B**).

c. Simultaneously execute an Inside Middle Block with left forearm.

Sixteenth Position: Inside Middle Block

a. Pivoting on right foot, slide left foot out and backward one step (toward **A**).

b. Assume Back Stance (facing **B**).

c. Simultaneously execute an Inside Middle Block with right forearm.

Seventeenth Position: Inside Middle Block

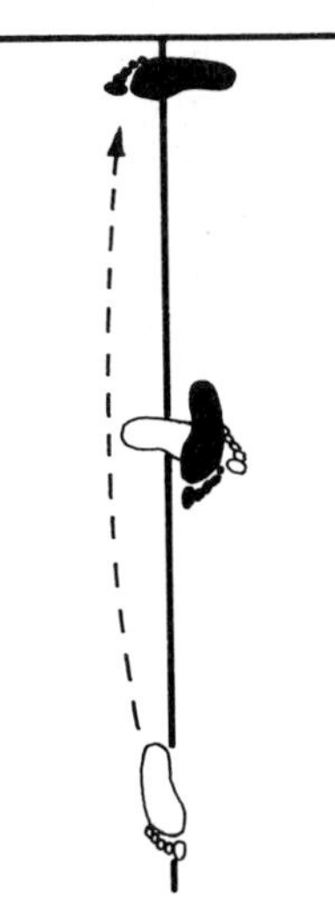

a. Pivoting on left foot, slide right foot out and backward one step (to **A**).

b. Assume Back Stance (facing **B**).

c. Simultaneously execute an Inside Middle Block with left forearm.

Eighteenth Position: Outside Middle Block

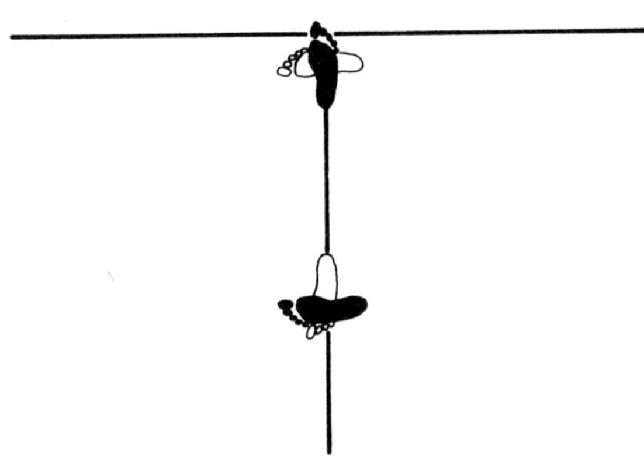

a. Pivoting on left foot, shift right foot out and back, turning about-face, to the center (remaining at point **A**).

b. Assume Back Stance (facing **A**).

c. Simultaneously execute an Outside Middle Block with right forearm.

Nineteenth Position: High Block

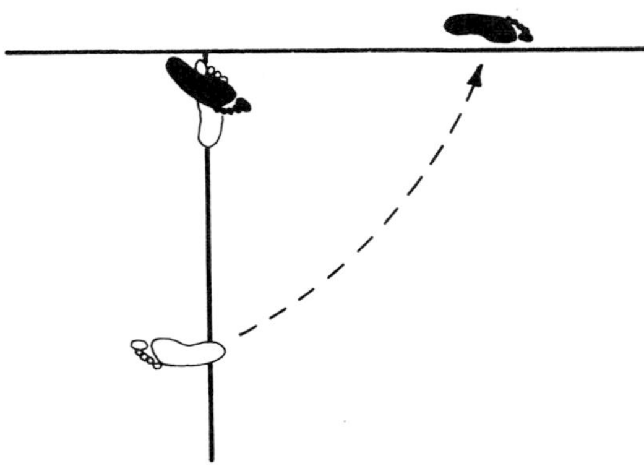

a. Pivoting on right foot, slide left foot out and back in a wide arc, turning 270° (to face **L–1**).

b. Assume Front Stance.

c. Simultaneously execute a High Block with left forearm.

Twentieth Position: High Punch

a. Slide right foot forward one step (to **L–1**).

b. Assume Front Stance.

c. Simultaneously execute a High Punch with right fist.

Twenty-First Position: High Block

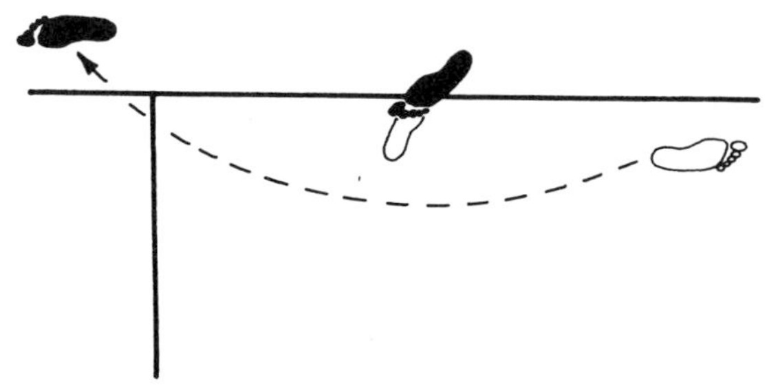

a. Pivoting on left foot, slide right foot out and back, turning 180° (to face **R–1**).

b. Assume Front Stance.

c. Simultaneously execute a High Block with right forearm.

Twenty-Second Position: High Punch and Yell

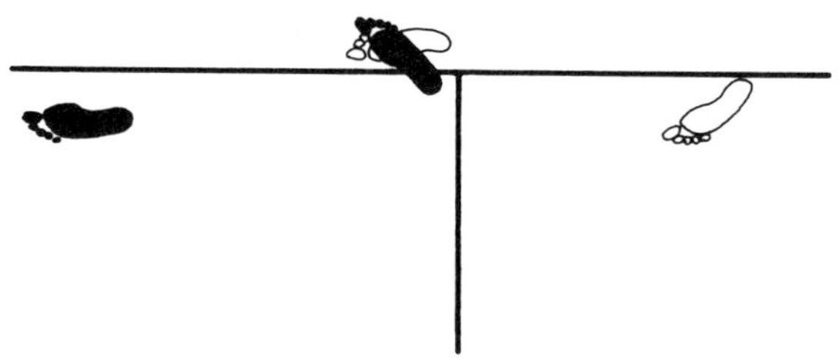

a. Slide left foot forward one step (to **R–1**).

b. Assume Front Stance.

c. Simultaneously execute a High Punch with left fist and yell.

Stop

Pivoting on right foot, slide left foot out and back, turning 90° (to resume Starting Point, **A**). Assume Ready Stance.

READY
1
2
3
4 (1)
6
5
4 (2)
7 (1)
7 (2)
8 (1)
PAL-GWE 4
8 (2)
9 (2)
13
12
11
9 (1)
10
14 (1)
14 (2)
15
16

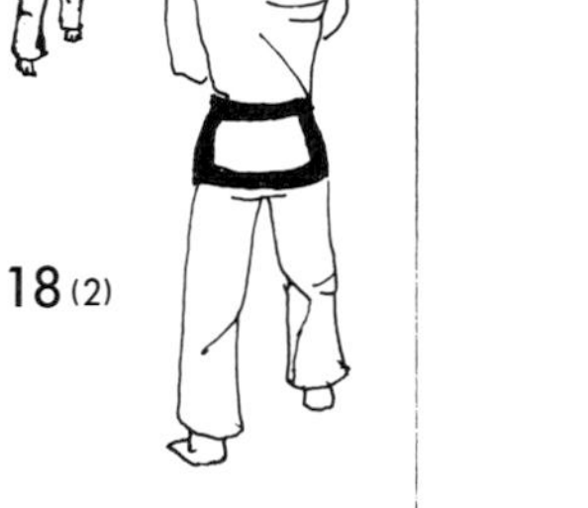

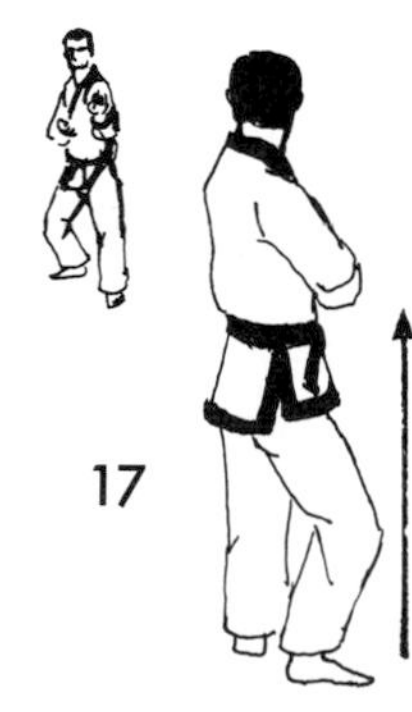

1. Double-Hand High Middle Block
2. Pull and Reverse Upper-Cut
3. Knife-Hand Strike
4. (1) Close-Step
   (2) Double-Hand High Middle Block
5. Pull and Reverse Upper-Cut
6. Knife-Hand Strike
7. (1) Close-Step
   (2) Knife-Hand Middle Block
8. (1) Front Kick
   (2) Palm-Heel Center Block
   and Spear-Hand Thrust
9. (1) Twist Spear-Hand and Turn
   (2) Hammer-Fist Strike (Outward)
10. Middle Punch and Yell
11. Double-Hand High Middle Block
12. Pull and Reverse Upper-Cut
13. Knife-Hand Strike
14. (1) Close-Step
    (2) Double-Hand High Middle Block
15. Pull and Reverse Upper-Cut
16. Knife-Hand Strike
17. (1) Close-Step
    (2) Knife-Hand Middle Block
18. (1) Front Kick
    (2) Palm-Heel Center Block
    and Spear-Hand Thrust
19. (1) Twist Spear-Hand and Turn
    (2) Hammer-Fist Strike (Outward)
20. Middle Punch and Yell
21. Low Block to the Left
    in Horseback Stance
22. Reverse Middle Punch
23. (1) Ready Stance
    (2) Low Block to the Right
    in Horseback Stance
24. Reverse Middle Punch

PAL-GWE 4 (*Pal-Gwe Sa-Chang*)

Number of positions: 24 (excluding Ready Stance and Stop)

Center
(Starting Point)

R-1 ◄——► A ◄——► L-1

▲
▼

R-2 ◄——► B ◄——► L-2

Movement proceeds in an H pattern, beginning at A:

Ready Stance

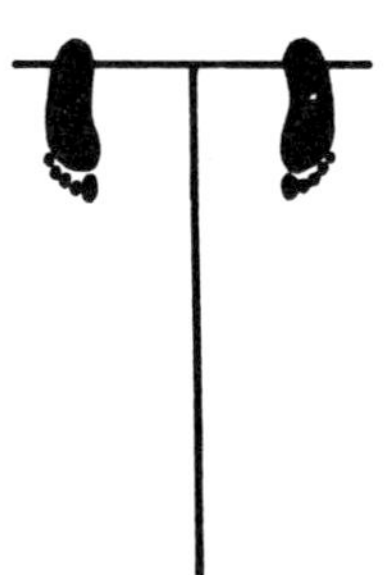

Stand at Attention at Starting Point, **A**.

First Position: Double-Hand High Middle Block

a. Pivoting on right foot, turn 90° to the left and slide left foot forward a half-step (toward **L–1**).

b. Assume Back Stance.

c. Simultaneously execute a Double-Hand High Middle Block (sweep left forearm up and out into position with fist, palm in, held out from left shoulder, as in normal Middle Block; simultaneously sweep right forearm up into position with right fist, palm out, held above and a little in front of forehead, as in normal High Block—except that head is turned to the left, toward **L–1.** The blocking surfaces are the inner edge of the lower left forearm and the outer edge of the lower right forearm).

Second Position: Pull and Reverse Upper-Cut

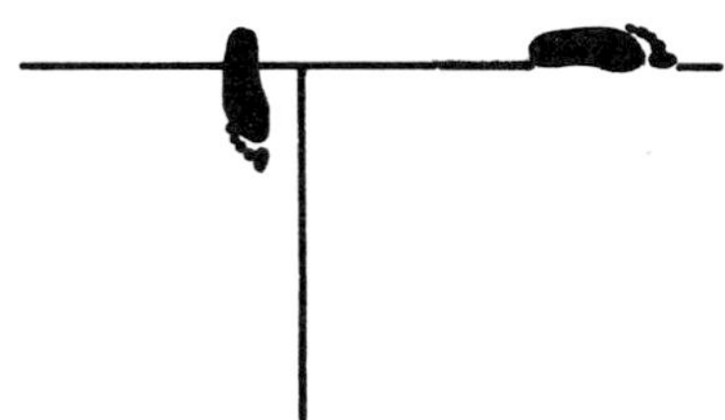

a. Maintain Back Stance (same position as above).

b. Execute a Pull and Reverse Upper-Cut (pull left fist sharply toward chest, palm in, as though grabbing and pulling the punching arm of imaginary opponent at **L–1**, and immediately thrust right fist forward, snapping wrist palm up, delivering an Upper-Cut to opponent's chin).

Third Position: Left Knife-Hand Strike

a. Draw left foot back into position parallel to, and one shoulder-width from, right foot, at **A.**

b. Assume Ready Stance, body facing forward (**B**), eyes still focused toward **L–1.**

c. Simultaneously execute a Left Knife-Hand Strike outward to the side with left hand (sweep left Knife Hand from right shoulder, palm in, outward to strike the neck of imaginary opponent at **L–1**, snapping wrist palm down. Simultaneously pull right fist back to hip, palm up).

Fourth Position: Close-Step, Double-Hand High Middle Block

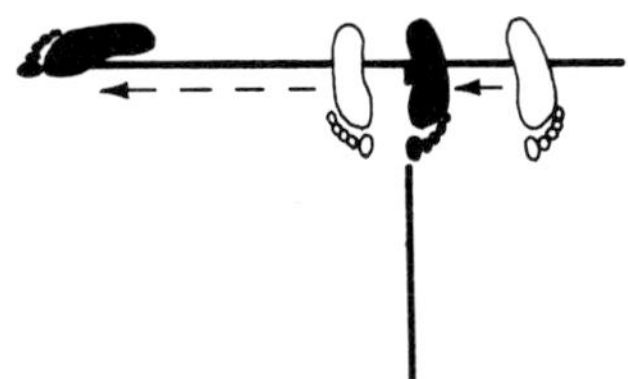

Note: The two motions, 1 and 2, are performed in continuous motion.

1. Close-Step

a. Draw left foot into position immediately next to right foot, at **A.**

b. Simultaneously lower both fists to left hip and focus eyes to the right (toward **R–1**).

2. Double-Hand High Middle Block

a. Immediately pivot on left foot and slide right foot forward one step (toward **R–1**).

b. Assume Back Stance.

c. Simultaneously execute a Double-Hand High Middle Block (a Middle Block, inside-to-outside, with right forearm and a High Block with left forearm).

Fifth Position: Pull and Reverse Upper-Cut

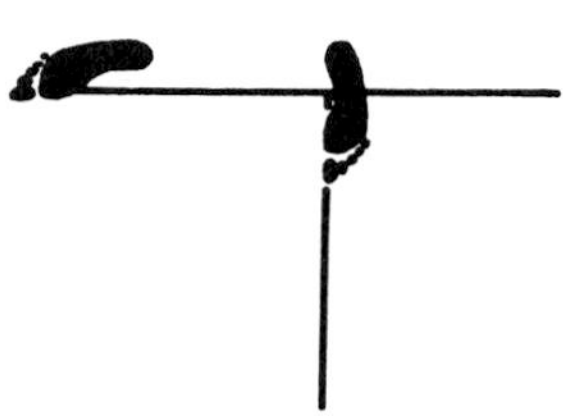

a. Maintain Back Stance (same position as above).

b. Execute a Pull and Reverse Upper-Cut (pulling right fist toward chest and punching at chin level with left fist).

Sixth Position: Right Knife-Hand Strike

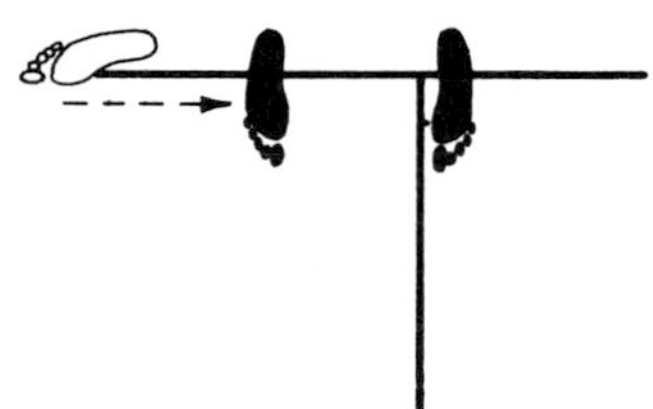

a. Draw right foot back into position parallel to, and one shoulder-width from, left foot, at **A**.

b. Assume Ready Stance, body facing forward, eyes still focused toward **R–1**.

c. Simultaneously execute a Right Knife-Hand Strike outward to the side with right hand, palm down.

Seventh Position: Close-Step, Knife-Hand Middle Block

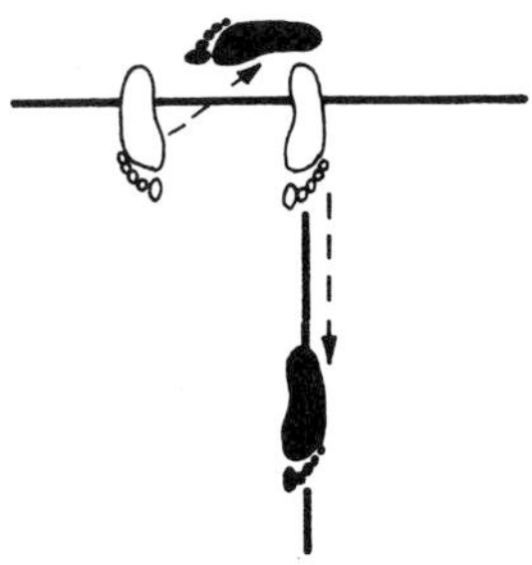

Note: The two motions, 1 and 2, are performed in continuous motion.

1. Close-Step

a. Draw right foot into position immediately next to left foot, at **A**, facing front, **B.**

b. Simultaneously move left Knife Hand to right ear, palm in, and right Knife Hand to right hip, palm down (in preparation for Knife-Hand Block). Stand facing front, **B**.

2. Knife-Hand Middle Block

a. Slide left foot forward one step (toward **B**).

b. Assume Back Stance.

c. Simultaneously execute a Knife-Hand Middle Block with left hand, right Knife Hand assisting.

Eighth Position: Front Kick, Palm-Heel Center Block and Spear-Hand Thrust

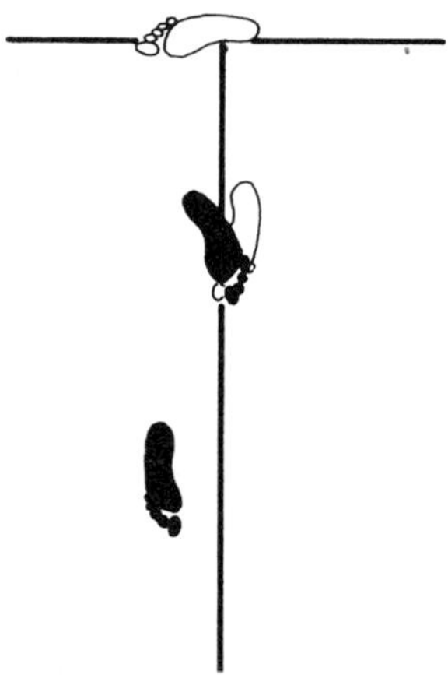

Note: The two motions, 1 and 2, are performed in continuous motion.

1. Front Kick

Execute a high Front Thrust Kick with right foot.

2. Palm-Heel Center Block and Spear-Hand Thrust

a. Bring right foot down one step forward (toward **B**).

b. Assume Front Stance.

c. Simultaneously execute a Palm-Heel Center Block with left hand and Spear-Hand Thrust with right hand (press Palm Heel of left hand downward in front of solar plexus, and immediately thrust fingertips of right hand—the hand held open, fingers together, palm facing left—to arm's length at solar plexus of imaginary opponent at **B**. At end of motion, right Spear Hand is extended at solar plexus level and left hand is open, palm down, immediately under right elbow).

Ninth Position: Twist Spear-Hand and Turn, and Hammer-Fist Strike

Note: The application of this motion is that if the opponent, at **B**, should grab your hand or wrist (when you attack with right Spear Hand), you spin, freeing yourself, and strike him with a side Hammer-Fist Strike at shoulder level. All the steps of this position should be performed as one smooth motion.

1. Twist Spear-Hand and Turn

a. Twist right Spear Hand palm down and pull it back sharply as a fist, into position with the back of the fist against the small of your back.

b. Simultaneously draw the ball of left foot close behind and to the right of right foot, bend at the knees, and, pivoting on the balls of the feet, turn 360° to the left (to face **B** again), closing left hand into a fist while turning.

2. Hammer-Fist Strike

a. As you are completing the turn, extend left fist, palm down, to arm's length at shoulder level.

b. Immediately upon completing the turn, slide left foot forward one step (toward **B**).

c. Assume Front Stance.

d. Simultaneously execute a Hammer-Fist Strike outward to the side with left fist, palm down, at shoulder level (striking imaginary opponent at **B**), and at the same time snap right fist, palm up, into position beside right hip.

Tenth Position: Middle Punch and Yell

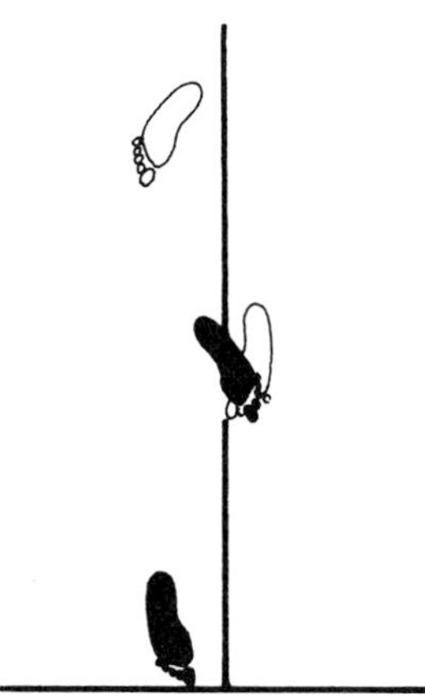

a. Slide right foot forward one step (to **B**).

b. Assume Front Stance.

c. Simultaneously execute a Middle Punch with right fist (pulling left fist back to hip, palm up) and yell.

Eleventh Position: Double-Hand High Middle Block

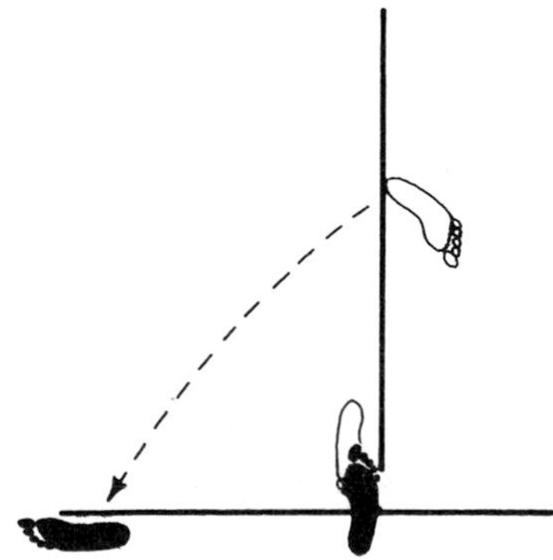

a. Pivoting on right foot, slide left foot out and back in a wide arc, turning 270° (three-quarters of a circle, to face **R–2**).

b. Assume Back Stance.

c. Simultaneously execute a Double-Hand High Middle Block (pull both fists back to right hip and execute a Middle Block, inside-to-outside, with left forearm and a High Block with right forearm).

Twelfth Position: Pull and Reverse Upper-Cut

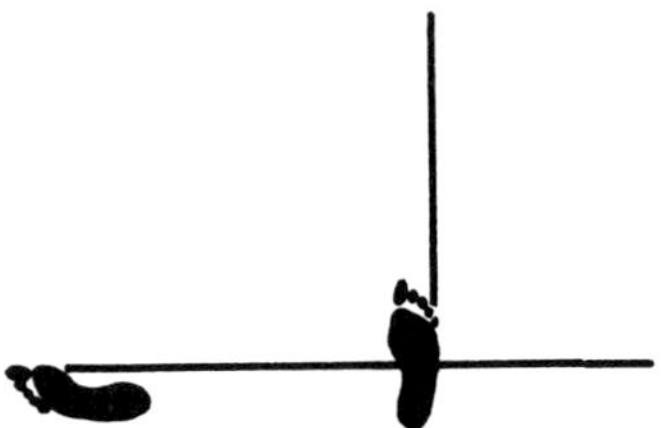

a. Maintain Back Stance (same position as above).

b. Execute a Pull and Reverse Upper-Cut (pulling left fist toward chest and punching at chin level with right fist).

Thirteenth Position: Left Knife-Hand Strike

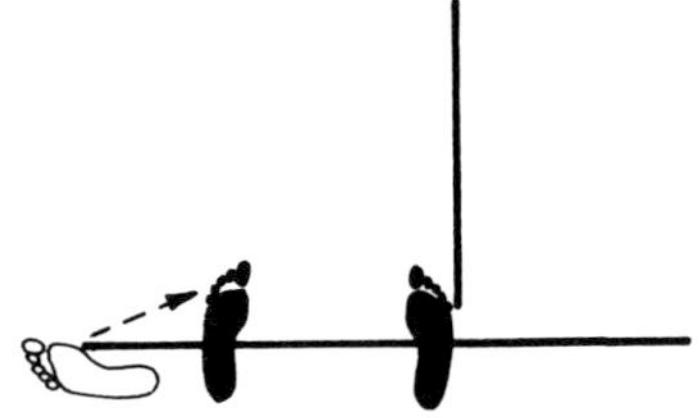

a. Draw left foot back into position parallel to, and one shoulder-width from, right foot, at **B**.

b. Assume Ready Stance, body facing the center, **A**, eyes still focused toward **R–2**.

c. Simultaneously execute a Left Knife-Hand Strike outward to the side with left hand, palm down.

Fourteenth Position: Close-Step, Double-Hand High Middle Block

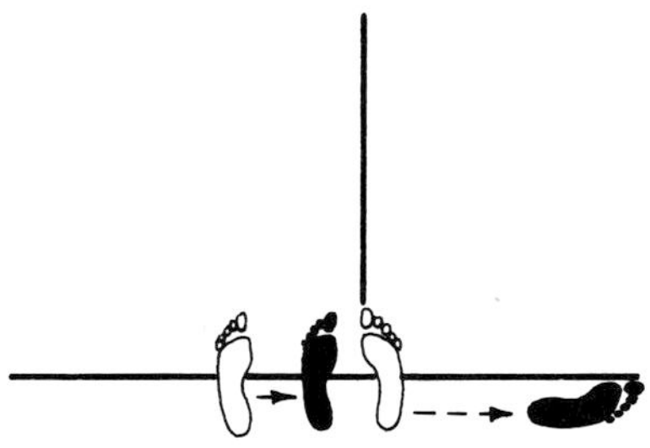

Note: The two motions, 1 and 2, are performed in continuous motion.

a. Draw left foot into position immediately next to right foot, at **B**.

b. Simultaneously lower fists to left hip, and focus eyes to the right (toward **L–2**).

c. Immediately pivot on left foot and slide right foot forward one step (toward **L–2**).

d. Assume Back Stance.

e. Simultaneously execute a Double-Hand High Middle Block (a Middle Block, inside-to-outside, with right forearm and a High Block with left forearm).

Fifteenth Position: Pull and Reverse Upper-Cut

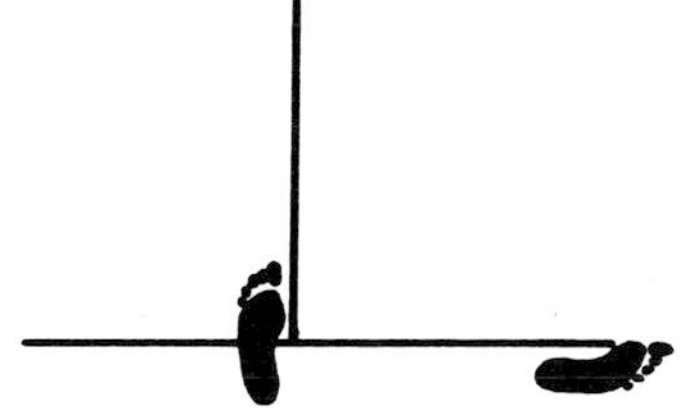

a. Maintain Back Stance (same position as above).

b. Execute a Pull and Reverse Upper-Cut (pulling right fist toward chest and punching at chin level with left fist).

Sixteenth Position: Right Knife-Hand Strike

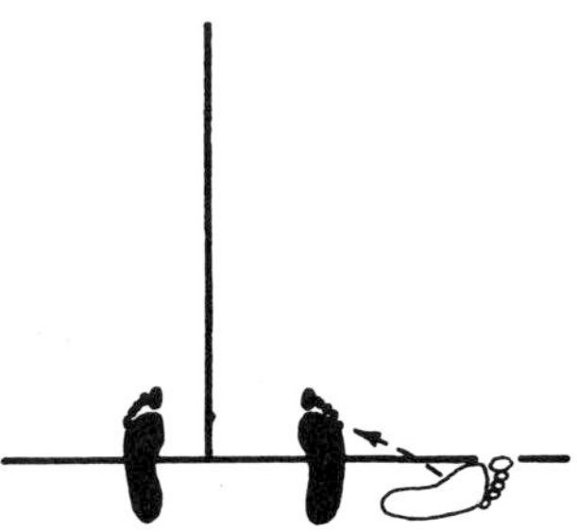

a. Draw right foot back into position parallel to, and one shoulder-width from, left foot, at **B**.

b. Assume Ready Stance, body facing the center, **A**, eyes still focused toward **L–2**.

c. Simultaneously execute a Right Knife-Hand Strike outward to the side with right hand, palm down.

Seventeenth Position: Close-Step, Knife-Hand Middle Block

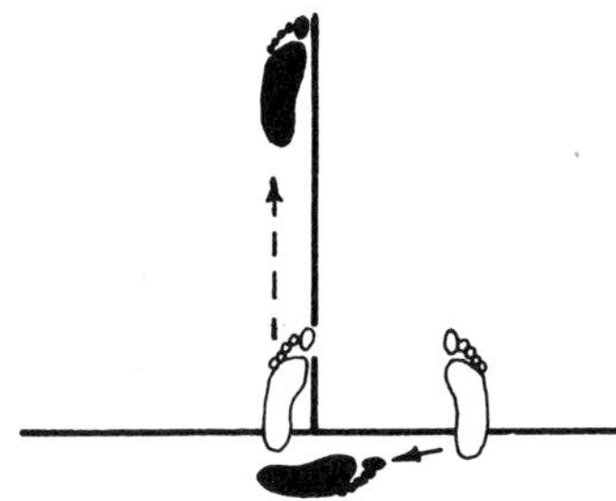

Note: The two motions, 1 and 2, are performed in continuous motion.

a. Draw right foot into position immediately next to left foot, at **B**.

b. Simultaneously move left Knife Hand to right ear, palm in, and right Knife Hand to right hip, palm down (in preparation for Knife-Hand Block). Stand facing the center, **A**.

c. Slide left foot forward one step (toward **A**).

d. Assume Back Stance.

e. Simultaneously execute a Knife-Hand Middle Block with left hand, right Knife Hand assisting.

Eighteenth Position: Front Kick, Palm-Heel Center Block and Spear-Hand Thrust

Note: The two motions, 1 and 2, are performed in continuous motion.

1. Front Kick

Execute a high Front Thrust Kick with right foot.

front view

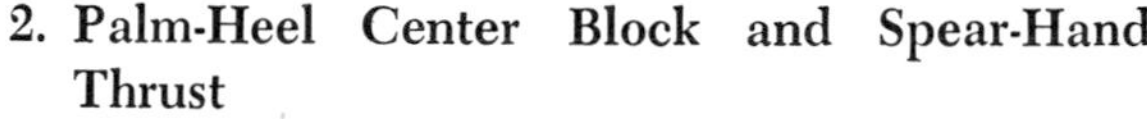

2. Palm-Heel Center Block and Spear-Hand Thrust

a. Bring right foot down one step forward (toward **A**).

b. Assume Front Stance.

c. Simultaneously execute a Palm-Heel Center Block with left hand and Spear-Hand Attack with right hand.

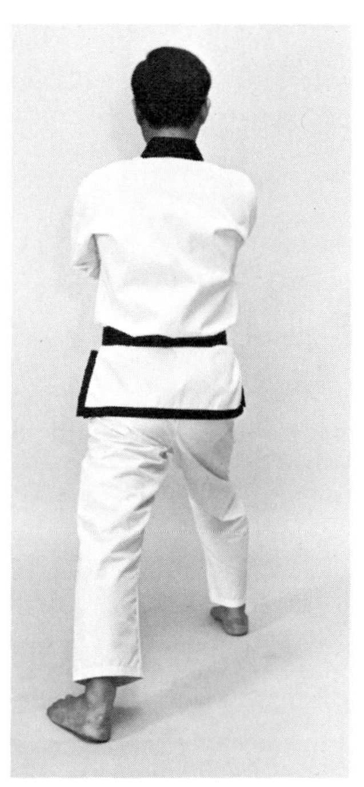

front view

Nineteenth Position: Twist Spear-Hand and Turn, and Hammer-Fist Strike

Note: The application of this motion is the same as that in Ninth Position. All the steps of this position should be performed as one smooth motion.

1. Twist Spear-Hand and Turn

a. Twist right Spear Hand palm up and pull it sharply up and back as a fist, palm down, next to right ear.

b. Simultaneously draw the ball of left foot close behind and to the right of right foot, bend at the knees, and, pivoting on the balls of the feet, turn 360° to the left (to face **A** again), closing left hand into a fist while turning.

front view

2. Hammer-Fist Strike

a. As you are completing the turn, extend left fist, palm down, to arm's length at shoulder level.

b. Immediately upon completing the turn, slide left foot forward one step (toward **A**).

c. Assume Front Stance.

d. Simultaneously execute a Hammer-Fist Strike outward to the side with left fist, palm down, at shoulder level (striking imaginary opponent at **A**), and at the same time pull right fist into position, palm up, beside right hip.

Twentieth Position: Middle Punch and Yell

front view

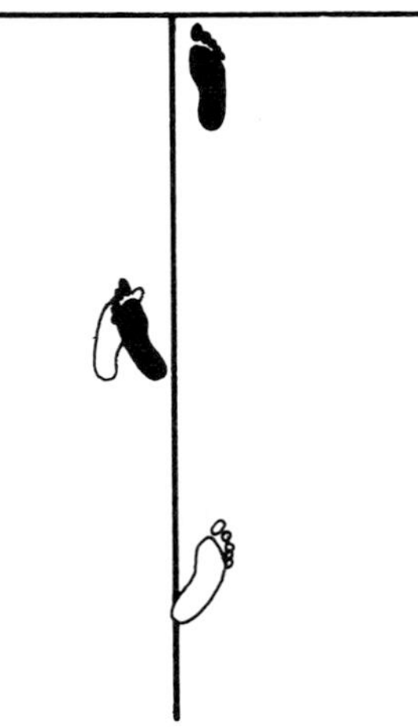

a. Slide right foot forward one step (to **A**).

b. Assume Front Stance.

c. Simultaneously execute a Middle Punch with right fist (pulling left fist back to hip palm up) and yell.

Twenty-First Position: Low Block to the Left in Horseback Stance

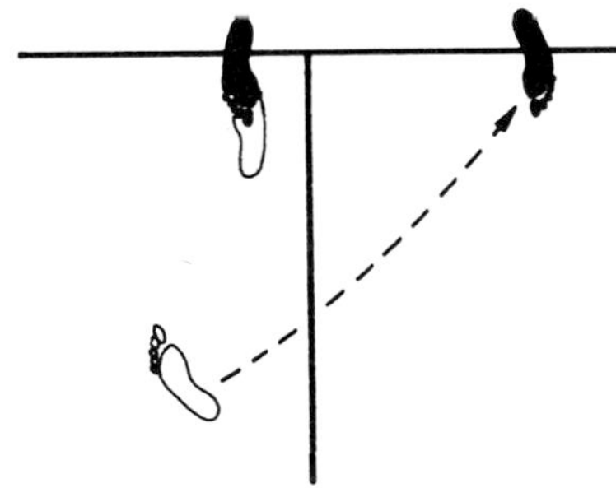

a. Pivoting on right foot, slide left foot out and back in a wide arc, turning 180° (to face **B**).

b. Assume Horseback Stance (feet two foot-lengths apart, toes pointed forward, both knees bent outward, weight evenly distributed on both legs). Stand with body facing front, **B**, and eyes focused left (toward **L–1**), crossing both forearms in front of chest.

c. Simultaneously execute a Low Block with left forearm (blocking kick of imaginary opponent at **L–1**), and at the same time pull right fist into position, palm up, beside right hip.

Twenty-Second Position: Reverse Middle Punch

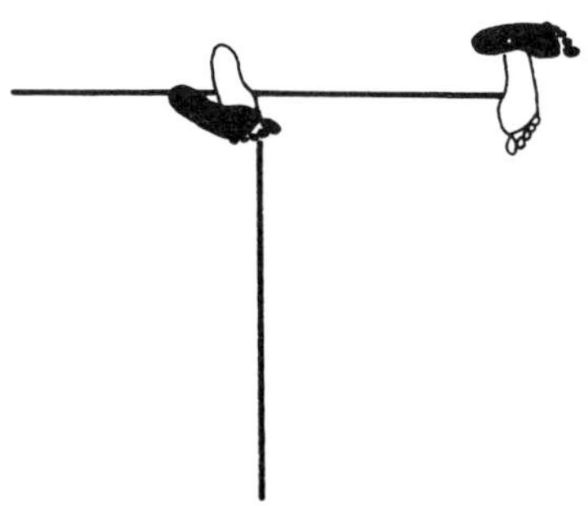

a. Shift left foot straight back a half-step.

b. Assume Front Stance (facing **L–1**).

c. Simultaneously execute a Reverse Middle Punch with right fist.

Twenty-Third Position: Ready Stance, Low Block to the Right in Horseback Stance

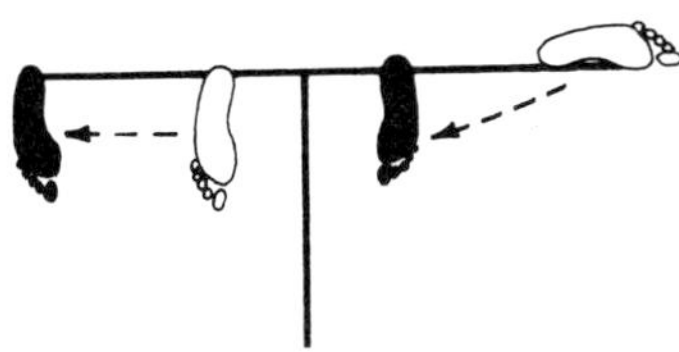

Note: The two motions, 1 and 2, are performed in continuous motion.

1. Ready Stance

a. Pivoting on right foot, turn 90° to face front, **B**.

b. Assume Ready Stance (slide left foot into position parallel to and one shoulder-width from right foot), crossing both forearms in front of chest.

2. Low Block

a. Immediately slide right foot one step out to the side.

b. Assume Horseback Stance (body facing front, eyes focused right, toward **R–1**).

c. Simultaneously execute a Low Block with right forearm (blocking kick of imaginary opponent at **R–1**).

Twenty-Fourth Position: Reverse Middle Punch

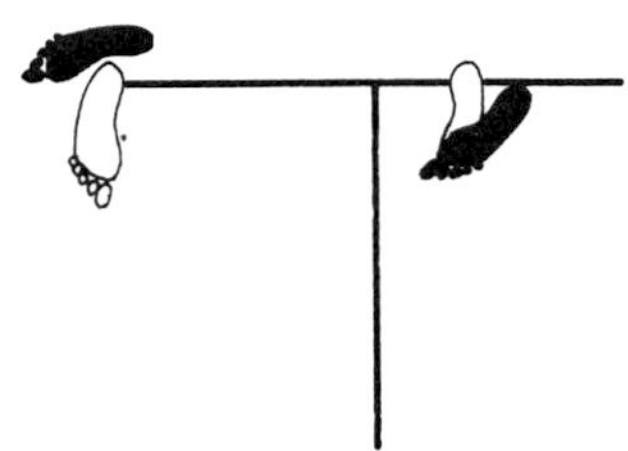

a. Shift right foot straight back a half-step.

b. Assume Front Stance (facing **R–1**).

c. Simultaneously execute a Reverse Middle Punch with left fist.

Stop

Pivoting on left foot, turn 90° to face front, **B**. Assume Ready Stance (slide right foot into position parallel to and one shoulder-width from left foot, at **A**, and stand at Attention).

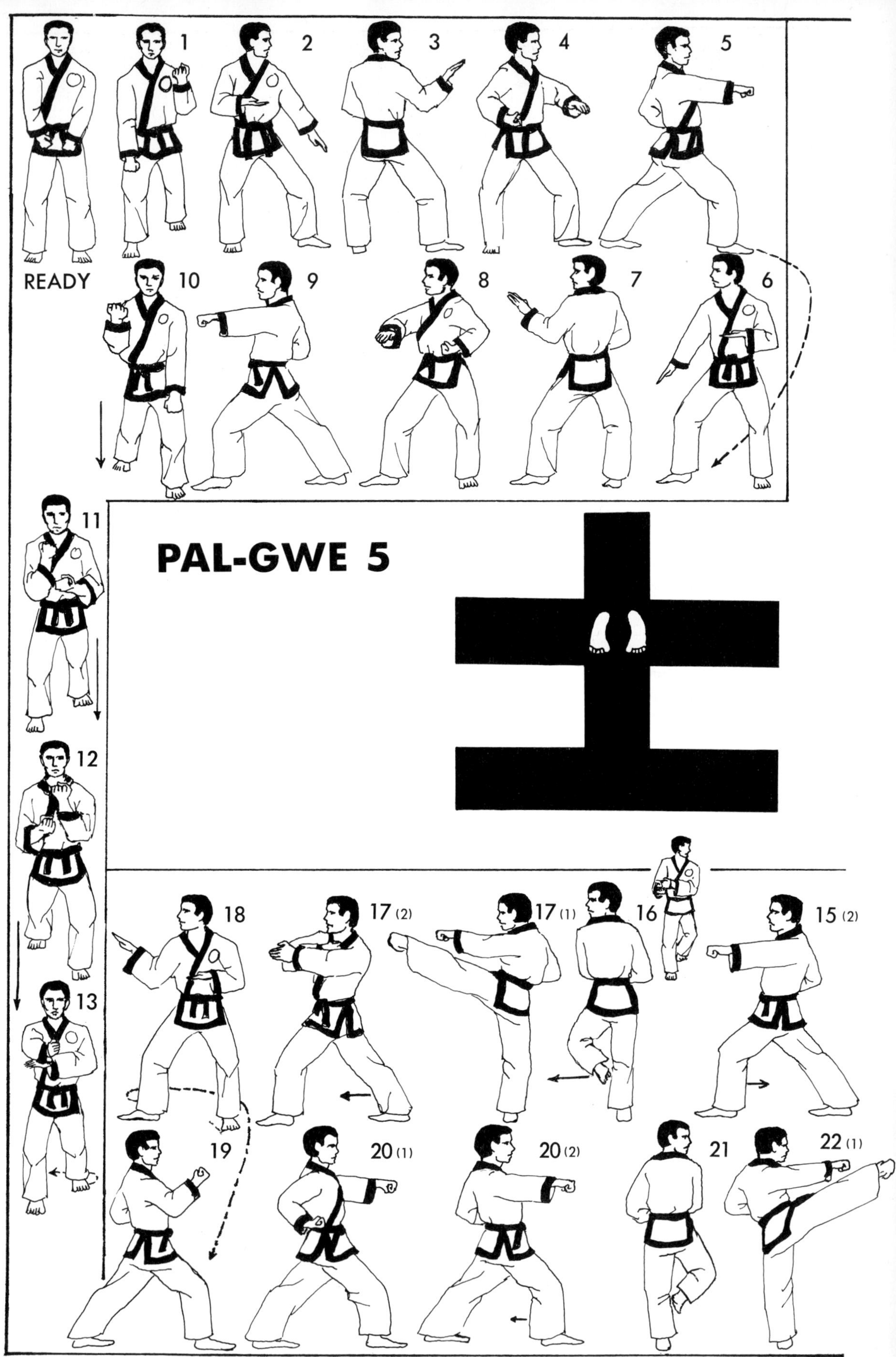
PAL-GWE 5
READY
1
2
3
4
5
6
7
8
9
10
11
12
13
15 (2)
16
17 (1)
17 (2)
18
19
20 (1)
20 (2)
21
22 (1)

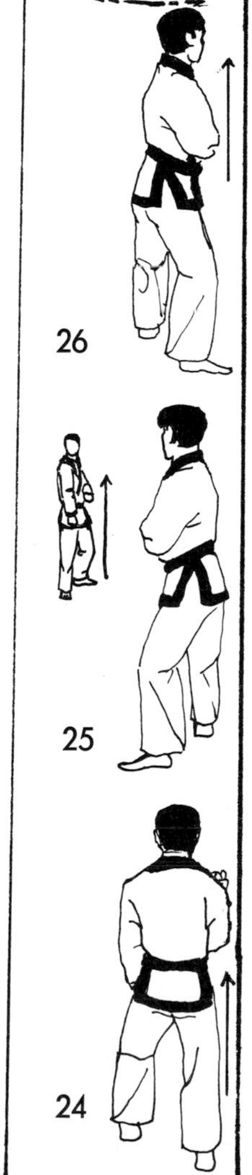

1. Scissors Block
2. Knife-Hand Low Block
3. Knife-Hand Middle Block
4. Palm-Heel Center Block
5. Middle Punch
6. Knife-Hand Low Block
7. Knife-Hand Middle Block
8. Palm-Heel Center Block
9. Middle Punch
10. Scissors Block
11. Double-Hand Middle Block
12. Double-Hand Middle Block
13. Palm-Heel Center Block and Spear-Hand Thrust and Yell
14. Outside Middle Block
15. (1) Middle Punch
    (2) Middle Punch
16. Crane Stance
17. (1) Side Kick
    (2) Elbow Strike
18. Knife-Hand Middle Block
19. Outside Middle Block
20. (1) Middle Punch
    (2) Middle Punch
21. Crane Stance
22. (1) Side Kick
    (2) Elbow Strike
23. Knife-Hand Middle Block
24. Scissors Block
25. Double-Hand Low Block (Palm Down)
26. Double-Hand Low Block (Palm Down)
27. Middle Punch and Yell
28. Knife-Hand Low Block
29. Knife-Hand Middle Block
30. Palm-Heel Center Block
31. Middle Punch
32. Knife-Hand Low Block
33. Knife-Hand Middle Block
34. Palm-Heel Center Block
35. Middle Punch

PAL-GWE 5 (*Pal-Gwe O-Chang*)

Number of positions: 35 (excluding Ready Stance and Stop)

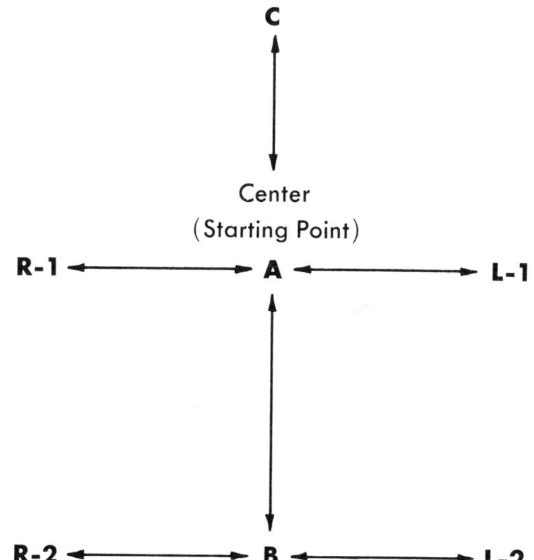

Movement proceeds in a ⊥ pattern, beginning at A:

Ready Stance

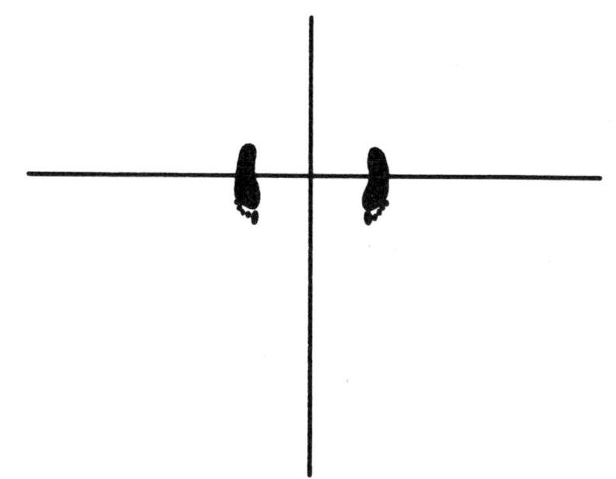

Stand at Attention at Starting Point, **A**.

First Position: Scissors Block

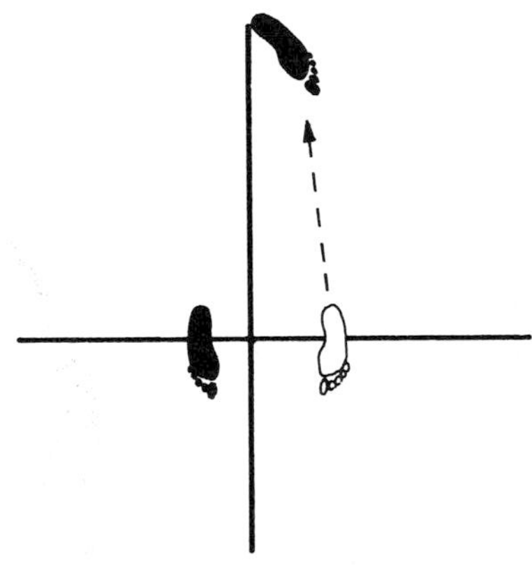

a. Slide left foot back one step (to **C**).

b. Assume Front Stance, facing front, **B**.

c. Simultaneously execute a Scissors Block (beginning with right fist palm in near left ear and left fist palm down under right elbow, sweep right forearm down in Low Block, snapping wrist palm down, and simultaneously sweep left forearm up and out—crossing outside of right forearm—in Outside Middle Block, snapping wrist palm in).

Second Position: Knife-Hand Low Block

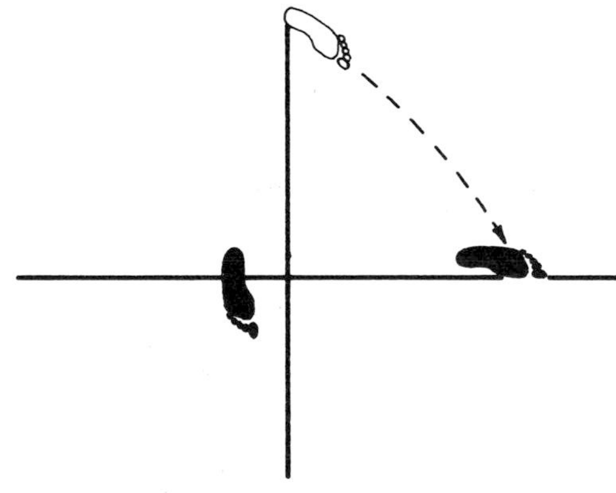

a. Pivoting on right foot, turn 90° to the left and slide left foot up into position one half-step forward (toward **L–1**).

b. Assume Back Stance.

c. Simultaneously execute a Knife-Hand Low Block with left hand, right Knife Hand assisting.

Third Position: Knife-Hand Middle Block

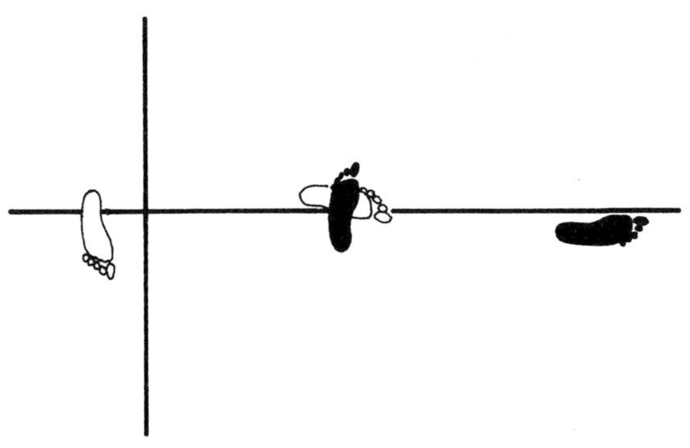

a. Slide right foot forward one step past left foot (to **L–1**).

b. Assume Back Stance.

c. Simultaneously execute a Knife-Hand Middle Block with right hand, left Knife Hand assisting.

Fourth Position: Palm-Heel Center Block

a. Slide right foot one step back past left foot (to **A**).

b. Assume Back Stance (still facing **L–1**).

c. Simultaneously execute a Palm-Heel Center Block with left hand (turn left Knife Hand palm down and press palm downward quickly just in front of chest and solar plexus, simultaneously pulling right fist back to hip, palm up. The blocking surface is the heel of the palm of the left Knife Hand, which serves to deflect a middle punch or kick from an imaginary opponent at **L–1**).

Fifth Position: Middle Punch

a. Slide right foot forward one step past left foot (to **L–1**).

b. Assume Front Stance.

c. Simultaneously execute a Middle Punch with right fist.

Sixth Position: Knife-Hand Low Block

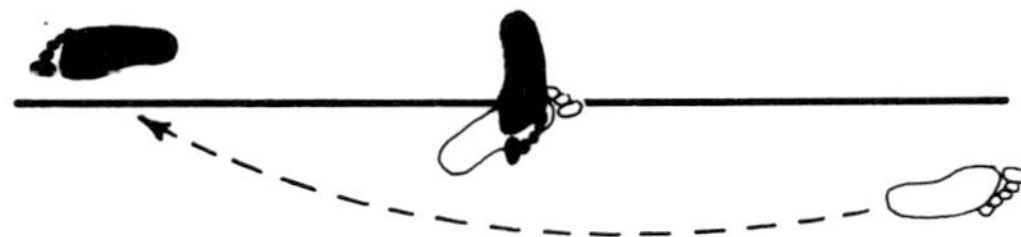

a. Pivoting on left foot, slide right foot out and back in a wide arc, turning 180° (to face **R–1**).

b. Assume Back Stance.

c. Simultaneously execute a Knife-Hand Low Block with right hand, left Knife Hand assisting.

Seventh Position: Knife-Hand Middle Block

a. Slide left foot forward one step past right foot (to **R–1**).

b. Assume Back Stance.

c. Simultaneously execute a Knife-Hand Middle Block with left hand, right Knife Hand assisting.

Eighth Position: Palm-Heel Center Block

a. Slide left foot one step back past right foot (to **A**).

b. Assume Back Stance (still facing **R–1**).

c. Simultaneously execute a Palm-Heel Center Block with right hand.

Ninth Position: Middle Punch

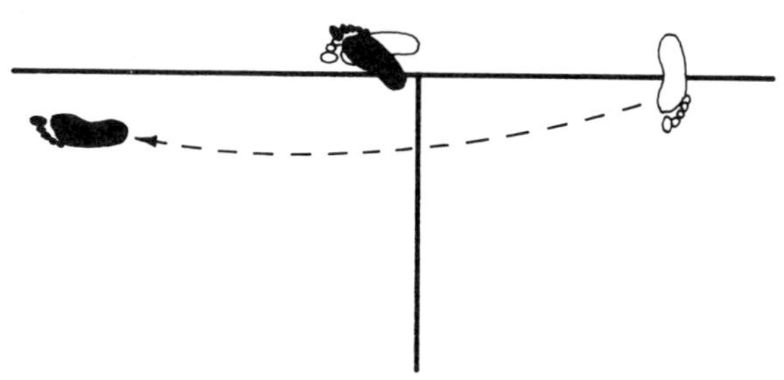

a. Slide left foot forward one step past right foot (to **R–1**).

b. Assume Front Stance.

c. Simultaneously execute a Middle Punch with left fist.

Tenth Position: Scissors Block

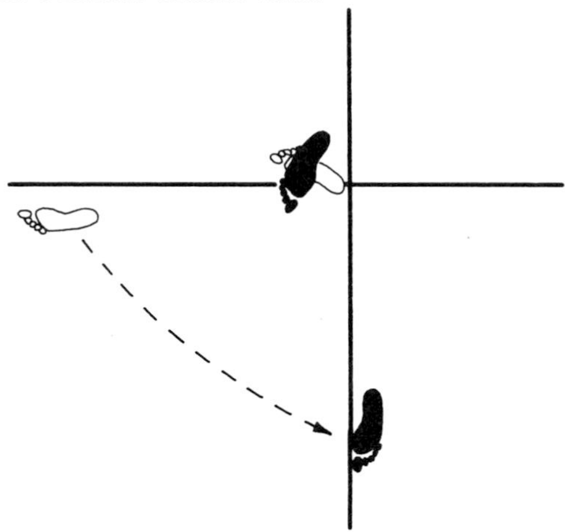

a. Pivoting on right foot, slide left foot out, turning 90° (toward **B**).

b. Assume Front Stance.

c. Simultaneously execute a Scissors Block (beginning with left fist palm in near right ear and right fist palm down under left elbow, sweep left forearm downward in Low Block and simultaneously sweep right forearm up and out—outside of left forearm—in Outside Middle Block).

Eleventh Position: Double-Hand Middle Block

a. Slide right foot forward one step (toward **R**).

b. Assume Front Stance.

c. Simultaneously execute a Double-Hand Middle Block with right forearm, left forearm assisting (pull right forearm back into position below left shoulder and parallel to floor, fist palm down, and left fist palm down at left hip, then sweep right forearm up and out into Outside Middle Block and simultaneously thrust left forearm into position with left fist palm up near outside edge—pinkie side—of upper right forearm. The blocking surfaces are the inner edges—thumb sides—of both lower forearms).

Twelfth Position: Double-Hand Middle Block

a. Slide left foot forward one step (toward **B**).

b. Assume Front Stance.

c. Simultaneously execute a Double-Hand Middle Block with left forearm, right forearm assisting.

Thirteenth Position: Palm-Heel Center Block and Spear-Hand Thrust and Yell

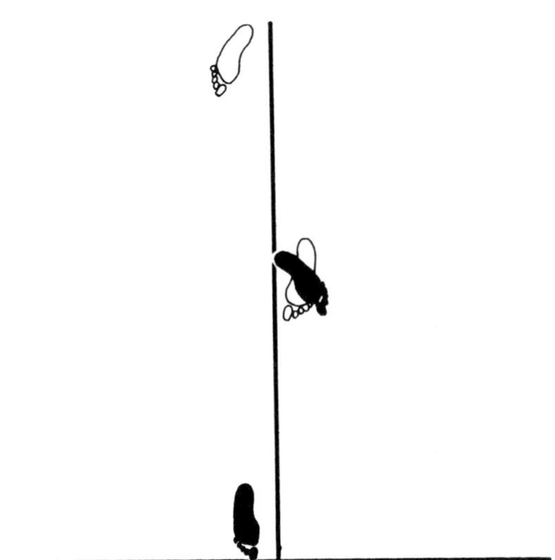

a. Slide right foot forward one step (to **B**).

b. Assume Front Stance.

c. Simultaneously execute a Palm-Heel Center Block with left hand and Spear-Hand Thrust with right hand (press Palm Heel of left hand downward in front of solar plexus and immediately thrust right Spear Hand forward—over left hand, held in position under right elbow—at solar plexus level) and yell.

Fourteenth Position: Outside Middle Block

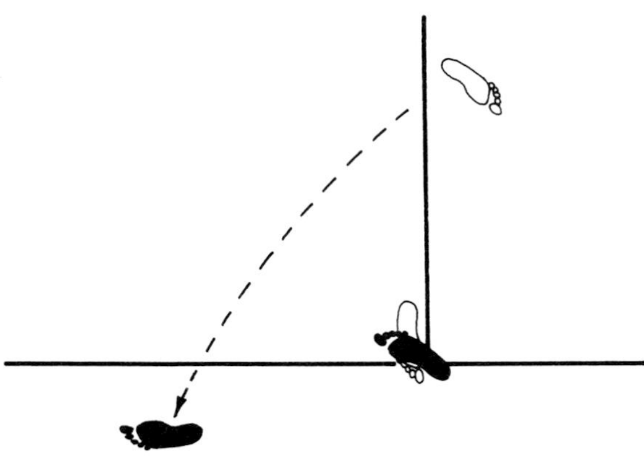

a. Pivoting on right foot, slide left foot out and back in a wide arc, turning 270° (three-quarters of a circle, to face **R–2**).

b. Assume Front Stance.

c. Simultaneously execute an Outside Middle Block with left forearm.

Fifteenth Position: Double Middle Punch

a. Maintain Front Stance (same position as above).

b. Execute a Double Middle Punch (two punches in rapid sequence):

(1) first with right fist,
(2) then with left fist.

Sixteenth Position: Crane Stance (for Side Kicking)

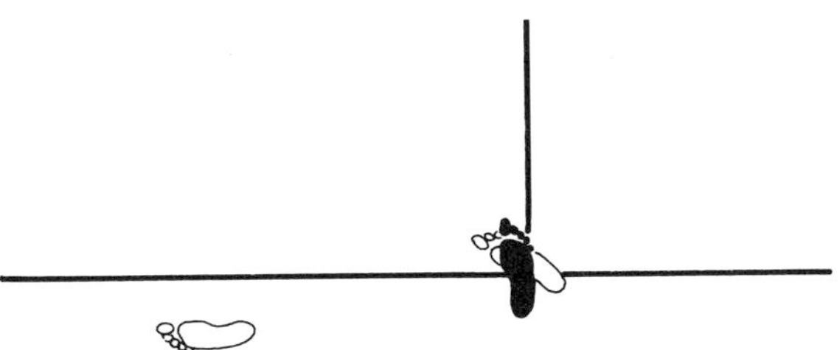

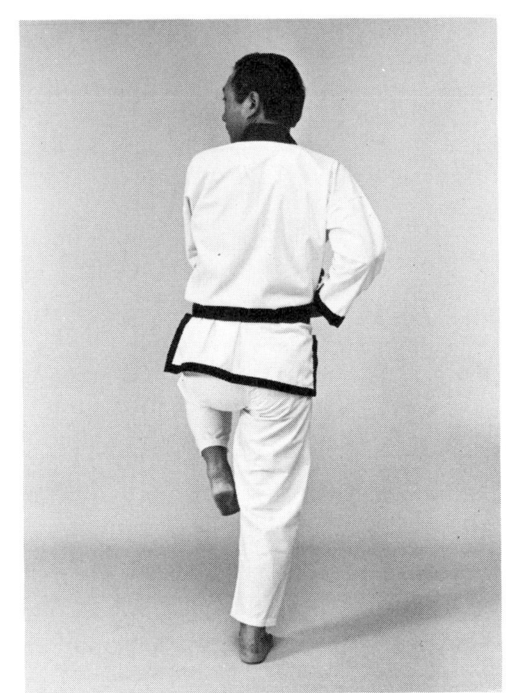

a. Pivoting on right foot, draw left foot up into position near right knee.

b. Simultaneously pull both fists back to right hip, left forearm in front of waist, left fist, palm in, held above right fist palm up.

c. Hold this position for a second (body facing **A**, eyes focused toward **R–2**).

Seventeenth Position: Side Kick, Elbow Strike

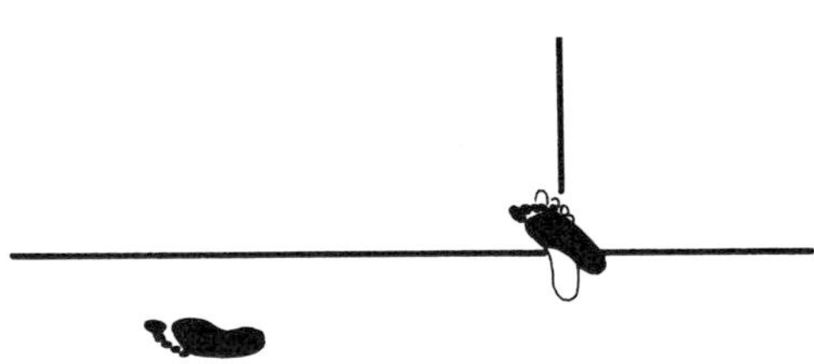

Note: The two motions, 1 and 2, are performed in continuous motion.

1. Side Kick

a. Execute a high Side Thrust Kick with left foot (toward **R–2**).

b. Simultaneously execute a High Punch with left fist (toward **R–2**).

2. Elbow Strike

a. Immediately bring left foot down one step forward (toward **R–2**).

b. Assume Front Stance.

c. Simultaneously execute an Elbow Strike with right elbow (striking left palm at shoulder level).

Eighteenth Position: Knife-Hand Middle Block

a. Slide right foot forward one step (to **R–2**).

b. Assume Back Stance.

c. Simultaneously execute a Knife-Hand Middle Block with right hand, left Knife Hand assisting.

Nineteenth Position: Outside Middle Block

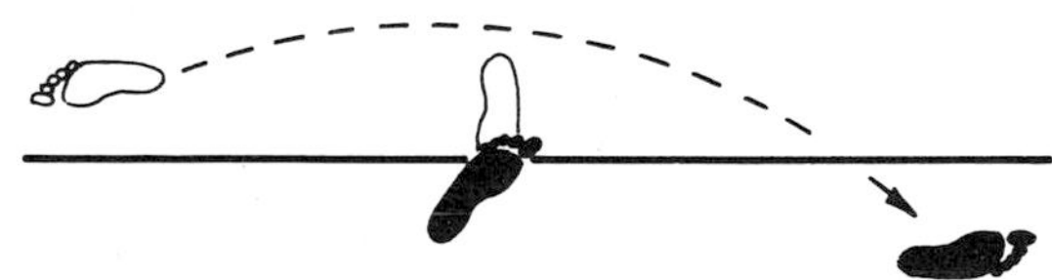

a. Pivoting on left foot, slide right foot out and back in a wide arc, turning 180° (to face **L–2**).

b. Assume Front Stance.

c. Simultaneously execute an Outside Middle Block with right forearm.

Twentieth Position: Double Middle Punch

a. Maintain Front Stance (same position as above).

b. Execute a Double Middle Punch:

(1) first with left fist,

(2) then with right fist.

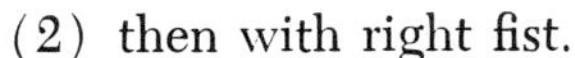

Twenty-First Position: Crane Stance (for Side Kicking)

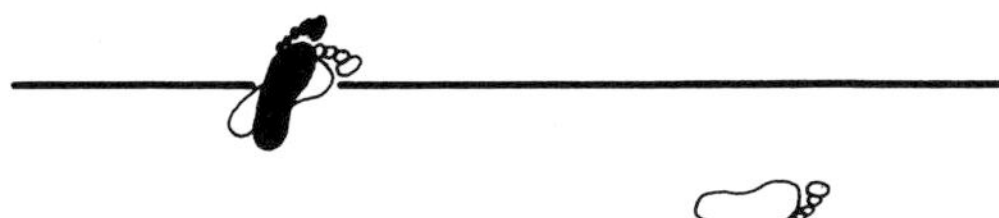

a. Pivoting on left foot, draw right foot up into position near left knee.

b. Simultaneously pull both fists back to left hip, right forearm in front of waist, right fist, palm in, held above left fist, palm up.

c. Hold this position for a second (body facing **A**, eyes focused toward **L–2**).

Twenty-Second Position: Side Kick, Elbow Strike

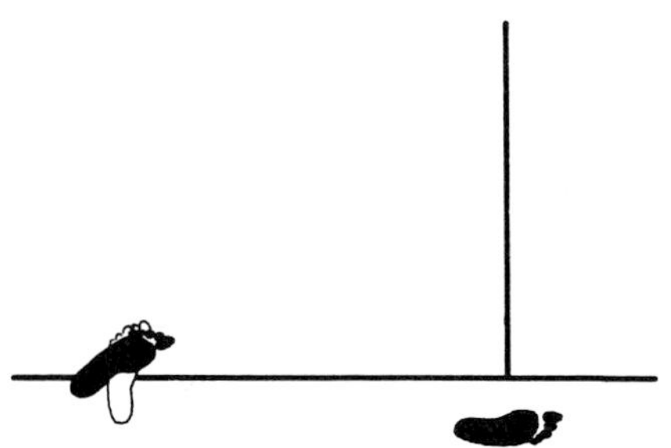

Note: The two motions, 1 and 2, are performed in continuous motion.

1. Side Kick

a. Execute a high Side Thrust Kick with right foot (toward **L–2**).

b. Simultaneously execute a High Punch with right fist (toward **L–2**).

2. Elbow Strike

a. Immediately bring right foot down one step forward (toward **L–2**).

b. Assume Front Stance.

c. Simultaneously execute an Elbow Strike with left elbow to right palm.

Twenty-Third Position: Knife-Hand Middle Block

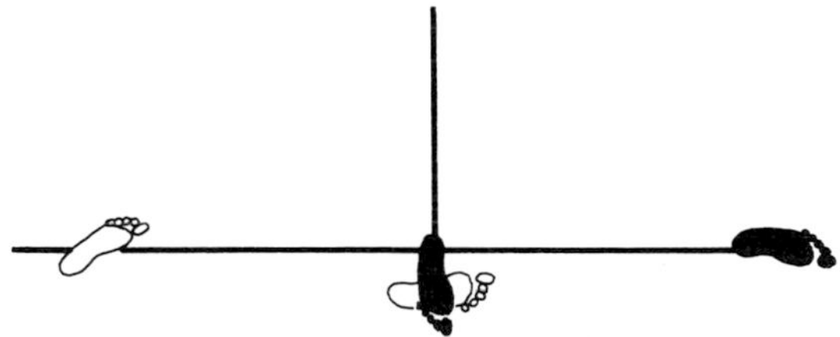

a. Slide left foot forward one step (to **L–2**).

b. Assume Back Stance.

c. Simultaneously execute a Knife-Hand Middle Block with left hand, right Knife Hand assisting.

Twenty-Fourth Position: Scissors Block

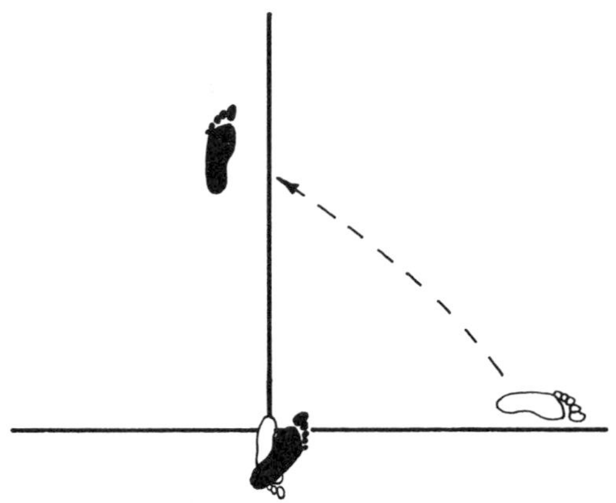

front view

a. Pivoting on right foot, slide left foot out, turning 90° (to face **A**).

b. Assume Front Stance.

c. Simultaneously execute a Scissors Block (a Low Block with left forearm and an Outside Middle Block with right forearm).

Twenty-Fifth Position: Double-Hand Low Block

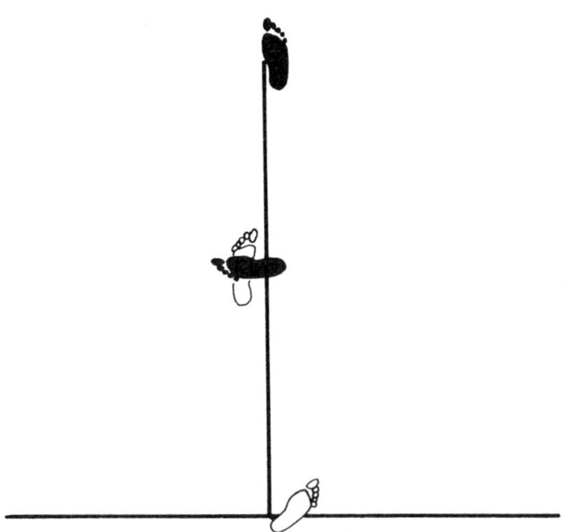

front view

a. Slide right foot one step forward (toward **A**).

b. Assume Back Stance.

c. Simultaneously execute a Double-Hand Low Block with right forearm, left fist assisting (sweep right forearm down into Low Block, palm down, and thrust left fist into position palm up just in front of solar plexus).

Twenty-Sixth Position: Double-Hand Low Block

front view

a. Slide left foot forward one step (toward **A**).

b. Assume Back Stance.

c. Simultaneously execute a Double-Hand Low Block with left forearm, right fist assisting (as you execute a Low Block with left forearm, palm down, thrust right fist into position palm up just in front of solar plexus).

Twenty-Seventh Position: Middle Punch and Yell

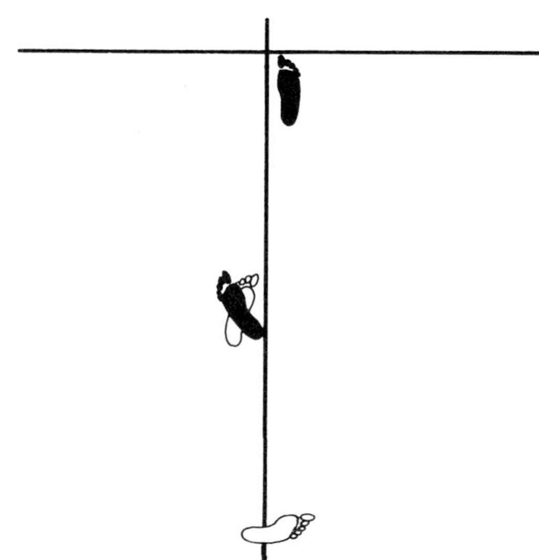

a. Slide right foot forward one step (to **A**).

b. Assume Front Stance.

c. Simultaneously execute a Middle Punch with right fist and yell.

Twenty-Eighth Position: Knife-Hand Low Block

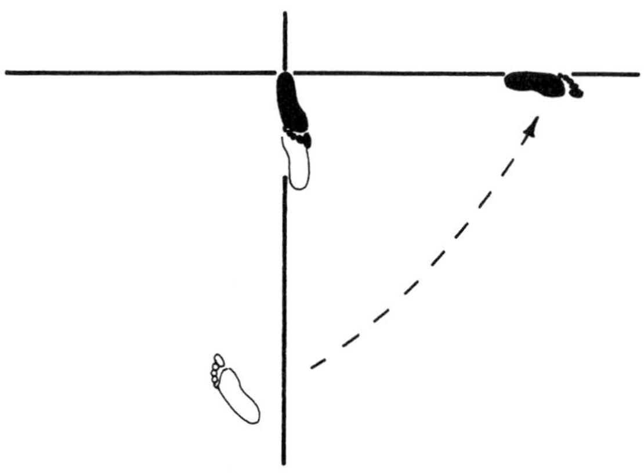

a. Pivoting on right foot, slide left foot out and back in a wide arc, turning 270° (to face **L–1**).

b. Assume Back Stance.

c. Simultaneously execute a Knife-Hand Low Block with left hand, right Knife Hand assisting.

Twenty-Ninth Position: Knife-Hand Middle Block

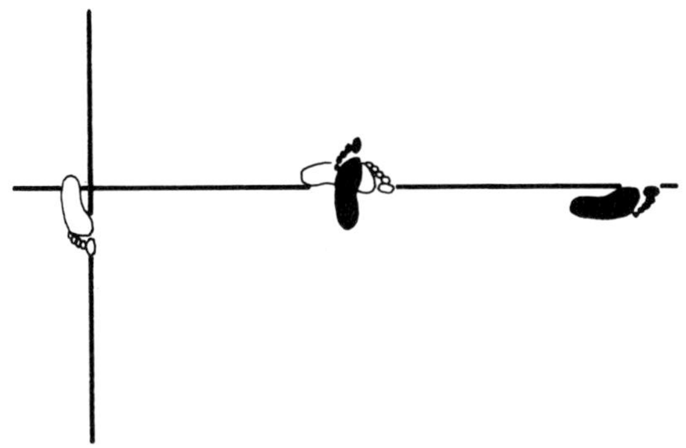

a. Slide right foot forward one step past left foot (to **L–1**).

b. Assume Back Stance.

c. Simultaneously execute a Knife-Hand Middle Block with right hand, left Knife Hand assisting.

Thirtieth Position: Palm-Heel Center Block

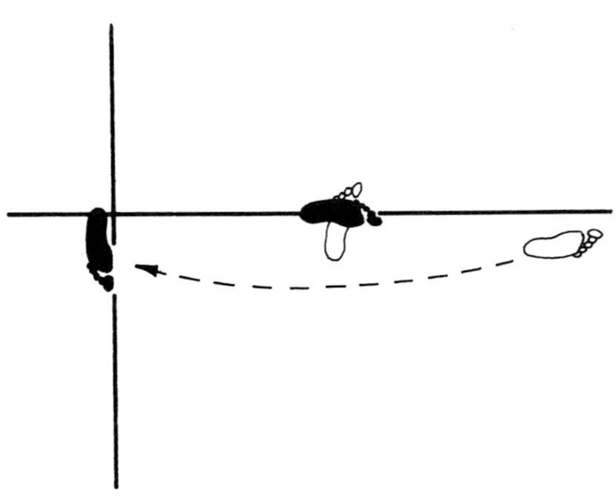

a. Slide right foot one step back past left foot (to **A**).

b. Assume Back Stance (still facing **L–1**).

c. Simultaneously execute a Palm-Heel Center Block with left hand.

Thirty-First Position: Middle Punch

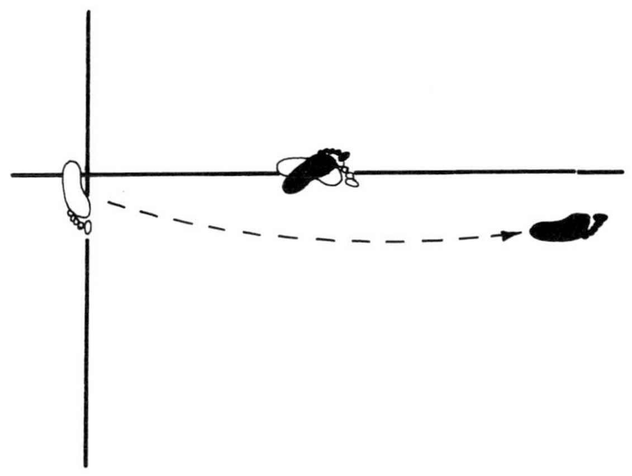

a. Slide right foot forward one step past left foot (to **L–1**).

b. Assume Front Stance.

c. Simultaneously execute a Middle Punch with right fist.

Thirty-Second Position: Knife-Hand Low Block

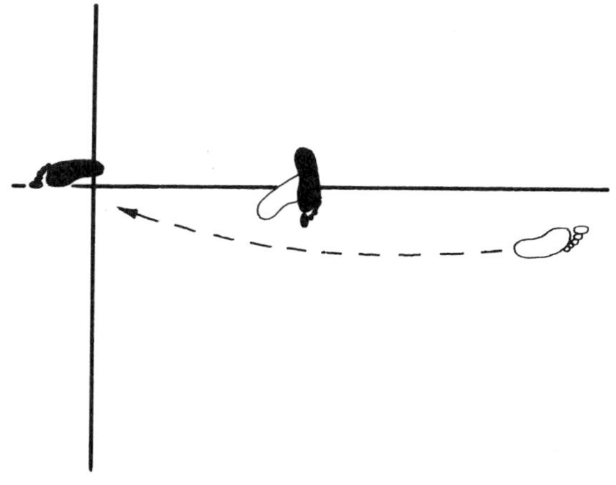

a. Pivoting on left foot, slide right foot out and back in a wide arc, turning 180° (to face **R–1**).

b. Assume Back Stance.

c. Simultaneously execute a Knife-Hand Low Block with right hand, left Knife Hand assisting.

Thirty-Third Position: Knife-Hand Middle Block

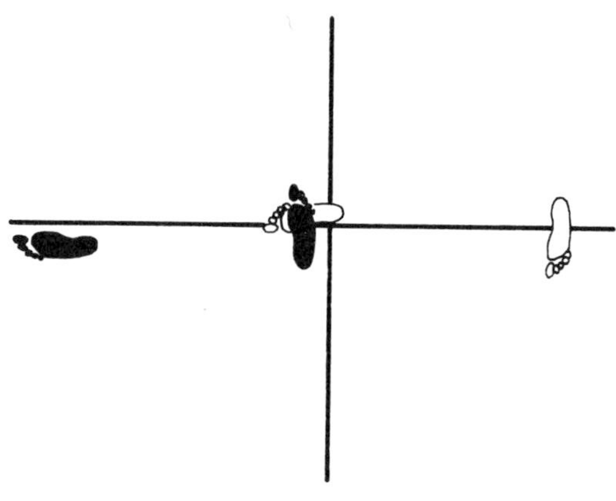

a. Slide left foot forward one step past right foot (to **R–1**).

b. Assume Back Stance.

c. Simultaneously execute a Knife-Hand Middle Block with left hand, right Knife Hand assisting.

Thirty-Fourth Position: Palm-Heel Center Block

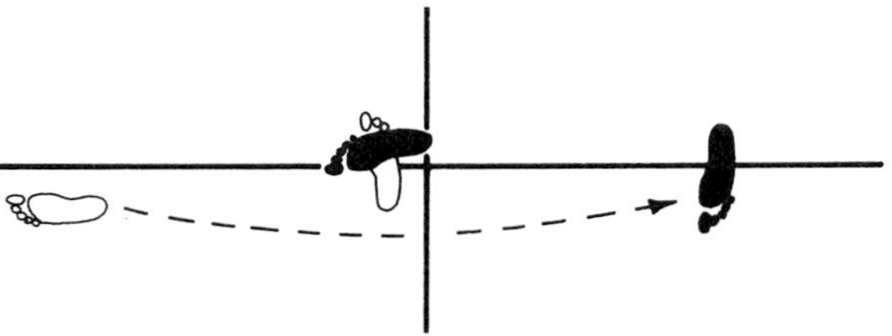

a. Slide left foot one step back past right foot (to **A**).

b. Assume Back Stance (still facing **R–1**).

c. Simultaneously execute a Palm-Heel Center Block with right hand.

Thirty-Fifth Position: Middle Punch

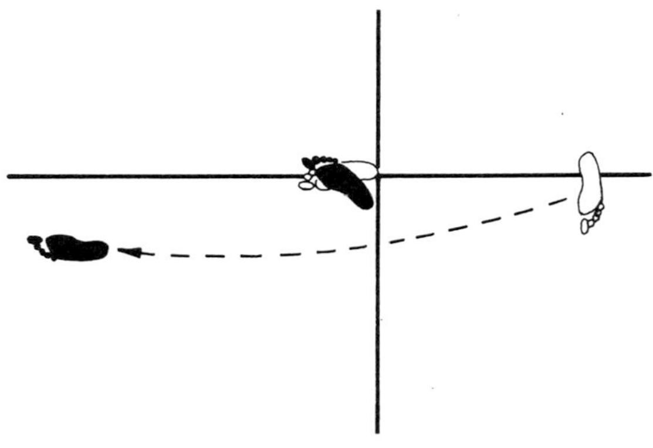

a. Slide left foot forward one step past right foot (to **R–1**).

b. Assume Front Stance.

c. Simultaneously execute a Middle Punch with left fist.

Stop

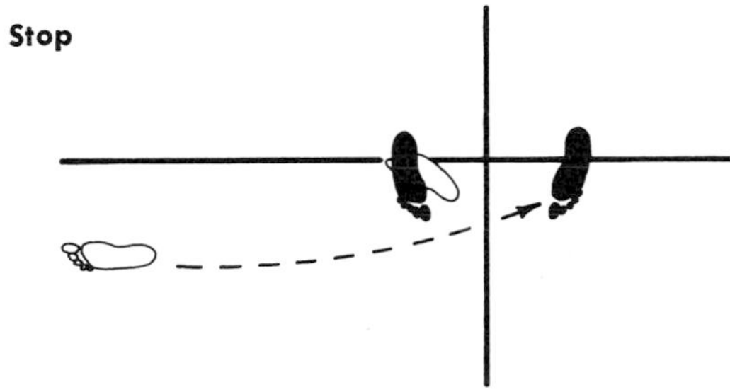

Pivoting on right foot, slide left foot out and back, turning 90° (to resume Starting Point, **A**). Assume Ready Stance.

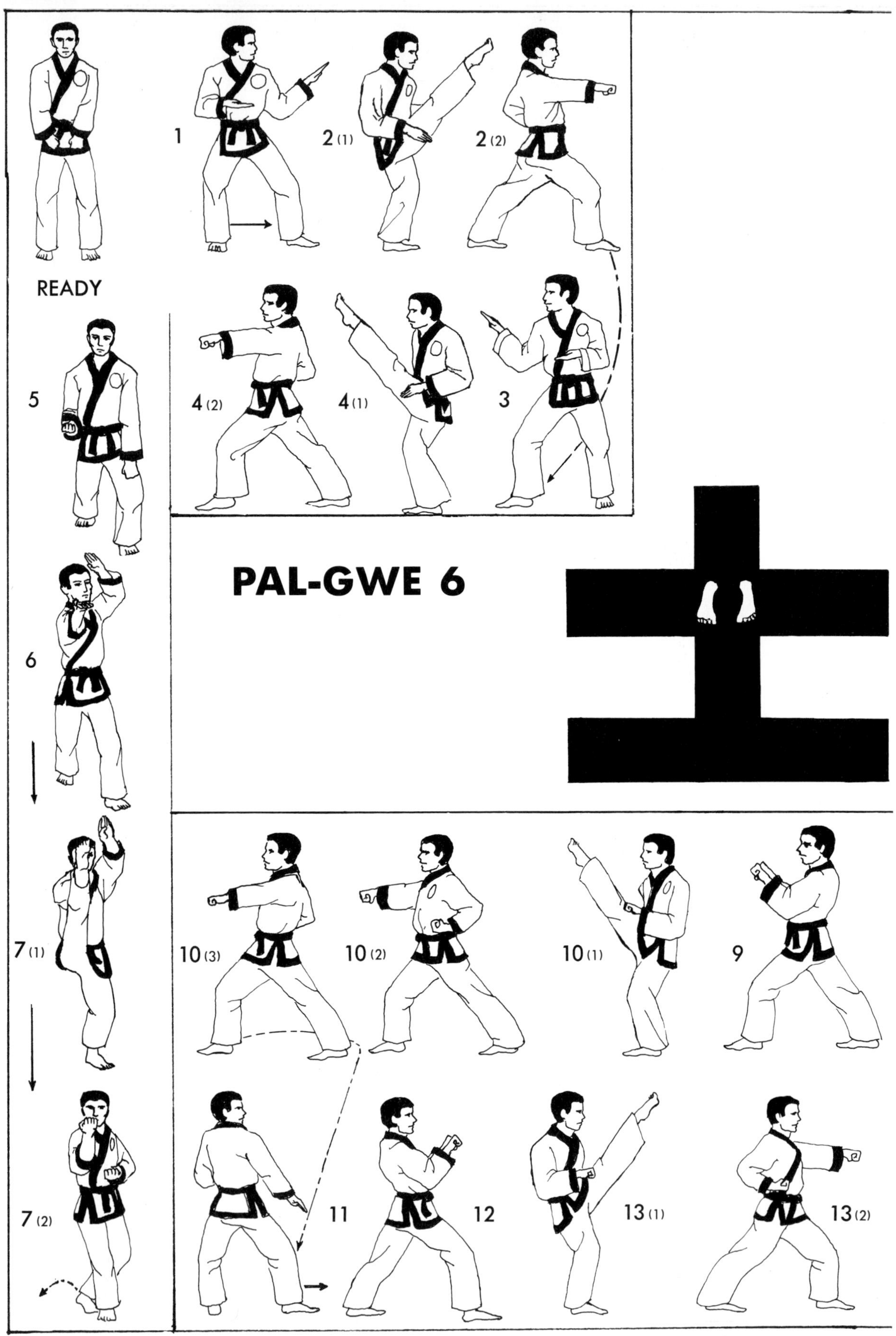
READY
1
2 (1)
2 (2)
3
4 (1)
4 (2)
5
6
7 (1)
7 (2)
PAL-GWE 6
9
10 (1)
10 (2)
10 (3)
11
12
13 (1)
13 (2)

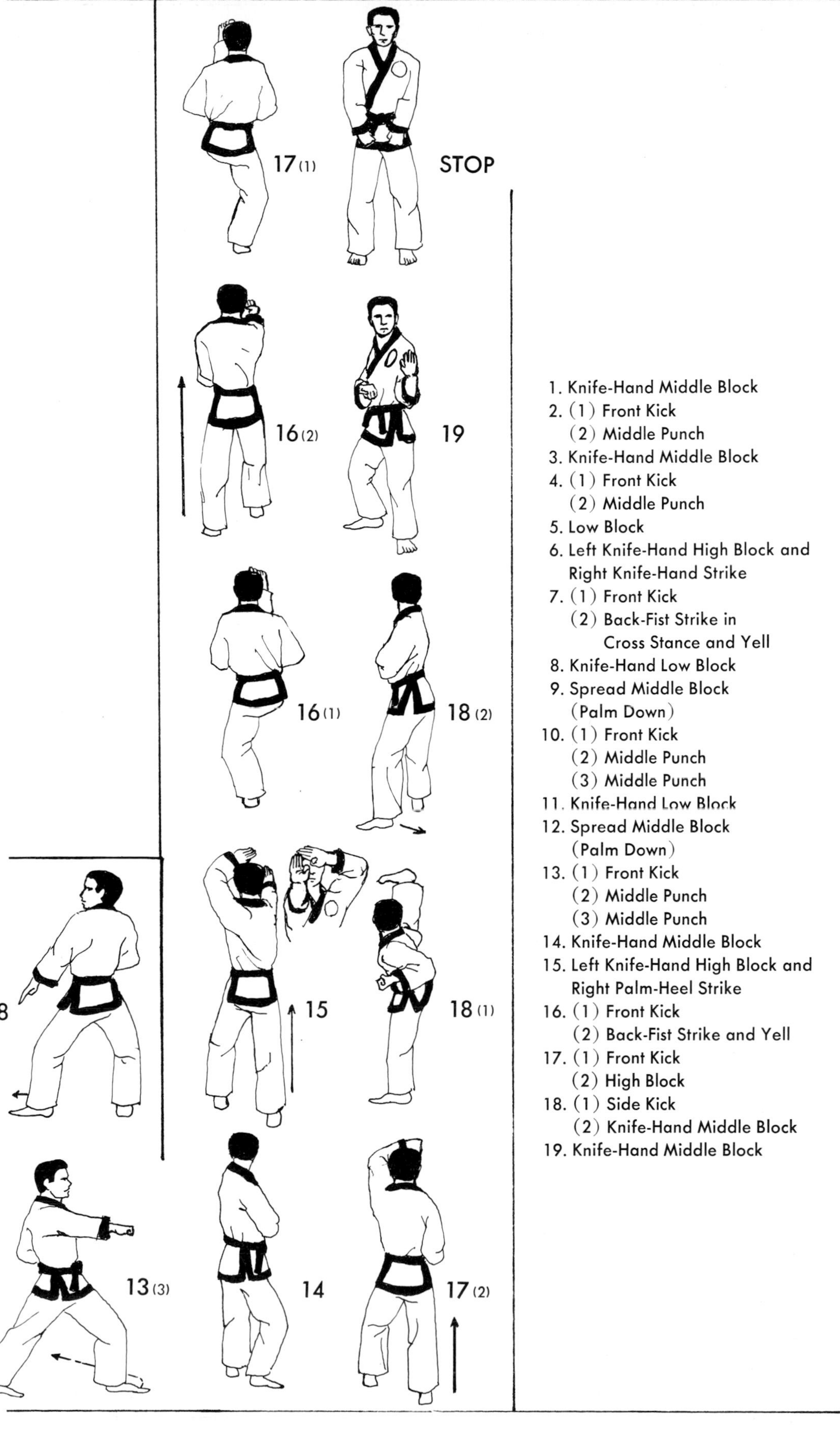

1. Knife-Hand Middle Block
2. (1) Front Kick
   (2) Middle Punch
3. Knife-Hand Middle Block
4. (1) Front Kick
   (2) Middle Punch
5. Low Block
6. Left Knife-Hand High Block and Right Knife-Hand Strike
7. (1) Front Kick
   (2) Back-Fist Strike in Cross Stance and Yell
8. Knife-Hand Low Block
9. Spread Middle Block (Palm Down)
10. (1) Front Kick
    (2) Middle Punch
    (3) Middle Punch
11. Knife-Hand Low Block
12. Spread Middle Block (Palm Down)
13. (1) Front Kick
    (2) Middle Punch
    (3) Middle Punch
14. Knife-Hand Middle Block
15. Left Knife-Hand High Block and Right Palm-Heel Strike
16. (1) Front Kick
    (2) Back-Fist Strike and Yell
17. (1) Front Kick
    (2) High Block
18. (1) Side Kick
    (2) Knife-Hand Middle Block
19. Knife-Hand Middle Block

PAL-GWE 6 (*Pal-Gwe Yook-Chang*)

Number of positions: 19 (excluding Ready Stance and Stop)

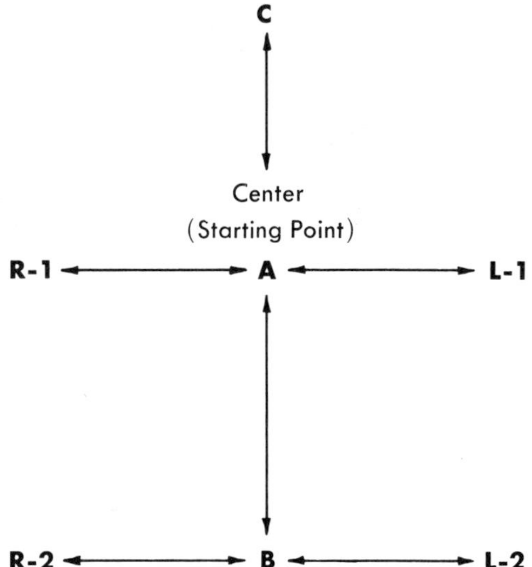

Movement proceeds in a ± pattern, beginning at A:

Ready Stance

Stand at Attention at Starting Point, **A.**

First Position: Knife-Hand Middle Block

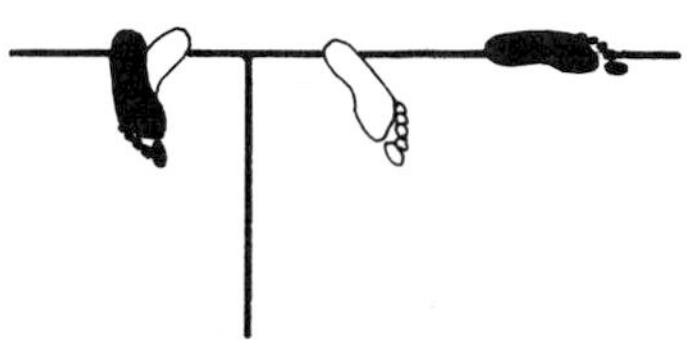

a. Pivoting on right foot, turn 90° to the left and slide left foot forward a half-step (toward **L–1**).

b. Assume Back Stance.

c. Simultaneously execute a Knife-Hand Middle Block with left hand, right Knife Hand assisting.

Second Position: Front Kick, Middle Punch

Note: The two motions, 1 and 2, are performed in continuous motion.

1. Front Kick

Execute a high Front Thrust Kick with right foot.

2. Middle Punch

a. Bring right foot down one step forward (to **L–1**).

b. Assume Front Stance.

c. Simultaneously execute a Middlc Punch with right fist.

Third Position: Knife-Hand Middle Block

a. Pivoting on left foot, slide right foot out and back in a wide arc, turning 180° (to face R–1).

b. Assume Back Stance.

c. Simultaneously execute a Knife-Hand Middle Block with right hand, left Knife Hand assisting.

Fourth Position: Front Kick, Middle Punch

Note: The two motions, 1 and 2, are performed in continuous motion.

1. Front Kick

Execute a High Front Kick with left foot.

2. Middle Punch

a. Bring left foot down one step forward (to R–1).

b. Assume Front Stance.

c. Simultaneously execute a Middle Punch with left fist.

Fifth Position: Low Block

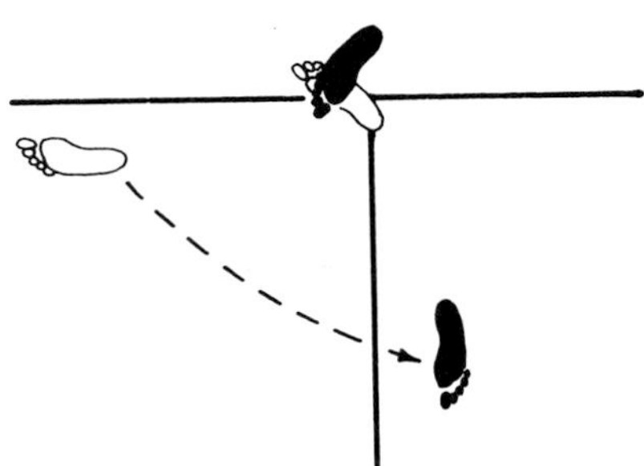

a. Pivoting on right foot, slide left foot out, turning 90° (toward **B**).

b. Assume Front Stance.

c. Simultaneously execute a Low Block with left forearm.

Sixth Position: Knife-Hand High Block and Knife-Hand Strike

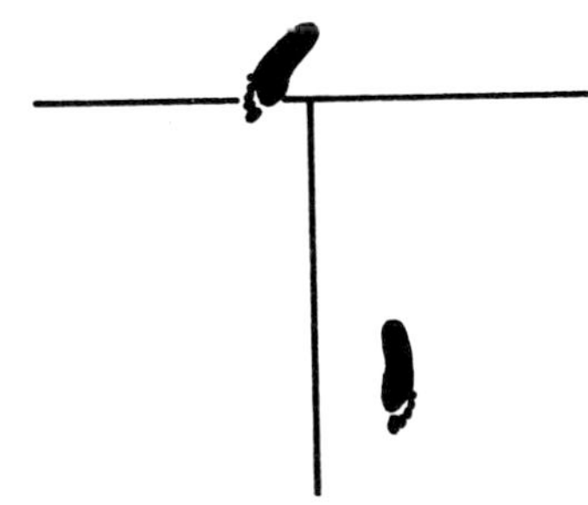

a. Maintain Front Stance (same position as above).

b. Without moving feet, twist upper torso to the left so that right shoulder is forward.

c. Simultaneously execute a Knife-Hand High Block with left hand and a Knife-Hand Strike to the neck of imaginary opponent, near **B**, with right hand (the blocking surface is the outer edge of left Knife Hand, palm out above forehead. The Knife-Hand Strike to the neck is made from outside to inside with the right hand palm up).

Seventh Position: Front Kick, Back-Fist Strike in Cross Stance and Yell

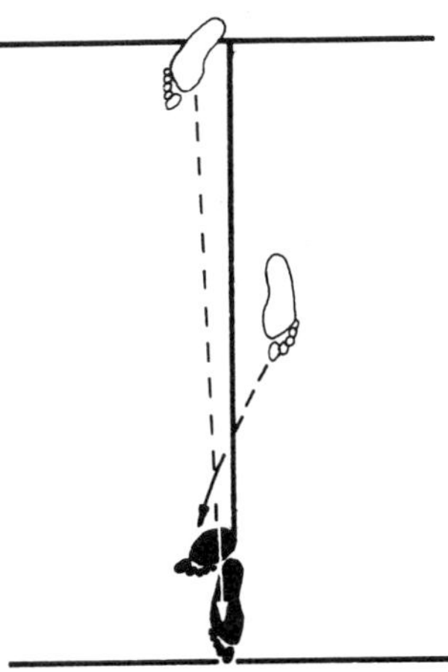

Note: The two motions, 1 and 2, are performed in continuous motion.

1. Front Kick

Execute a high Front Thrust Kick with right foot. (Keep left Knife-Hand up in High Block position and right Knife-Hand extended, as in Sixth Position.)

2. Back-Fist Strike (in Cross Stance) and Yell

a. Immediately lunge a long step forward (to **B**), bringing weight down on right foot with a stamp and drawing ball of left foot close into position behind and to the right of right heel, standing with knees slightly bent in Cross Stance. (The application of this motion would be to lunge and stamp on the instep of an opponent at **B**.)

b. Simultaneously as you stamp into position with right foot, execute a Back-Fist Strike at face level with right Back Fist, left fist assisting, and yell. (The Back-Fist Strike is performed with right elbow pointed downward and right fist palm in at face level with wrist slightly bent back. The striking surface is the back of the first two knuckles of the right fist. The left fist assists in that as you strike with the right Back Fist, you thrust left fist into position palm up just in front of solar plexus.)

Eighth Position: Knife-Hand Low Block

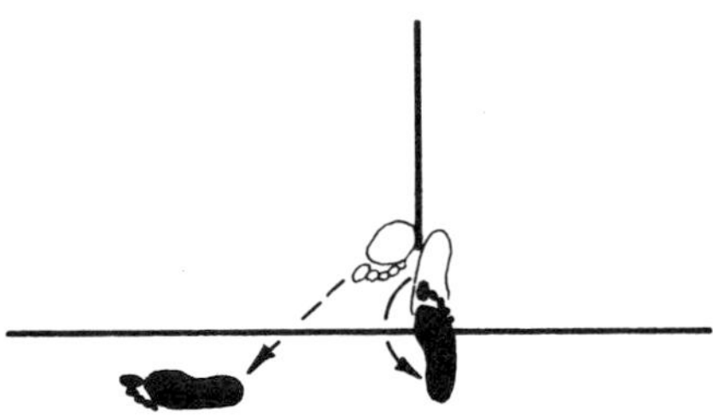

a. Pivoting on right heel, slide left foot out and back in a wide arc, turning 270° (three-quarters of a circle, to face **R–2**).

b. Assume Back Stance.

c. Simultaneously execute a Knife-Hand Low Block with left hand, right Knife Hand assisting.

Ninth Position: Spread Middle Block

a. Pivoting on ball of right foot, slide left foot forward a half-step (toward **R–2**).

b. Assume Front Stance.

c. Simultaneously execute a Spread Middle Block, inside-to-outside (cross both wrists in front of chest, fists palm in, right wrist inside left, then sweep both forearms outward simultaneously, snapping both wrists palm down, into position with fists on a level with and out in front of shoulders. The blocking surfaces are the outer edges of both lower forearms).

Tenth Position: Front Kick, Double Middle Punch

Note: The two motions, 1 and 2, are performed in continuous motion.

1. Front Kick

Execute a high Front Thrust Kick with right foot.

2. Double Middle Punch

a. Bring right foot down one step forward (to **R–2**).

b. Assume Front Stance.

c. Simultaneously execute a Double Middle Punch (in rapid sequence):

(1) first with right fist,

(2) then with left fist.

Eleventh Position: Knife-Hand Low Block

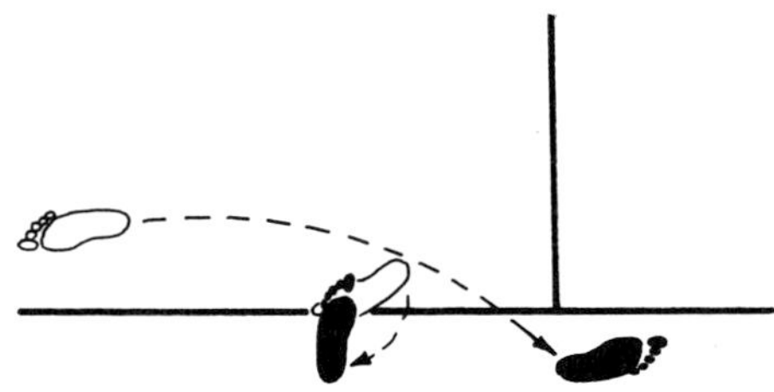

a. Pivoting on left foot, slide right foot out and back in a wide arc, turning 180° (to face **L–2**).

b. Assume Back Stance.

c. Simultaneously execute a Knife-Hand Low Block with right hand, left Knife Hand assisting.

Twelfth Position: Spread Middle Block

a. Pivoting on ball of left foot, slide right foot forward a half-step (toward **L–2**).

b. Assume Front Stance.

c. Simultaneously execute a Spread Middle Block, inside-to-outside.

Thirteenth Position: Front Kick, Double Middle Punch

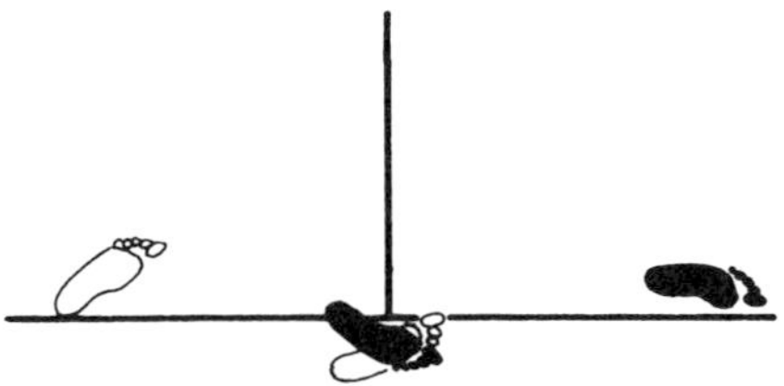

Note: The two motions, 1 and 2, are performed in continuous motion.

1. Front Kick

Execute a high Front Thrust Kick with left foot.

2. Double Middle Punch

a. Bring left foot down one step forward (to **L–2**).

b. Assume Front Stance.

c. Simultaneously execute a Double Middle Punch (in rapid sequence):

(1) first with left fist,

(2) then with right fist.

Fourteenth Position: Knife-Hand Middle Block

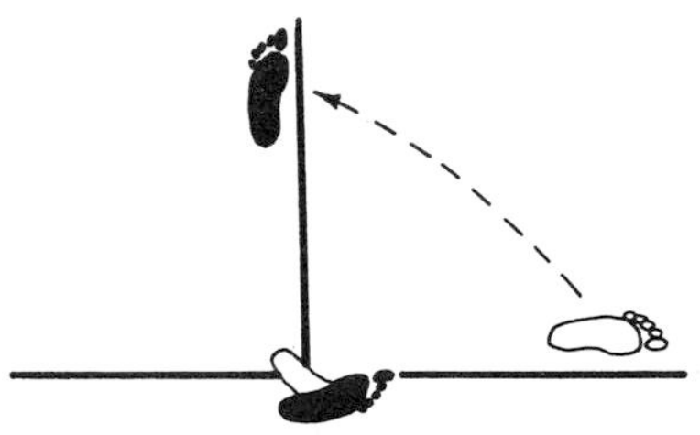

front view

a. Pivoting on right foot, slide left foot out, turning 90° (to face **A**).

b. Assume Back Stance.

c. Simultaneously execute a Knife-Hand Middle Block with left hand, right Knife Hand assisting.

Fifteenth Position: Knife-Hand High Block and Palm-Heel Strike

front view

a. Pivoting on ball of right foot, slide left foot forward a half-step (toward **A**).

b. Assume Front Stance.

c. Simultaneously execute a Knife-Hand High Block with left hand and a high Palm-Heel Strike with right hand. (Palm-Heel Strike is delivered with fingers of right hand pointing up and the heel of the hand striking to the chin of imaginary opponent near **A**.)

Sixteenth Position: Front Kick, Back-Fist Strike and Yell

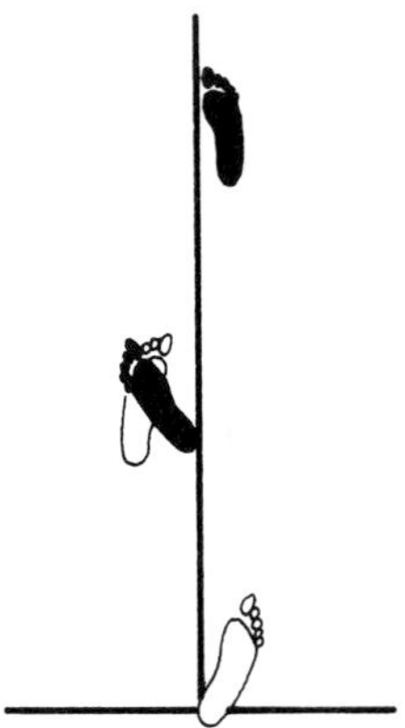

Note: The two motions, 1 and 2, are performed in continuous motion.

1. Front Kick

Execute a high Front Thrust Kick with right foot. (Keep left Knife Hand up in High Block position and right Palm Heel extended, as in Fifteenth Position.)

front view

2. Back-Fist Strike and Yell

a. Bring right foot down one step forward (to **A**), and at the same time cross forearms in front of chest, right forearm outside left.

b. Assume Front Stance.

c. Simultaneously execute a Back-Fist Strike at face level with right Back Fist (pulling left fist back to hip) and yell.

Seventeenth Position: Front Kick, High Block

front view

Note: The two motions, 1 and 2, are performed in continuous motion.

1. Front Kick

Execute a high Front Thrust Kick with left foot.

front view

2. High Block

a. Bring left foot down one step forward (toward **C**).

b. Assume Front Stance.

c. Simultaneously execute a High Block with left forearm.

Eighteenth Position: Side Kick, Knife-Hand Middle Block

Note: The two motions, 1 and 2, are performed in continuous motion.

1. Side Kick

a. Execute a high Side Thrust Kick with right foot (toward **C**).

b. Simultaneously execute a High Punch with right fist (toward **C**).

front view

2. Knife-Hand Middle Block

a. Bring right foot down one step forward (to **C**).

b. Assume Back Stance.

c. Simultaneously execute a Knife-Hand Middle Block with right hand, left Knife Hand assisting.

front view

Nineteenth Position: Knife-Hand Middle Block

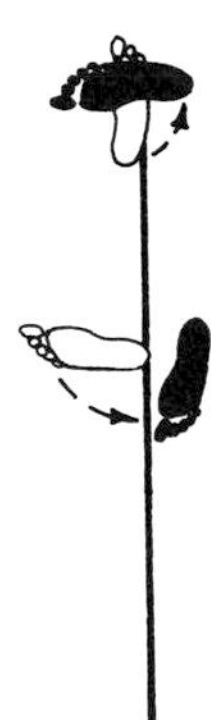

a. Pivoting on the ball of right foot, shift left foot back, turning about-facc (to face **A**).

b. Assume Back Stance.

c. Simultaneously execute a Knife-Hand Middle Block with left hand, right Knife Hand assisting.

Stop

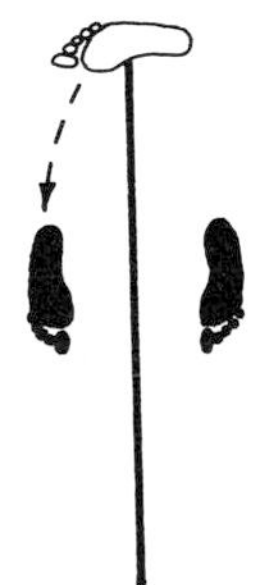

Slide right foot forward into position parallel to left foot to face front at Starting Point, **A**. Assume Ready Stance.

PAL-GWE 7

1. Spread Low Block
2. (1) Front Kick
   (2) Spread Middle Block (Palm In)
3. (1) Front Kick
   (2) Double-Fist High X Block
4. (1) Side Kick
   (2) Knife-Hand Middle Block
5. Outside Middle Block
6. Reverse High Punch
7. High Block
8. (1) Side Kick
   (2) Knife-Hand Low Block
9. Reverse Middle Punch
10. Outside Middle Block
11. Reverse High Punch
12. High Block
13. (1) Side Kick
    (2) Knife-Hand Low Block
14. Reverse Middle Punch
15. Double-Fist Low X Block
16. Double-Fist High X Block
17. Grab, High Punch and Yell
18. Low Block to the Front in Horseback Stance
19. Knife-Hand Strike
20. (1) Crescent Kick
    (2) Elbow Strike
21. High Side Block-Low Block in Horseback Stance
22. Knife-Hand Middle Block
23. Reverse Middle Punch and Yell

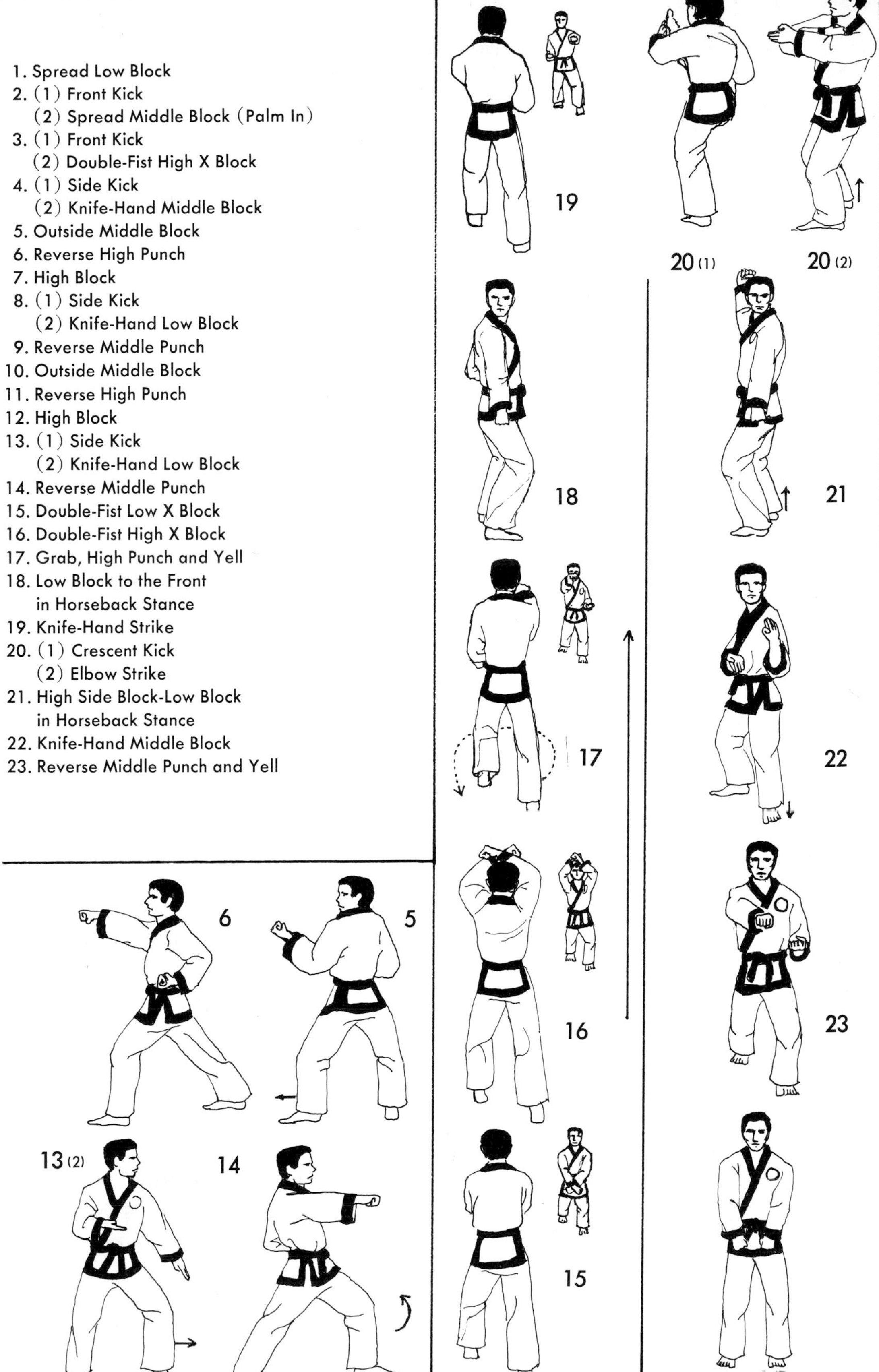

PAL-GWE 7 (*Pal-Gwe Chil-Chang*)

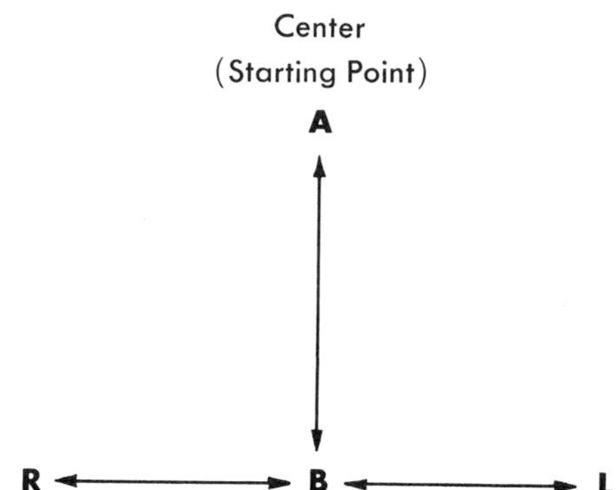

Number of positions: 23 (excluding Ready Stance and Stop)

Movement proceeds in a ⊥ pattern, beginning at A:

Ready Stance

Stand at Attention at Starting Point, **A**.

First Position: Spread Low Block

a. Slide left foot forward one step (toward **B**).

b. Assume Front Stance.

c. Simultaneously execute a Spread Low Block with both forearms (cross both wrists, right over left, in front of chest, fists palm in, then sweep both forearms down and outward, snapping wrists around, into position with fists palm in at arms' length a little in front and out to the sides of the thighs. The blocking surfaces are the outer edges of both lower forearms).

Second Position: Front Kick, Spread Middle Block

Note: The two motions, 1 and 2, are performed in rapid sequence.

1. Front Kick

Execute a high Front Thrust Kick with right foot.

2. Spread Middle Block

a. Bring right foot down one step forward (toward **B**).

b. Assume Front Stance.

c. Simultaneously execute a Spread Middle Block with both forearms (cross both wrists, right over left, in front of chest, fists palm down, then sweep both forearms outward, snapping wrists around, into position with fists palm in on a level with and out in front of shoulders. The blocking surfaces are the inner edges of both lower forearms).

Third Position: Front Kick, Double-Fist High X Block

Note: The two motions, 1 and 2, are performed in continuous motion.

1. Front Kick

Execute a high Front Thrust Kick with left foot.

2. Double-Fist High X Block

a. Bring left foot down one step forward (toward **B**).

b. Assume Front Stance.

c. Simultaneously execute a Double-Fist High X Block (thrust both fists up and forward into position with wrists crossed and fists back-to-back above and out in front of forehead. The blocking surface is the V formed by the backs of the crossed wrists).

Fourth Position: Side Kick and Knife-Hand Middle Block

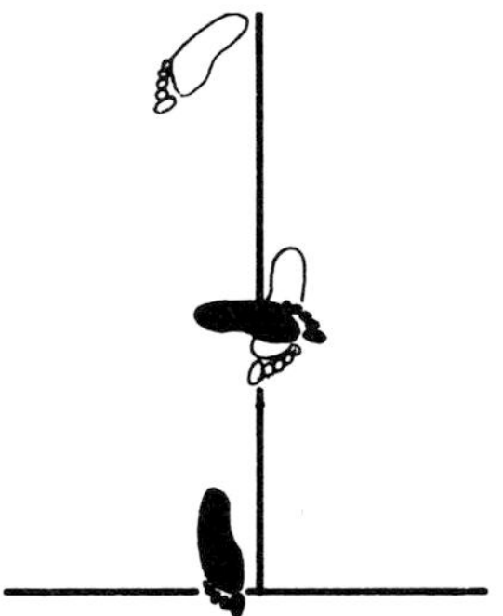

Note: The two motions, 1 and 2, are performed in continuous motion.

1. Side Kick

a. Execute a high Side Thrust Kick with right foot (toward **B**).

b. Simultaneously execute a High Punch with right fist (toward **B**).

2. Knife-Hand Middle Block

a. Bring right foot down one step forward (to **B**).

b. Assume Back Stance.

c. Simultaneously execute a Knife-Hand Middle Block with right hand, left Knife Hand assisting.

Fifth Position: Outside Middle Block

Note: The three positions, Five, Six, and Seven, should be performed in rapid sequence.

a. Pivoting on right foot, slide left foot out and back in a wide arc, turning 270° (three-quarters of a circle, to face **R**).

b. Assume Back Stance.

c. Simultaneously execute an Outside Middle Block with left forearm.

Sixth Position: Reverse High Punch

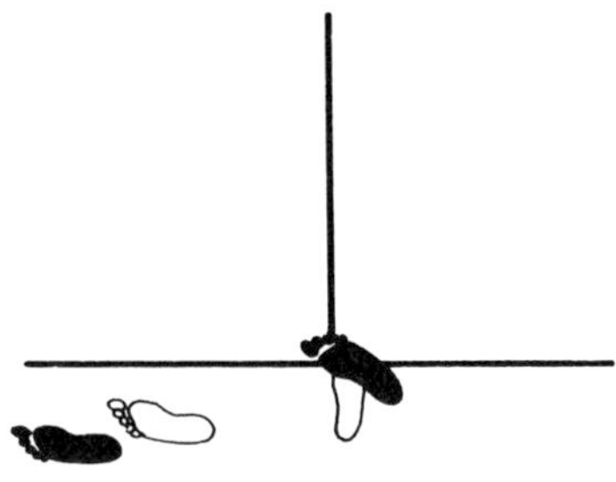

Note: The three positions, Five, Six, and Seven, should be performed in rapid sequence.

a. Pivoting on ball of right foot, slide left foot forward a half-step (toward **R**).

b. Assume Front Stance.

c. Simultaneously, execute a Reverse High Punch with right fist.

Seventh Position: High Block

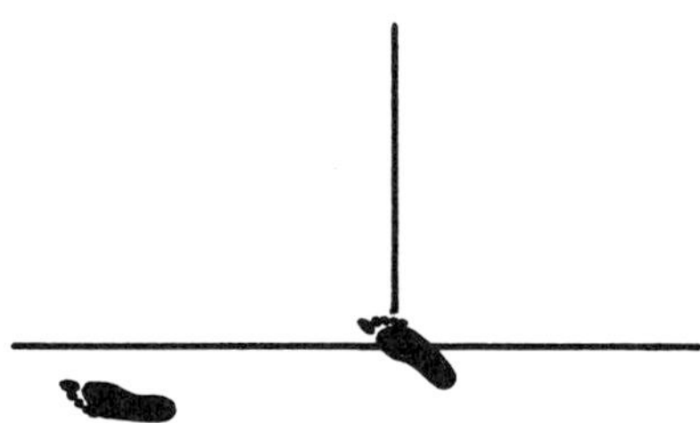

Note: The three positions, Five, Six, and Seven, should be performed in rapid sequence.

a. Maintain Front Stance (same position as above).

b. Execute a High Block with left forearm.

Eighth Position: Side Kick, Knife-Hand Low Block

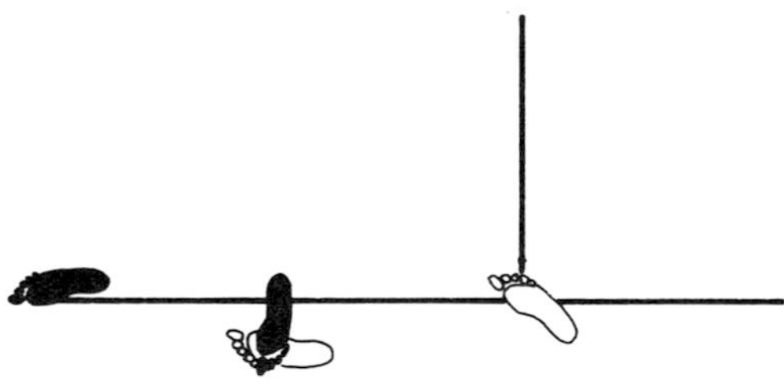

1. Side Kick

a. Execute a high Side Thrust Kick with right foot (toward **R**).

b. Simultaneously execute a High Punch with right fist (toward **R**).

2. Knife-Hand Low Block

Note: The two motions of Eighth Position, No. 2, Knife-Hand Low Block, and Ninth Position should be performed in rapid sequence.

a. Immediately bring right foot down one step forward (toward **R**).

b. Assume Back Stance.

c. Simultaneously execute a Knife-Hand Low Block with right hand, left Knife Hand assisting.

Ninth Position: Reverse Middle Punch

Note: The two motions of Eighth Position, No. 2, Knife-Hand Low Block, and Ninth Position should be performed in rapid sequence.

a. Pivoting on ball of left foot, slide right foot a half-step forward (to **R**).

b. Assume Front Stance.

c. Simultaneously execute a Reverse Middle Punch with left fist.

Tenth Position: Outside Middle Block

Note: The three positions, Ten, Eleven, and Twelve, should be performed in rapid sequence.

a. Pivoting on left foot, slide right foot out and back in a wide arc, turning 180° (to face **L**).

b. Assume Back Stance.

c. Simultaneously execute an Outside Middle Block with right forearm.

Eleventh Position: Reverse High Punch

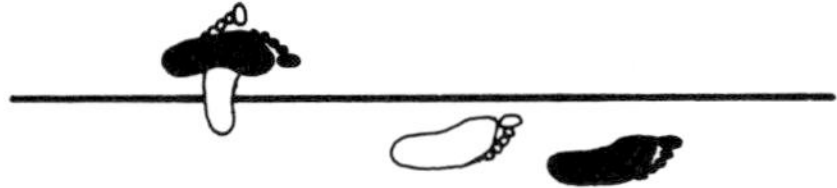

Note: The three positions, Ten, Eleven, and Twelve, should be performed in rapid sequence.

a. Pivoting on ball of left foot, slide right foot forward a half-step (toward **L**).

b. Assume Front Stance.

c. Simultaneously execute a Reverse High Punch with left fist.

Twelfth Position: High Block

Note: The three positions, Ten, Eleven, and Twelve, should be performed in rapid sequence.

a. Maintain Front Stance (same position as above).

b. Execute a High Block with right forearm.

Thirteenth Position: Side Kick, Knife-Hand Low Block

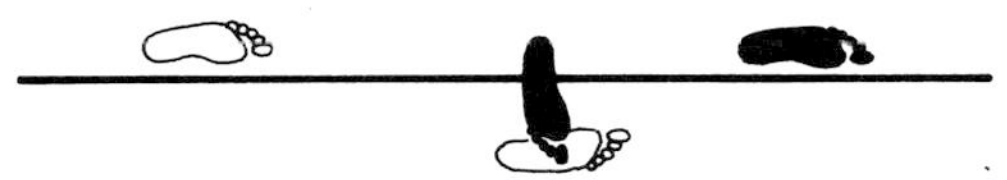

1. Side Kick

a. Execute a high Side Thrust Kick with left foot (toward **L**).

b. Simultaneously execute a High Punch with left fist (toward **L**).

2. Knife-Hand Low Block

Note: This motion and the following position, Fourteen, should be performed in rapid sequence.

a. Immediately bring left foot down one step forward (toward **L**).

b. Assume Back Stance.

c. Simultaneously execute a Knife-Hand Low Block with left hand, right Knife Hand assisting.

Fourteenth Position: Reverse Middle Punch

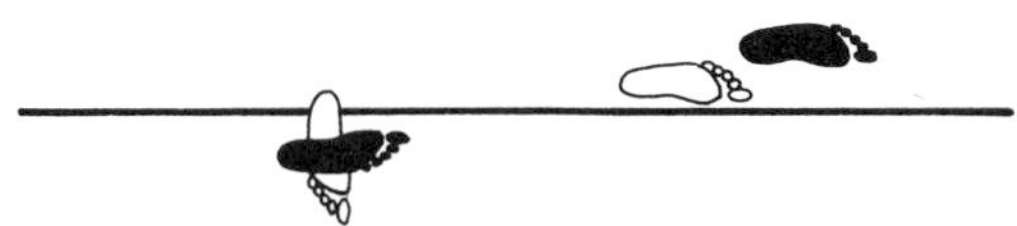

Note: The second motion, Knife-Hand Low Block, of the Thirteenth Position and the Reverse Middle Punch of this position should be performed in rapid sequence.

a. Pivoting on ball of right foot, slide left foot a half-step forward (to **L**).

b. Assume Front Stance.

c. Simultaneously execute a Reverse Middle Punch with right fist.

Fifteenth Position: Double-Fist Low X Block

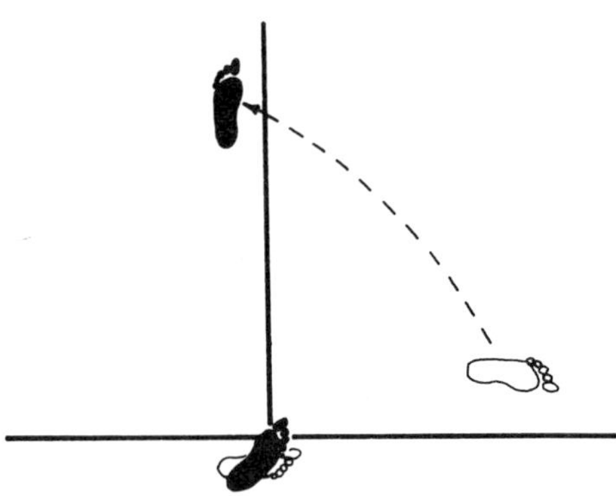

front view

a. Pivoting on right foot, slide left foot out, turning 90° (to face **A**).

b. Assume Front Stance.

c. Simultaneously execute a Double-Fist Low X Block (thrusting both fists down and forward into position with wrists crossed, right over left).

Sixteenth Position: Double-Fist High X Block

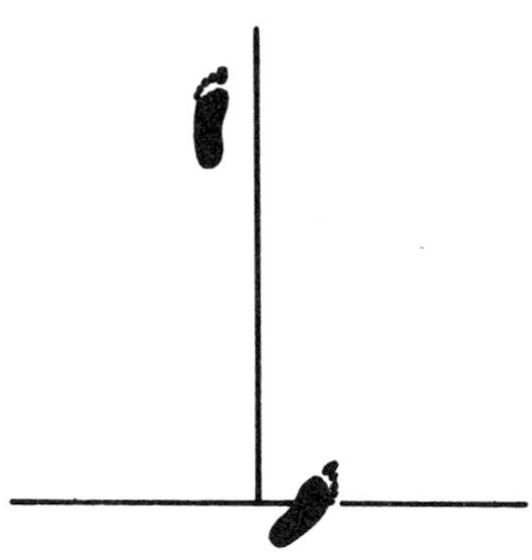

a. Maintain Front Stance (same position as above).

b. Execute a Double-Fist High X Block.

Seventeenth Position: Grab, High Punch and Yell

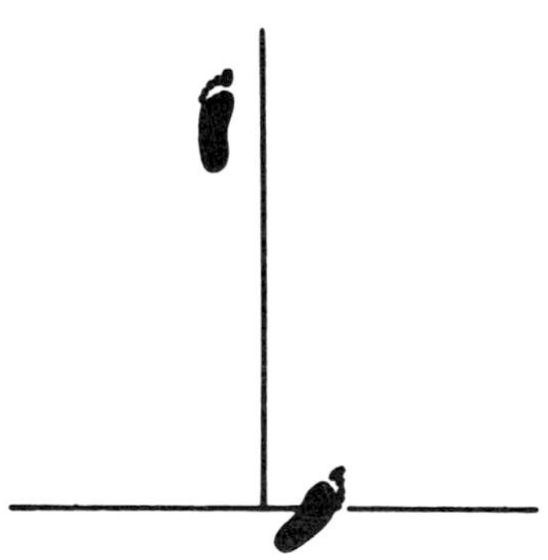

front view

a. Maintain Front Stance (same position as above).

b. Open and close hands and turn left wrist over right (grabbing and twisting wrist of imaginary opponent near **A**).

c. Immediately execute a High Punch with right fist (pulling left fist back to hip) and yell.

Eighteenth Position: Low Block to the Front

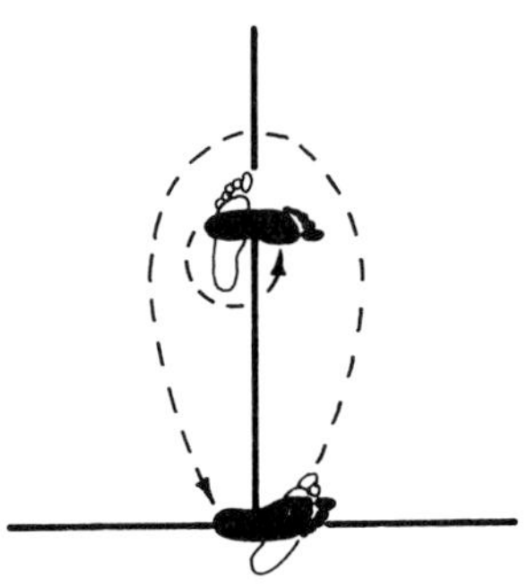

a. Pivoting on left foot, raise right foot and turn 360° to the left, bringing right foot down with a stamp (at Point **B** again).

b. Assume Horseback Stance (body facing **L**, eyes focused front, toward **B**).

c. Simultaneously execute a Low Block with right forearm (blocking kick of imaginary opponent at **B**).

Nineteenth Position: Knife-Hand Strike

front view

a. Pivot on ball of right foot and shift left foot back, turning about-face (to face **A**).

b. Assume Front Stance.

c. Simultaneously execute a Knife-Hand Strike outward with left hand at neck level (striking neck of imaginary opponent near **A** with left Knife Hand palm down).

Twentieth Position: Crescent Kick, Elbow Strike

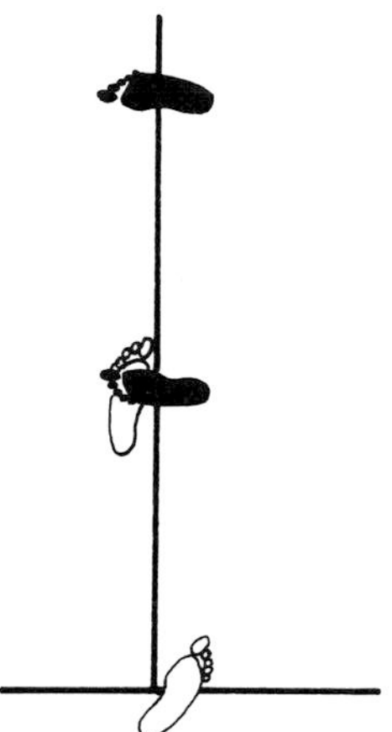

front view

Note: The two motions, 1 and 2, are performed in continuous motion.

1. Crescent Kick

Execute a Crescent Kick with right foot to palm of left hand (raise right leg as for a Front Kick—but keep knee bent and swing right foot sharply to the left at chest level, simultaneously extending left hand forward, thumb uppermost, and strike left palm with sole of right foot).

2. Elbow Strike

a. Bring right foot down one step forward (toward **A**).

b. Assume Horseback Stance (facing **R**).

c. Simultaneously execute an Elbow Strike with right elbow (striking left palm at shoulder level).

Twenty-First Position: High Side Block–Low Block

a. Slide both feet a half-step to your right (toward **A**).

b. Assume Horseback Stance (body still facing **R**, but eyes focused toward **B**).

c. Simultaneously execute a high Side Block–Low Block (beginning with forearms crossed in front of chest, left fist palm in near right ear and right fist palm down under left elbow, sweep left forearm down and out to the left and simultaneously sweep right forearm up and out to the right, snapping both wrists around. At end, left fist is palm down out to the left of left thigh, and right fist is palm in with right forearm perpendicular to the floor and right elbow level with and straight out to the right of right shoulder. The blocking surfaces are the outer edge of the lower left forearm and the inner—thumb-side—edge of the lower right forearm).

Twenty-Second Position: Knife-Hand Middle Block

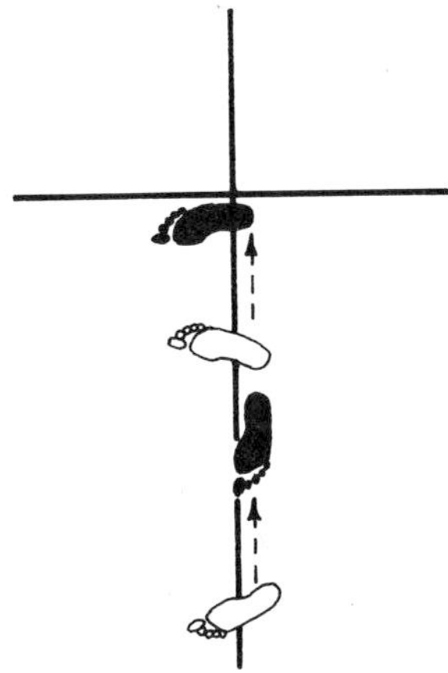

a. Slide both feet a half-step to your right (to **A**).

b. Assume Back Stance (facing front, toward **B**).

c. Simultaneously execute a Knife-Hand Middle Block with left hand, right Knife Hand assisting.

Twenty-Third Position: Reverse Middle Punch and Yell

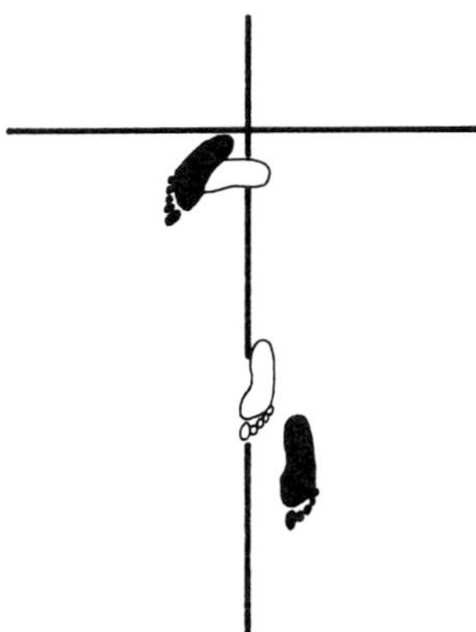

a. Pivoting on ball of right foot, slide left foot a half-step forward (toward **B**).

b. Assume Front Stance.

c. Simultaneously, execute a Reverse Middle Punch with right fist and yell.

Stop

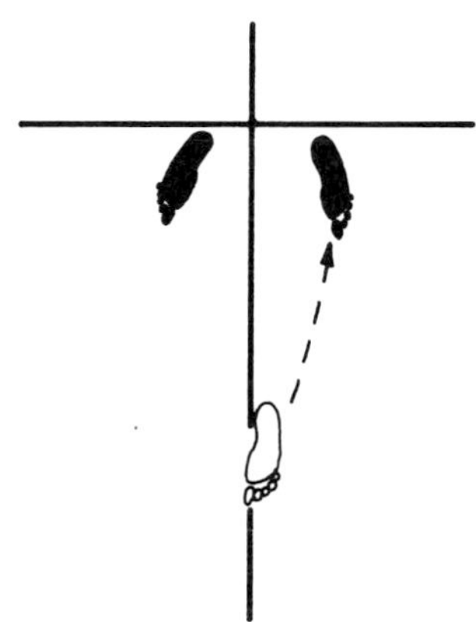

Slide left foot back into position parallel to right foot to face front, at Starting Point, **A**. Assume Ready Stance.

PAL-GWE 8

1. Low Block
2. Pull Free and Hammer-Fist Strike (Downward)
3. Middle Punch
4. Low Block
5. Pull Free and Hammer-Fist Strike (Downward)
6. Middle Punch
7. Knife-Hand Middle Block
8. Palm-Heel Center Block and Spear-Hand Thrust
9. (1) Twist Spear-Hand and Turn
   (2) Back-Fist Strike
10. High Punch and Yell
11. Knife-Hand Strike
12. Twist and Pull Free
13. Elbow Strike in Horseback Stance

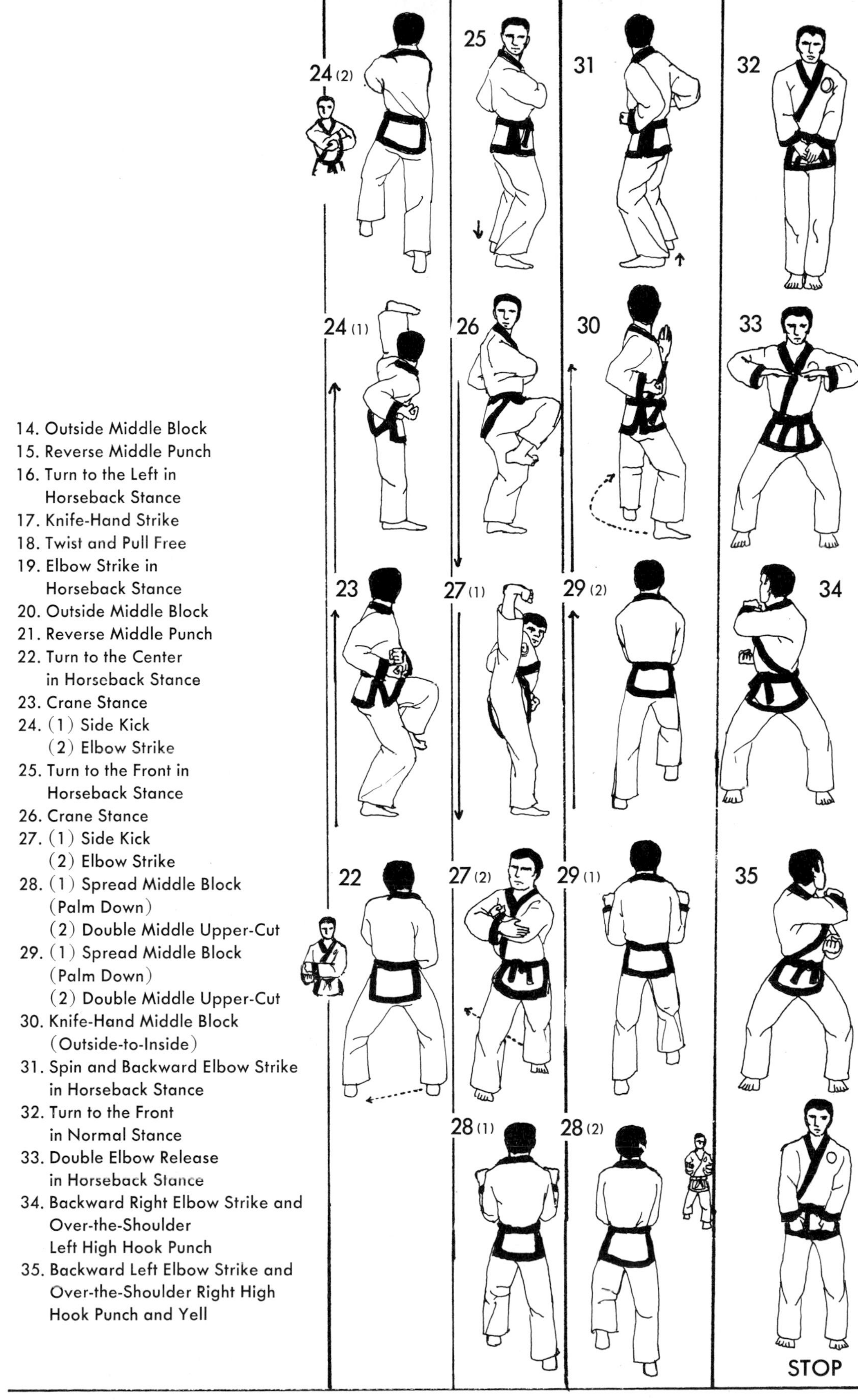

14. Outside Middle Block
15. Reverse Middle Punch
16. Turn to the Left in Horseback Stance
17. Knife-Hand Strike
18. Twist and Pull Free
19. Elbow Strike in Horseback Stance
20. Outside Middle Block
21. Reverse Middle Punch
22. Turn to the Center in Horseback Stance
23. Crane Stance
24. (1) Side Kick
    (2) Elbow Strike
25. Turn to the Front in Horseback Stance
26. Crane Stance
27. (1) Side Kick
    (2) Elbow Strike
28. (1) Spread Middle Block (Palm Down)
    (2) Double Middle Upper-Cut
29. (1) Spread Middle Block (Palm Down)
    (2) Double Middle Upper-Cut
30. Knife-Hand Middle Block (Outside-to-Inside)
31. Spin and Backward Elbow Strike in Horseback Stance
32. Turn to the Front in Normal Stance
33. Double Elbow Release in Horseback Stance
34. Backward Right Elbow Strike and Over-the-Shoulder Left High Hook Punch
35. Backward Left Elbow Strike and Over-the-Shoulder Right High Hook Punch and Yell

PAL-GWE 8 (*Pal-Gwe Pal-Chang*)

Number of positions: 35 (excluding Ready Stance and Stop)

Center
(Starting Point)

R-1 ←——→ **A** ←——→ **L-1**

R-2 ←——→ **B** ←——→ **L-2**

C

Movement proceeds in a 干 pattern, beginning at A:

Ready Stance

Stand at Attention at Starting Point, **A**.

First Position: Low Block

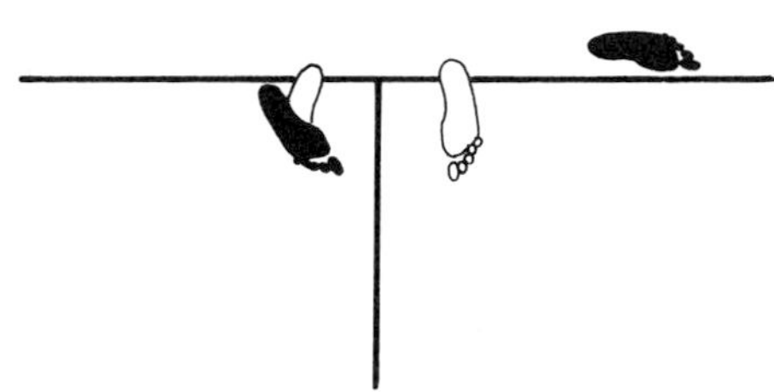

a. Turn 90° to the left, pivoting on right foot and sliding left foot one step forward (toward **L–1**).

b. Assume Front Stance.

c. Simultaneously execute a Low Block with left forearm.

Second Position: Pull Free and Hammer-Fist Strike

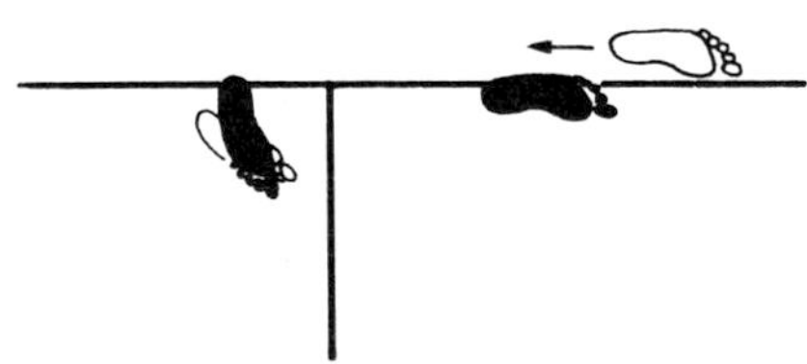

a. Draw left foot in a half-step toward right foot.

b. Stand with feet one shoulder-width apart, as in Back Stance, but with knees straight, eyes still focused toward **L–1**.

c. Simultaneously twist left fist palm up and pull it sharply inward and up, in front of body (as if pulling wrist free of opponent's grasp), and, in a continuous circular motion, swing left fist up past right shoulder, over head, outward to the left, and down, at arm's length, delivering a Hammer-Fist Strike, at shoulder level, toward **L–1**.

Third Position: Middle Punch

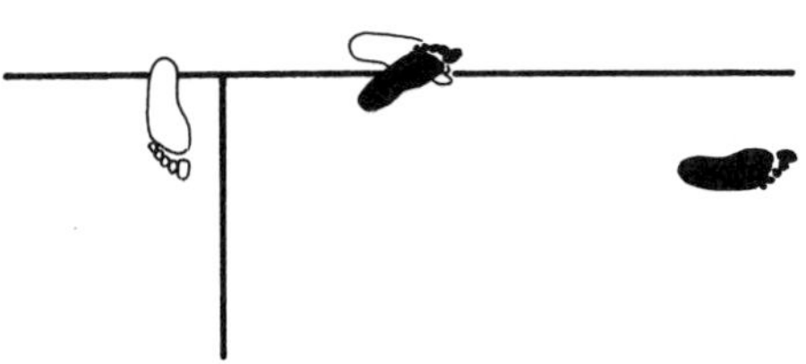

a. Slide right foot forward one step (to **L–1**).

b. Assume Front Stance.

c. Simultaneously execute a Middle Punch with right fist (pulling left fist back to hip, palm up).

Fourth Position: Low Block

a. Pivoting on left foot, slide right foot out and back in a wide arc, turning 180° (to face **R–1**).

b. Assume Front Stance.

c. Simultaneously execute a Low Block with right forearm.

Fifth Position: Pull Free and Hammer-Fist Strike

a. Draw right foot in a half-step toward left foot.

b. Stand with feet one shoulder-width apart, as in Back Stance, but with knees straight, eyes still focused toward **R–1**.

c. Simultaneously twist right fist palm up and pull it sharply inward and up, in front of body, and, in a continuous circular motion, swing right fist up, over head, outward to the right, and down, at arm's length, delivering a Hammer-Fist Strike, at shoulder level, toward **R–1**.

Sixth Position: Middle Punch

a. Slide left foot forward one step (to **R–1**).

b. Assume Front Stance.

c. Simultaneously execute a Middle Punch with left fist (pulling right fist back to hip, palm up).

Seventh Position: Knife-Hand Middle Block

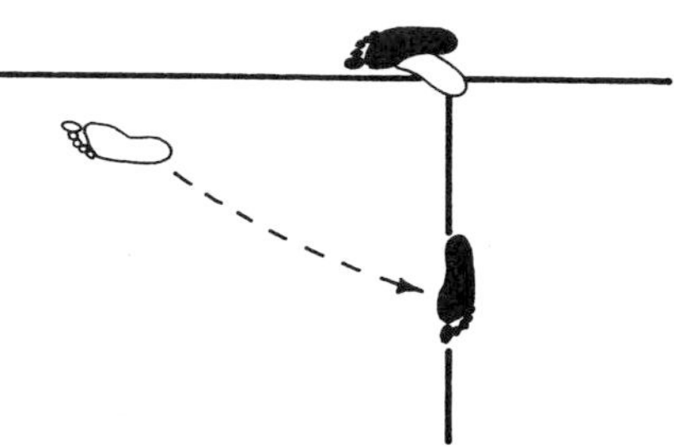

a. Pivoting on right foot, slide left foot out, turning 90° (to face **B**).

b. Assume Back Stance.

c. Simultaneously execute a Knife-Hand Middle Block with left hand, right Knife Hand assisting.

Eighth Position: Palm-Heel Center Block and Spear-Hand Thrust

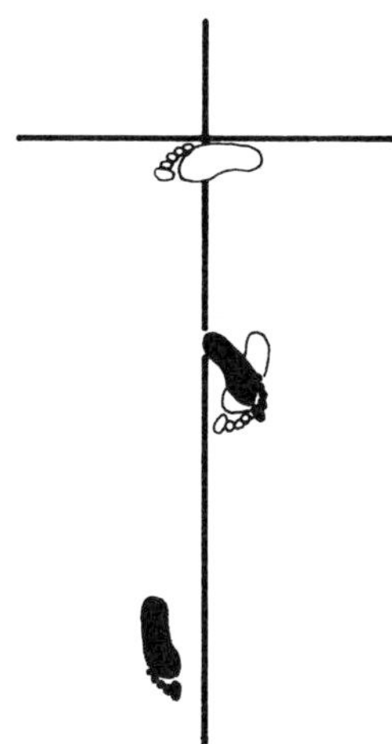

a. Slide right foot forward one step (toward **B**).

b. Assume Front Stance.

c. Simultaneously execute a Palm-Heel Center Block with left hand and Spear-Hand Thrust with right hand (at end of motion, back of left hand is immediately under right elbow).

Ninth Position: Twist Spear-Hand and Turn, and Back-Fist Strike

Note: The two motions, 1 and 2, are performed in continuous motion.

1. Twist Spear-Hand and Turn

a. Twist right Spear Hand palm down and pull it back sharply into position with back of open hand flat against the small of your back.

b. Simultaneously draw ball of left foot close behind and to the right of right foot, bend at the knees, and, pivoting on the balls of the feet, turn 360° to the left (to face **B** again), closing left hand into a fist while turning.

2. Back-Fist Strike

a. Immediately upon completing the turn, slide left foot forward a half-step (toward **B**).

b. Assume Back Stance.

c. Simultaneously execute a Back-Fist Strike with left fist at shoulder level (swinging left inverted fist outward horizontally to strike at arm's length).

Tenth Position: High Punch and Yell

a. Slide right foot forward one step (to **B**).

b. Assume Front Stance.

c. Simultaneously execute a High Punch with right fist and yell.

Eleventh Position: Left Knife-Hand Strike

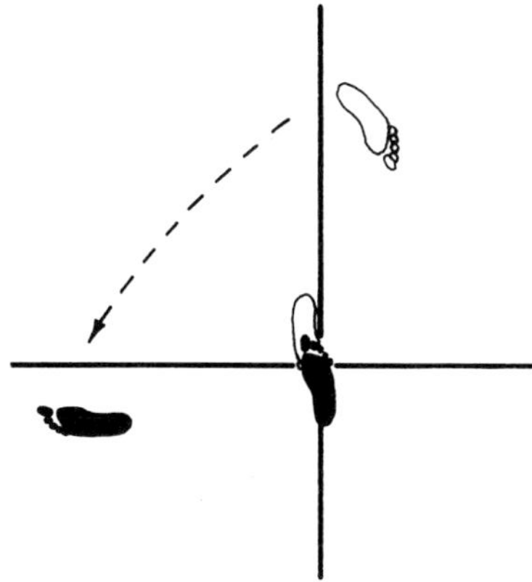

a. Pivoting on right foot, slide left foot out and back in a wide arc, turning 270° (three-quarters of a circle, to face **R–2**).

b. Assume Back Stance.

c. Simultaneously execute a high Knife-Hand Strike outward to the side with left hand, palm down, at neck level.

Twelfth Position: Twist and Pull Free

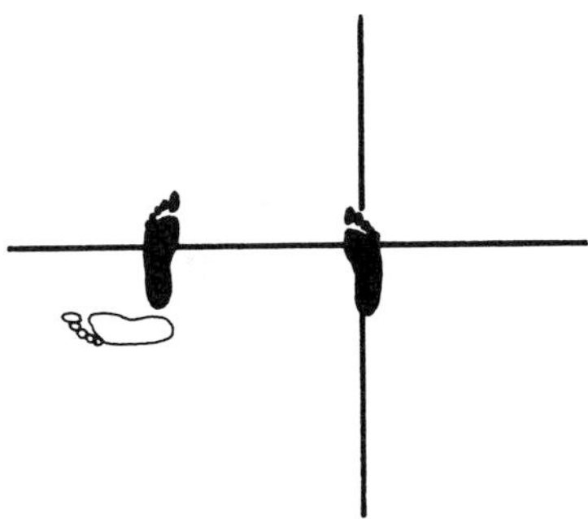

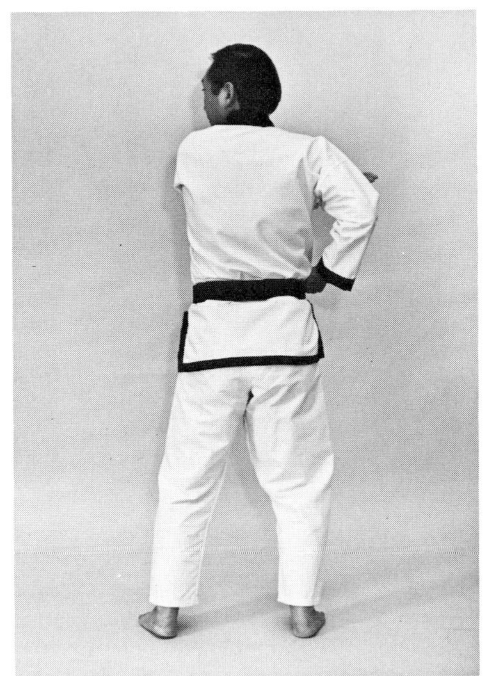

Note: Positions Twelve through Fifteen are performed in rapid sequence.

a. Draw left foot slightly in and forward (as an aid in pulling the left wrist free).

b. Simultaneously twist left Knife Hand and pull it sharply inward to chest, palm up (as if pulling the left wrist free of an opponent's grasp). Keep eyes focused toward **R–2**.

Thirteenth Position: Left Elbow Strike

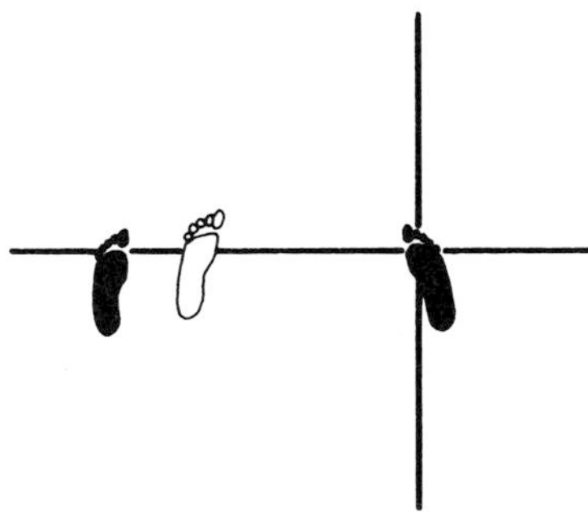

Note: This action is performed as part of the rapid sequence of Positions Twelve through Fifteen.

a. Slide left foot out a half-step sideways (toward **R–2**).

b. Assume Horseback Stance, body facing the center, **A**, eyes still focused toward **R–2**.

c. Simultaneously execute an Elbow Strike with left elbow to the ribs of imaginary opponent at **R–2**. In striking with the left elbow, the left hand is held open, palm up.

Fourteenth Position: Outside Middle Block

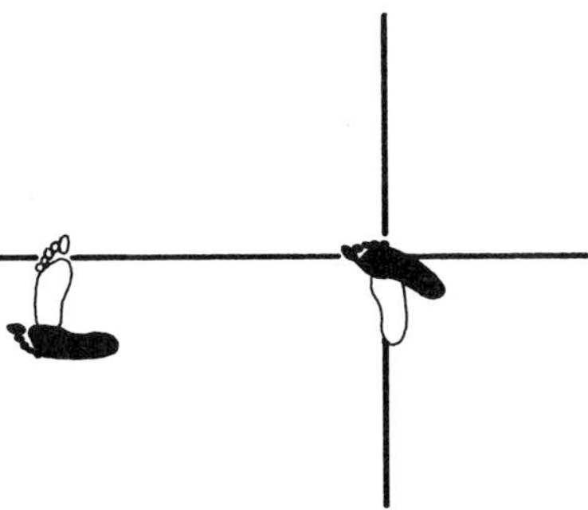

Note: This action is performed as part of the rapid sequence of Positions Twelve through Fifteen.

a. Pivoting on ball of right foot, shift left foot slightly back.

b. Assume Front Stance (facing **R–2**).

c. Simultaneously execute an Outside Middle Block with left forearm.

Fifteenth Position: Reverse Middle Punch

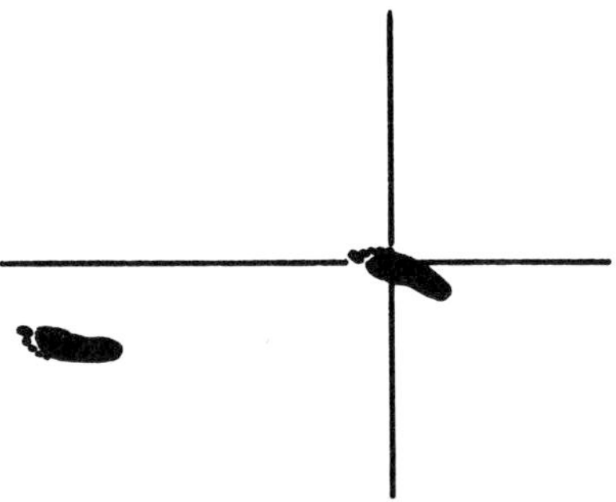

Note: This action is performed as part of the rapid sequence of Positions Twelve through Fifteen.

a. Maintain Front Stance (same position as above).

b. Execute a Reverse Middle Punch with right fist.

Sixteenth Position: Turn to the Left in Horseback Stance

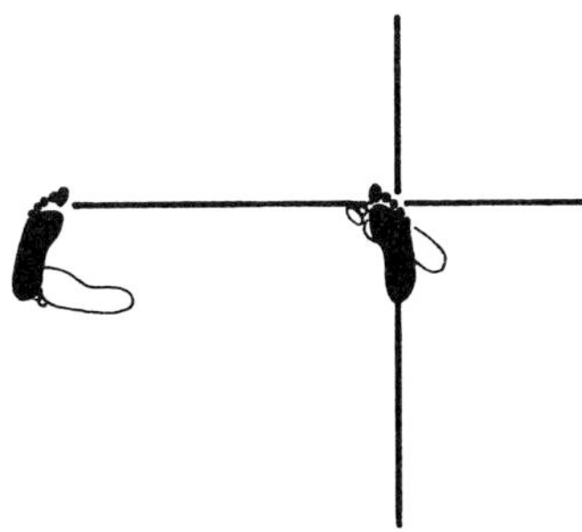

a. Pivoting on ball of right foot, shift left foot into line with—i.e., directly in front of—right foot, and turn 90° to your right.

b. Assume Horseback Stance, body facing the center, **A**, eyes focused toward **L–2**.

c. Simultaneously pull right fist into position, palm in, on top of left fist, palm up, at left hip.

Seventeenth Position: Close-Step, Right Knife-Hand Strike

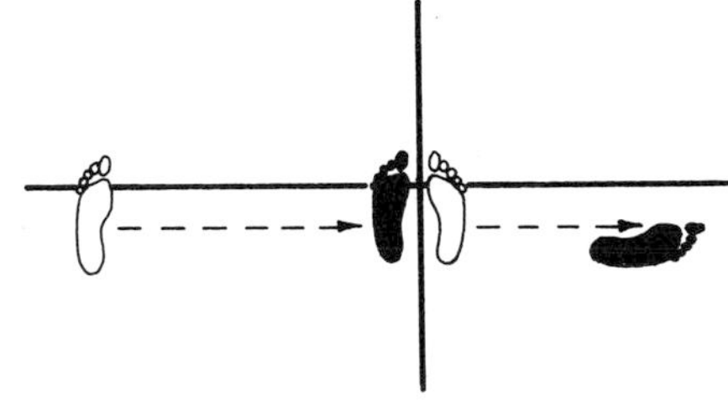

Note: Perform **a** through **d** in continuous motion.

a. Draw left foot into position immediately next to right foot, at **B**.

b. Immediately slide right foot a half-step to the side (toward **L–2**).

c. Assume Back Stance.

d. Simultaneously execute a right Knife-Hand Strike outward with right hand, palm down, toward **L–2** at neck level.

Eighteenth Position: Twist and Pull Free

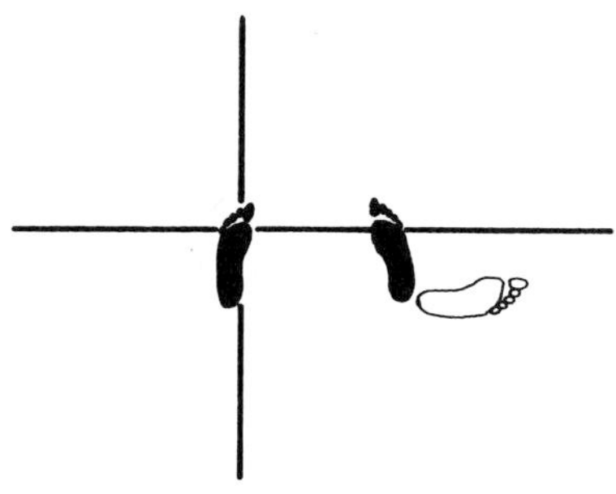

Note: Positions Eighteen through Twenty-One are performed in rapid sequence.

a. Draw right foot slightly in and forward.

b. Simultaneously twist right Knife Hand and pull it sharply inward to chest, palm up. Keep eyes focused toward **L–2**.

Nineteenth Position: Right Elbow Strike

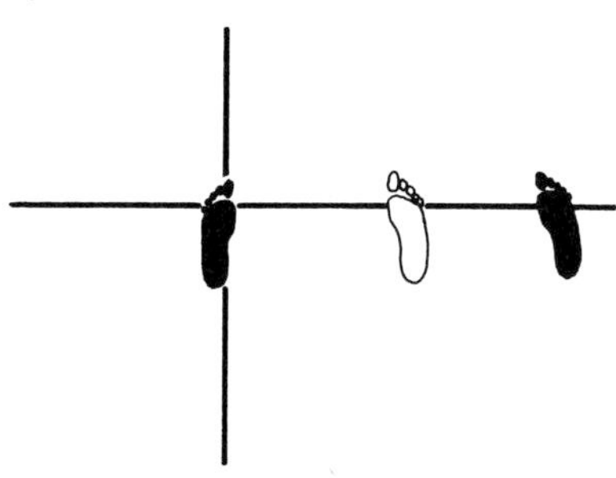

Note: This action is performed as part of the rapid sequence of Positions Eighteen through Twenty-One.

a. Slide right foot out a half-step sideways (toward **L–2**).

b. Assume Horseback Stance, body facing the center, **A**, eyes still focused toward **L–2**.

c. Simultaneously execute an Elbow Strike with left elbow to the ribs of imaginary opponent at **L–2**, holding right hand open, palm up.

Twentieth Position: Outside Middle Block

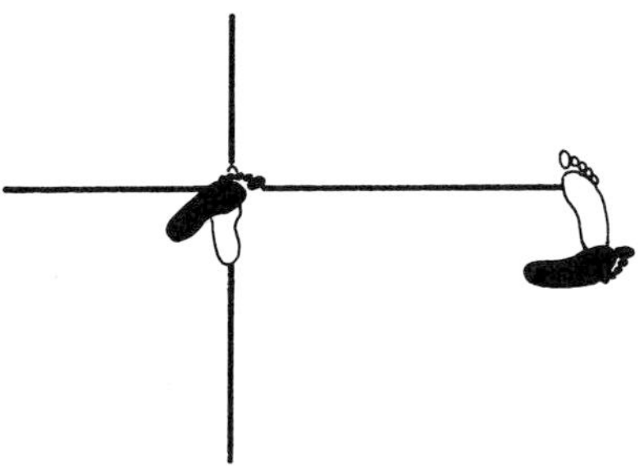

Note: This action is performed as part of the rapid sequence of Positions Eighteen through Twenty-One.

a. Pivoting on ball of left foot, shift right foot slightly back.

b. Assume Front Stance (facing **L–2**).

c. Simultaneously execute an Outside Middle Block with right forearm.

Twenty-First Position: Reverse Middle Punch

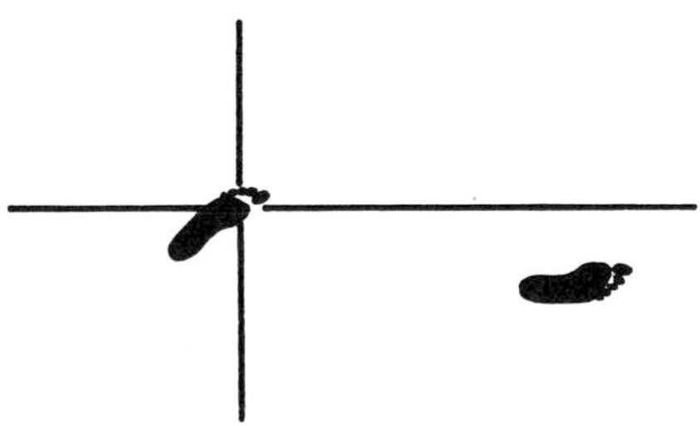

Note: This action is performed as part of the rapid sequence of Positions Eighteen through Twenty-One.

a. Maintain Front Stance (same position as above).

b. Execute a Reverse Middle Punch with left fist.

Twenty-Second Position: Turn to the Center in Horseback Stance

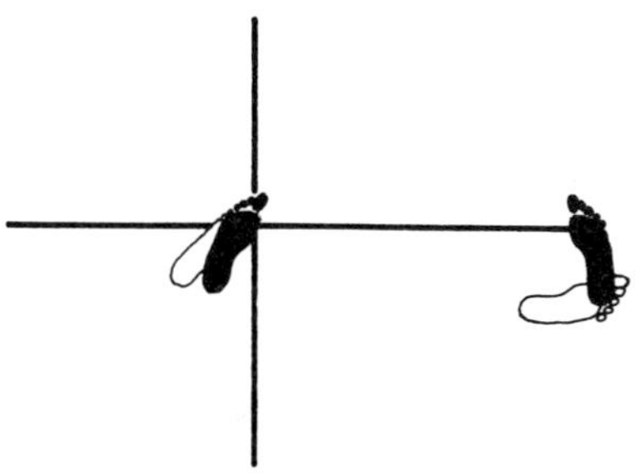

a. Pivoting on ball of left foot, shift right foot into line with—i.e., directly in front of—left foot, and turn 90° to your left.

b. Assume Horseback Stance, facing the center, **A**.

c. Simultaneously pull left fist into position, palm in, on top of right fist, palm up, at right hip.

Twenty-Third Position: Crane Stance (for Side Kick)

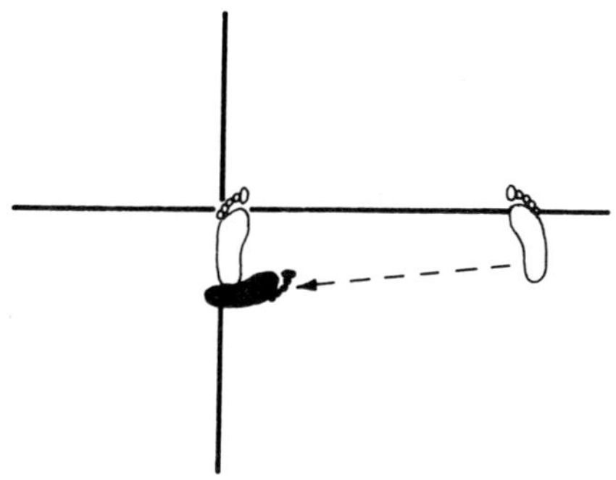

Note: Perform **a** through **c** as one smooth motion.

a. Draw right foot into position with arch immediately behind left heel.

b. Raise left foot into position next to right knee, and stand with right knee slightly bent, body turned to your right (toward **L–2**), eyes still focused toward the center, **A**.

c. Hold this position, with left fist on top of right fist at right hip, in preparation for a Side Kick toward the center, **A**.

Twenty-Fourth Position: Side Kick, Elbow Strike

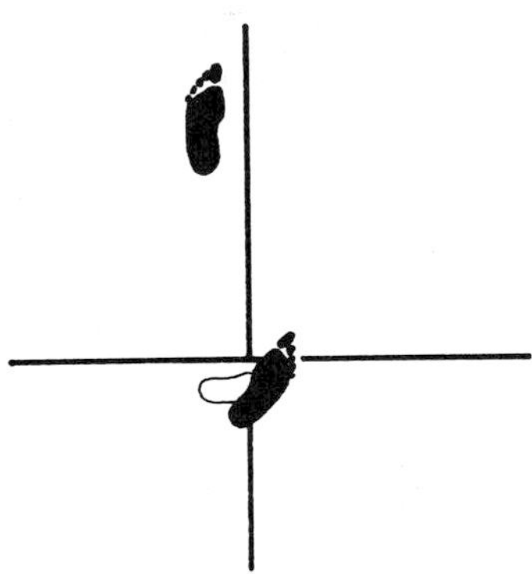

Note: The two motions, 1 and 2, are performed in continuous motion.

1. Side Kick

a. Execute a high Side Thrust Kick with left foot toward **A**.

b. Simultaneously execute a High Punch with left fist toward **A**.

2. Elbow Strike

a. Immediately bring left foot down one step forward (toward **A**).

b. Assume Front Stance.

c. Simultaneously execute an Elbow Strike with right elbow to left palm.

front view

Twenty-Fifth Position: Turn to the Front in Horseback Stance

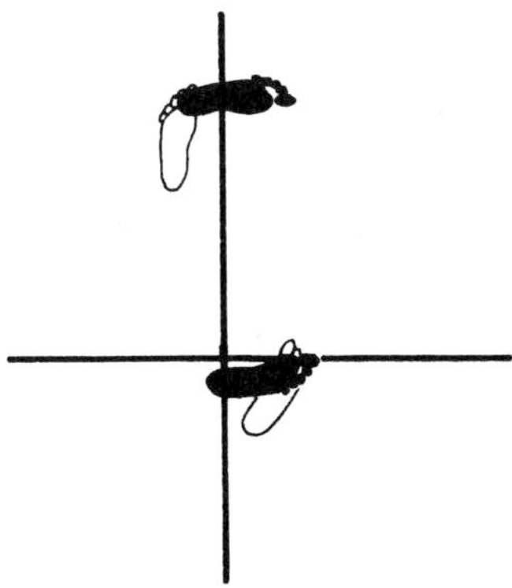

a. Pivoting on ball of right foot, shift left foot into line with—i.e., directly in front of—right foot, and turn 90° to your right.

b. Assume Horseback Stance, facing **L–2**, eyes focused front (toward **C**).

c. Simultaneously pull right fist into position, palm in, on top of left fist, palm up, at left hip.

Twenty-Sixth Position: Crane Stance (for Side Kick)

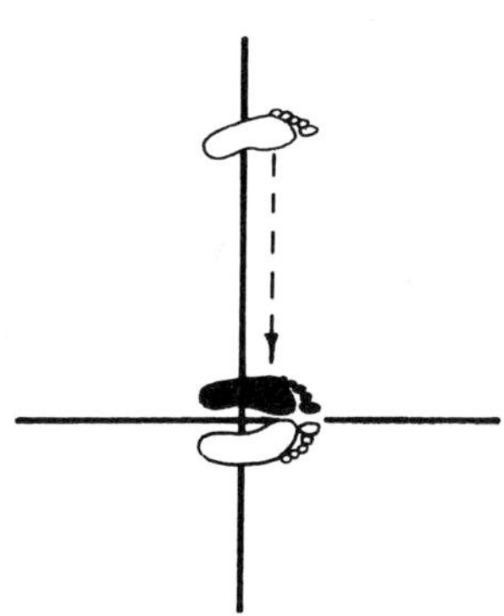

Note: Perform **a** through **c** as one smooth motion.

a. Draw left foot into position next to right foot.

b. Raise right foot into position next to left knee, and stand with left knee slightly bent.

c. Hold this position, with right fist on top of left fist at left hip, in preparation for a Side Kick toward **C**.

Twenty-Seventh Position: Side Kick, Elbow Strike

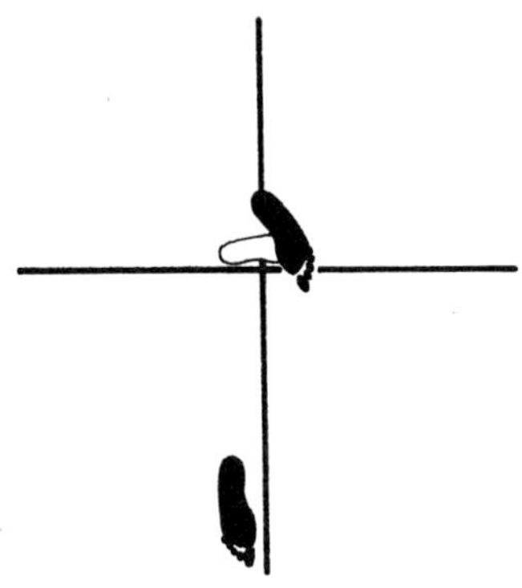

Note: The two motions, 1 and 2, are performed in continuous motion.

1. Side Kick

a. Execute a high Side Thrust Kick with right foot toward **C**.

b. Simultaneously execute a High Punch with right fist toward **C**.

2. Elbow Strike

a. Immediately bring right foot down one step forward (toward **C**).

b. Assume Front Stance.

c. Simultaneously execute an Elbow Strike with left elbow to right palm.

Twenty-Eighth Position: Spread Middle Block (Palm Down), Double Middle Upper-Cut

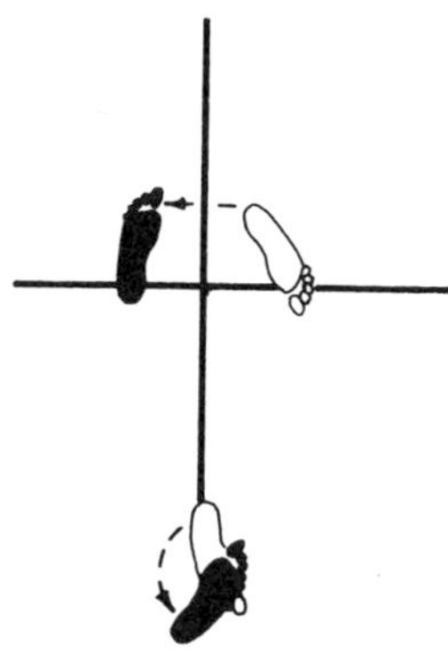

Note: The two motions, 1 and 2, are performed in rapid sequence.

1. Spread Middle Block (Palm Down)

a. Pivoting on right foot, shift left foot to the right, crossing it behind right foot, and turn about-face toward the center, **A**.

b. Assume Front Stance.

c. Simultaneously execute a Spread Middle Block with both forearms (cross forearms in front of chest and sweep them outward, fists palm down).

2. Double Middle Upper-Cut

a. Maintain Front Stance (same position as above).

b. Immediately pull both fists back to chest and thrust them out again in a Double Middle Upper-Cut (snapping both fists palm up, thrust left and right fists simultaneously forward and up in a short double punch, striking just under, and up into, rib cage of imaginary opponent near **A**).

front view

Twenty-Ninth Position: Spread Middle Block (Palm Down), Double Middle Upper-Cut

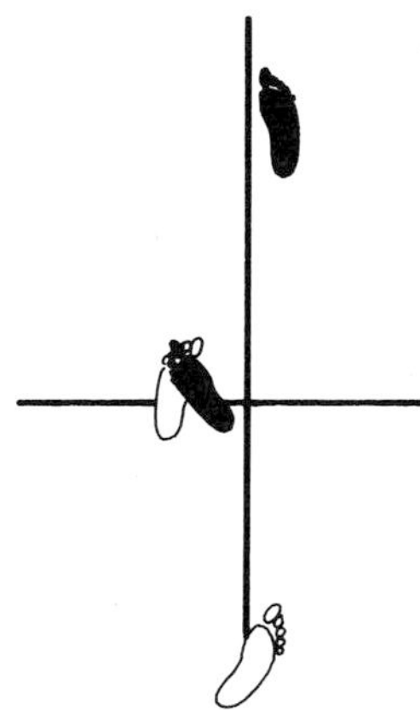

Note: The two motions, 1 and 2, are performed in rapid sequence.

1. Spread Middle Block (Palm Down)

a. Slide right foot one step forward (toward **A**).

b. Assume Front Stance.

c. Simultaneously execute a Spread Middle Block with both forearms (fists palm down).

2. Double Middle Upper-Cut

a. Maintain Front Stance (same position as above).

b. Immediately pull both fists back to chest and thrust them out again, palm up, in a Double Middle Upper-Cut.

front view

Thirtieth Position: Knife-Hand Middle Block (Outside-to-Inside)

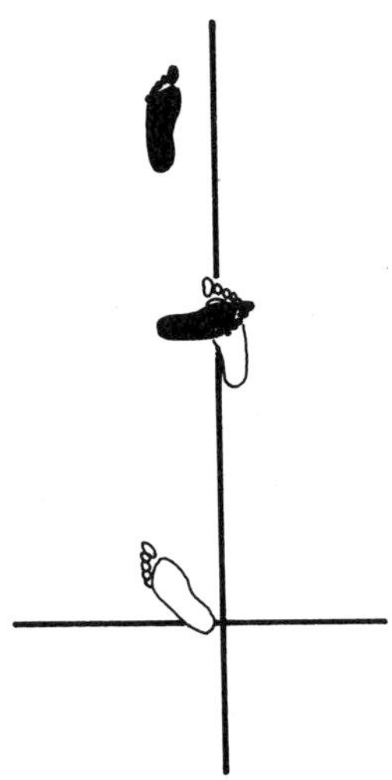

front view

a. Slide left foot forward one step (toward **A**).

b. Assume Back Stance.

c. Simultaneously execute a Knife-Hand Middle Block (outside-to-inside), with left hand.

Thirty-First Position: Spin and Backward Elbow Strike

a. With left hand, grab and twist hand of imaginary opponent at **A**, and pull it in to your left side.

b. Simultaneously pivot on ball of left foot and slide right foot backward in a wide arc, spinning 180° to your right (bringing right foot down at **A**).

c. Assume Horseback Stance (body facing **R–1**), with head turned to look back over right shoulder.

d. Simultaneously execute a Backward Elbow Strike with right elbow, right hand held open, palm up.

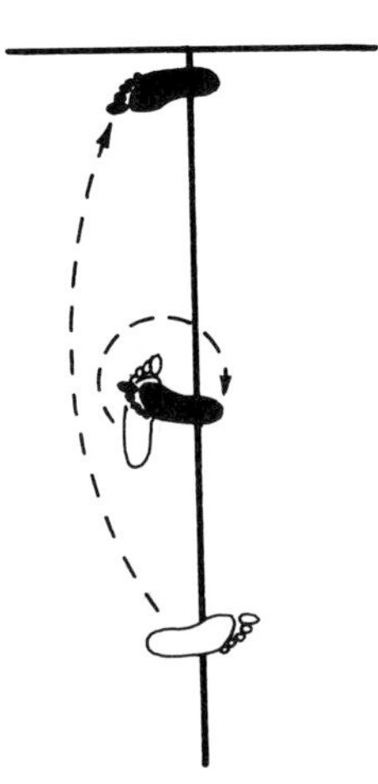

Thirty-Second Position: Turn to the Front in Normal Stance

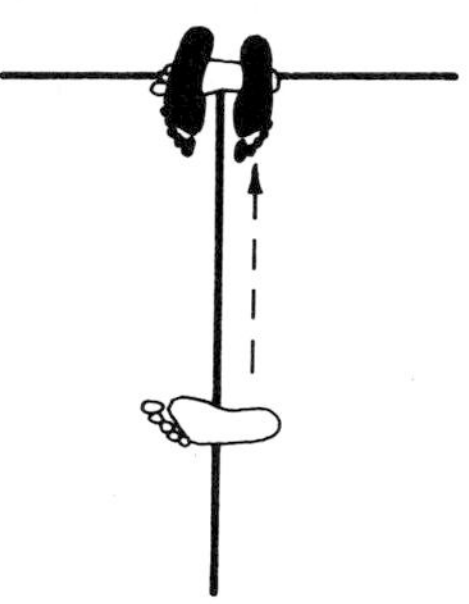

a. Draw left foot into position with arch immediately behind right heel, and turn 90° to the left, to face front, **B**.

b. Stand straight with feet together, eyes focused front in Normal Stance.

c. Simultaneously place hands together, left palm on the back of right hand, in front of abdomen.

Thirty-Third Position: Double Elbow Release

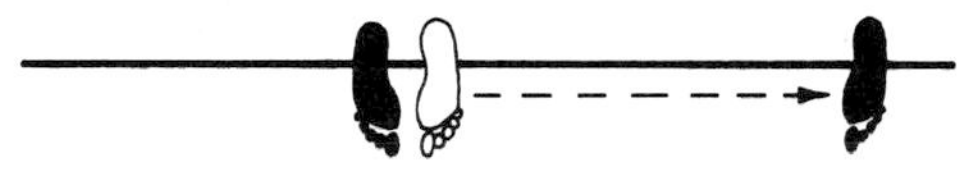

Note: The application of this action is to free oneself from the hug-hold of an opponent standing behind one.

a. Slide left foot out sideways one step (toward **L–1**).

b. Assume Horseback Stance (still facing front).

c. Simultaneously execute a Double Elbow Release (raise both elbows sharply outward and up to shoulder level, with both hands, palm down, in front of chest).

Thirty-Fourth Position: Backward Right Elbow Strike and Over-the-Shoulder Left High Hook Punch

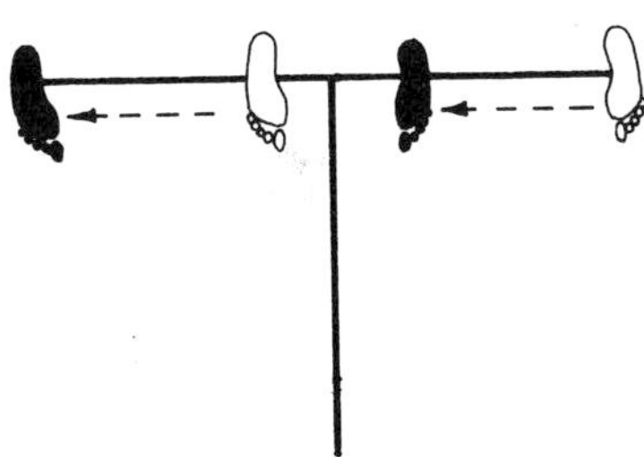

a. Raise right foot slightly and execute a sliding step sideways to the right (toward **R–1**).

b. Assume Horseback Stance, body still facing front, **A**, and turning head to look over right shoulder.

c. Simultaneously execute an Elbow Strike backward with right elbow (right hand held open palm up at the waist) and a High Hook Punch over the right shoulder with left fist, palm down.

Thirty-Fifth Position: Backward Left Elbow Strike and Over-the-Shoulder Right High Hook Punch and Yell

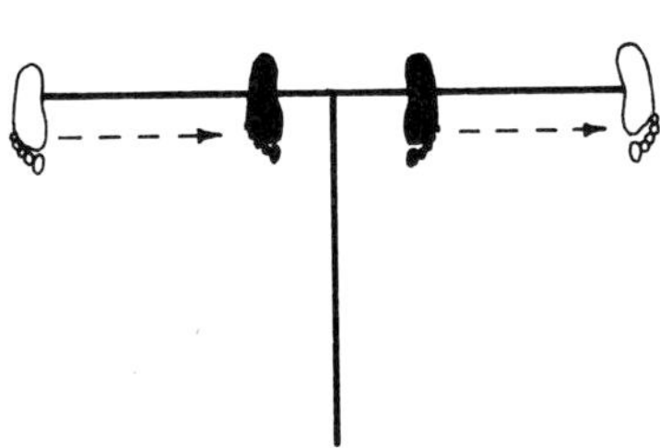

a. Raise left foot slightly and execute a sliding step sideways to the left (toward **L–1**).

b. Assume Horseback Stance, body still facing front, **A**, and turning head to look over left shoulder.

c. Simultaneously execute an Elbow Strike backward with left elbow (left hand held open palm up at the waist) and a High Hook Punch over the left shoulder with right fist, palm down, and yell.

Stop

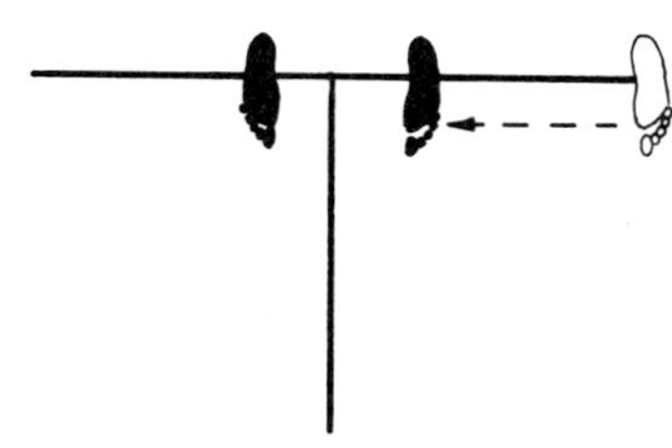

Draw left foot into position one shoulder-width from and parallel to right foot at Starting Point, **A**. Assume Ready Stance.

General Index

About the Author

Richard Chun is an acknowledged master in the art of Tae Kwon Do. In 1967, Mr. Chun received Seventh Dan from the Korea Tae Kwon Do Association and Kuk Ki Won (the Korea National Central Gymnasium). He was then appointed International Master Instructor in February of 1972 by the Korea Tae Kwon Do Association.

During the same year, he was promoted to Eighth Dan by Moo Duk Kwan, thus establishing him as one of the highest ranking instructors in this country. Since that time, Mr. Chun has been promoting the art of Tae Kwon Do in the U.S. by organizing the Annual Universal Tae Kwon Do Championship and serving as its president. In 1973, Mr. Chun was appointed Head Coach of the U.S.A. Tae Kwon Do team for the first World Tae Kwon Do Championship in Seoul, Korea, in which the U.S.A. team won second place.

In 1975 he served as Technical Advisor to the Second World Tae Kwon Do Championship in Seoul, Korea, and was appointed International Referee by the Korea Tae Kwon Do Association and World Tae Kwon Do Federation. He currently teaches the martial arts at his own schools in New York City and is technical adviser to many Tae Kwon Do schools throughout the U.S. He is also Assistant Professor of Martial Arts at the City University of New York and author of *Moo Duk Kwan Tae Kwon Do.*